Acclaim for

A Thousand Lives

"Riveting . . . You will not be able to look away."

—*San Francisco Chronicle*

"Julia Scheeres's book sheds startling new light on this murky, mini-chapter of contemporary history. . . . the narrative is [a] compelling . . . psychological mystery."

—*The Wall Street Journal*

"Julia Scheeres' *A Thousand Lives* . . . tells the tragic tale of Jonestown—in its way, a peculiarly American apocalypse."

—*Los Angeles Times*

"A gripping account of how decent people can be taken in by a charismatic and crazed tyrant."

—*The New York Times Book Review*

"How do you tell a new story about Jim Jones and his followers, when everyone knows how it ends? . . . Julia Scheeres' riveting *A Thousand Lives* gives us reason to look again. "

—*The Miami Herald*

"Almost unbearably chilling . . . but tempered with enormous sympathy."

—*The Boston Globe*

"A work of deep empathy for so many lives lost in the name of different shades of hope."

—*Los Angeles Times*

"The first solid history of the Temple . . . less a warning about the dangers of religiosity than a clear headed chronology."

—*San Francisco* magazine

"The revelations of [*A Thousand Lives*] shine through our everyday relationships to war, our politics, our beliefs and our own actions. This is a strikingly relevant book ."

—*San Francisco Sunday Chronicle Book Review*

"Gripping."

—*The Globe and Mail*

"Chilling and heart-wrenching, this is a brilliant testament to Jones's victims, so many of whom were simply in the wrong place at the wrong time."

—*Publishers Weekly*, starred review

"Scheeres shows great compassion and journalistic skill in reconstructing Jonestown's last months and the lives of many Temple members (including a few survivors) . . . [*A Thousand Lives* is a] well-written, disturbing tale of faith and evil."

—*Kirkus Reviews*

"Her account is notably levelheaded in a field where sensationalism, conspiracy theories and bizarre reasoning run free."

—*Salon*

"Jonestown has become a grim metaphor for blind obedience—for fanaticism without regard to consequences. In the aptly titled *A Thousand Lives*, Julia Scheeres captures the humanity within this terrible story, vividly depicting individuals trapped in a vortex of hope and fear, faith and loss of faith, not to mention the changes sweeping America in the 1960s and '70s. She makes their journeys to that unfathomable tragedy all too real; what was truly incredible, she shows, was the escape from death by a tiny handful of survivors. Drawing on a mountain of sources compiled and recently released by the FBI, she changes forever the way we think about this dark chapter of our history."

—T. J. Stiles, author of the Pulitzer Prize–winning
The First Tycoon: The Epic Life of Cornelius Vanderbilt

"For those who can picture only the gory end of Jonestown, Julia Scheeres offers a heartbreaking and often inspiring glimpse of what might have been. Her masterfully told and exhaustively researched *A Thousand Lives* should stand not only as the definitive word on Jones's horrific machinations, but on the utopian dreams of a bygone generation. A worthy follow-up to her superb memoir, *Jesus Land*."

—Tom Barbash, author of *On Top of the World: Cantor Fitzgerald, Howard Lutnick, and 9/11: A Story of Loss and Renewal*

"The definitive book on Jonestown and the *Danse Macabre* of suicide and murder orchestrated by mad Jim Jones. Julia Scheeres takes us by the hand and leads us gently, inexorably, into the darkness."

—Tim Cahill, author of *Lost in My Own Backyard*

"This the best book in a good long time on the dangers of fanatical faith, the power of group belief and lure of deep certainties. These demons that haunt the human mind can be countered only by facing them with courage and honesty. This is precisely what Scheeres has done."

—Ethan Watters, author of *Crazy Like Us*

"I thought I knew the story of Jonestown, but in reading *A Thousand Lives* discovered that much of what I'd read and heard was pure myth. Through meticulous research, beautiful writing, and great compassion, Scheeres presents an engrossing account of how Jim Jones's followers—eager parishioners who yearned for a more purposeful life and were willing to work for it—found themselves trapped in a nightmare of unfathomable proportions. This book serves as testimony to the seductiveness of religious fervor and how in the wrong hands it can be used to nefarious ends. It is also a poignant and unforgettable tribute to those who lost their lives and to those few who survived."

—Allison Hoover Bartlett, author of the bestselling *The Man Who Loved Books Too Much: The True Story of a Thief, a Detective, and a World of Literary Obsession*

Tommy Bogue

Zipporah Edwards

Marceline Jones

Janice Clayton

Carolyn Layton

Christine Bates

Mike Prokes

Marilee Bogue

Paula Adams

Monique Bacon

Harriet Tropp

Dick Tropp

Michael Rozynko

Eddie Crenshaw

Larry Schacht

Phyllis Chaikin

Vera Talley

Maya Ijames

Anne Moore

Tom Partak

Rose McKnight

Ron Talley

Eddie Washington

Katherine Domineck

Norya Blair

Dana Truss

Irvin Perkins

Leanndra Dennis McCoy

Jair Baker

Shanda James

Alleane Tucker

Michaeleen Brady

Brenda Warren

Crystal Simon

Lovie Jean Lucas

Jimmy Cordell

Garry (Poncho) Johnson

Jim McElvane

Thurman Guy

Julie Ann Runn

*f*P

ALSO BY JULIA SCHEERES

Jesus Land: A Memoir

A
THOUSAND
LIVES

THE UNTOLD STORY OF JONESTOWN

JULIA SCHEERES

FREE PRESS

NEW YORK   LONDON   TORONTO   SYDNEY   NEW DELHI

Free Press
A Division of Simon & Schuster, Inc.
1230 Avenue of the Americas
New York, NY 10020

First Free Press trade paperback edition November 2012

FREE PRESS and colophon are trademarks of Simon & Schuster, Inc.

For information about special discounts for bulk purchases,
please contact Simon & Schuster Special Sales at
1-866-506-1949 or business@simonandschuster.com.

The Simon & Schuster Speakers Bureau can bring authors to your live event.
For more information or to book an event, contact the Simon & Schuster Speakers Bureau at
1-866-248-3049 or visit our website at www.simonspeakers.com.

Designed by Carla Jayne Jones

Manufactured in the United States of America

1   3   5   7   9   10   8   6   4   2

The Library of Congress has cataloged the hardcover edition as follows:
Scheeres, Julia.
A thousand lives : the untold story of Jonestown / by Julia Scheeres. — 1st Free Press
hardcover ed.
p. cm.
1. Jonestown Mass Suicide, Jonestown, Guyana, 1978. I. Title.
BP605.P46S34 2011
289.9—dc22
2011012169

ISBN 978-1-4165-9639-4
ISBN 978-1-4165-9640-0 (pbk)
ISBN 978-1-4516-2896-8 (ebook)

Opening and closing images used with permission from
Peoples Temple Collection, California Historical Society.

FOR THE PEOPLE OF JONESTOWN

I love socialism, and I'm willing to die to bring it about, but if I did, I'd take a thousand with me.

—Jim Jones, September 6, 1975

CONTENTS

Contents

INTRODUCTION

H ad I walked by 1859 Geary Boulevard in San Francisco when Peoples Temple was in full swing, I certainly would have been drawn to the doorway.

I grew up in a conservative Christian family with an adopted black brother; race and religion were the dominant themes of my childhood. In our small Indiana town, David and I often felt self-conscious walking down the street together. Strangers scowled at us, and sometimes called us names. I wrote about the challenges of our relationship in my memoir, *Jesus Land*.

Suffice it to say, David and I would have been thrilled and amazed by Peoples Temple, a church where blacks and whites worshipped side by side, the preacher taught social justice instead of damnation, and the gospel choir transported the congregation to a loftier realm. We longed for such a place.

Unfortunately, the laudable aspects of Peoples Temple have been forgotten in the horrifying wake of Jonestown.

I stumbled onto writing this book by accident. I was writing a satirical novel about a charismatic preacher who takes over a fictional Indiana town, when I remembered Jim Jones was from Indiana, and Googled him. I learned that the FBI had released fifty thousand pages of documents, including diaries, meeting notes, and crop reports, as well as one thousand audiotapes that agents found in Jonestown after the massacre, and that no one had used this material to write a comprehensive history of the doomed community. Once I started digging through the files, I couldn't tear myself away.

It was easy to set my novel aside. I believe that true stories are more powerful, in a meaningful, existential way, than made-up ones. Learning about other people's lives somehow puts one's own life in sharper relief.

Aside from race and religion, there were other elements of the Peoples Temple story that resonated with me. When David and I were teenagers, our parents sent us to a Christian reform school in the Dominican Republic that had some uncanny parallels with Jonestown. I could empathize with the residents' sense of isolation and desperation.

You won't find the word *cult* in this book, unless I'm directly citing a source that uses the word. My aim here is to help readers understand the reasons that people were drawn to Jim Jones and his church, and how so many of them ended up dying in a mass-murder suicide on November 18, 1978. The word *cult* only discourages intellectual curiosity and empathy. As one survivor told me, nobody joins a cult.

To date, the Jonestown canon has veered between sensational media accounts and narrow academic studies. In this book, I endeavor to tell the Jonestown story on a grander, more human, scale.

Julia Scheeres
Berkeley, California, March 24, 2011

CHAPTER 1

AN ADVENTURE

The journey up the coastline was choppy, the shrimp trawler too far out to get a good look at the muddy shore. While other passengers rested fitfully in sleeping bags spread out on the deck or in the berths below, fifteen-year-old Tommy Bogue gripped the slick railing, bracing himself against the waves. He'd already puked twice, but was determined not to miss a beat of this adventure. The constellations soared overhead, clearer than he'd ever seen them. He wiped salt spray from his eyes with an impatient hand and squinted at the horizon. He was still boy enough to imagine a pirate galleon looming toward them, the Jolly Roger flapping in the Caribbean breeze.

This was his first sea journey. His first trip outside the United States. He squinted at South America as it blurred by, vague and mysterious, imagining the creatures that roamed there. A few years earlier, he'd devoured DC Comics' *Bomba, The Jungle Boy* series, and now imagined himself the hero of his own drama.

The very name of his destination was exotic: Guyana. None of his school friends had ever heard of it, nor had he before his church established an agricultural mission there. After his pastor made the announcement, Tommy read and reread the Guyana entry in the *Encyclopaedia Britannica* until he could spout Guyanese trivia to anyone who showed the slightest interest in what the lanky, bushy-haired teen had to say. Aboard the *Cudjoe,* he ticked off this book knowledge to himself. Jaguars. Howler monkeys. One of the world's largest snakes, the green anaconda, growing up to twenty feet long and reaching 350 pounds. The country was home to several of the world's largest beasts: the giant anteater, the giant sea otter, the giant armadillo, the fifteen-foot black caiman. He knew a few things about the strangeness surrounding him, and those few things comforted him.

The plane ride from San Francisco to Georgetown had been another first for Tommy. He sat next to another teenager from his church, Vincent Lopez, and the two boys took turns gaping out the small convex window as they soared over the Sierra Nevada, the Great Plains, the farm belt—the entire breadth of America. The cement mass of New York City astounded him; skyscrapers bristled toward every horizon. At JFK International Airport, Pastor Jones, who was going down to visit the mission himself, kept a tight hand on the boys as he herded them toward their connecting flight.

Everything about Tommy Bogue was average—his height, his build, his grades—except for his penchant for trouble. His parents couldn't control him. Neither could the church elders. He hated the long meetings the congregation was required to attend, and was always sneaking off to smoke weed or wander the tough streets of the Fillmore District. Ditching church became a game, one he was severely punished for, but which proved irresistible.

They'd only told him two days ago that he was being sent to the mission field. His head was still spinning with the quickness of it all. The counselors told him he should feel honored to be chosen, but he was wise to them. He overheard people talking about manual labor, separation from negative peers, isolation, culture shock: All these things were supposed to be good for him. He knew he was being sent away, but at least he'd get out of the never-ending meetings, and more important, he'd see his father, for the first time in two years.

His dad left for Guyana in 1974, one of the pioneers. He'd called home a few times over the mission's ham radio, and in brief, static-filled reports, he sounded proud of what the settlers had accomplished: clearing the bush by hand, planting crops, building cottages. Tommy was eager to see it himself.

Finally, as the sun blazed hot and high overhead, the *Cudjoe* shifted into low gear and swung toward land. The other church members crowded Tommy as the boat nosed up a muddy river, the wake lifting the skirts of the mangroves as it passed. In the high canopy, color flashed: parrots, orchids, bromeliads.

The travelers slipped back in time, passing thatched huts stilted on the river banks and Amerindians, who eyed them warily from dug-out canoes. This was their territory. Late in the afternoon, the passengers arrived at a village named Port Kaituma and excitement rippled through them. The deck hands tied the *Cudjoe* to a pole in the water and Tommy helped unload cargo up the steep embankment. Pastor Jones, who'd spent most of the trip secluded in the deck house, welcomed them to the village as if he owned it. There wasn't much to it beyond a few stalls selling produce and secondhand clothes. As he spoke, Tommy listened attentively along with the others; Guyana was a fresh start for him, and he planned to stay out of trouble. Jones told the small group that the locals were grateful for the church's assistance—the mission's farm would put food on their tables.

After a short delay, a tractor pulling a flatbed trailer motored up and the newcomers climbed aboard with their gear. The tractor slipped and lurched down the pitted road to the mission, and the passengers grabbed the high sides and joked as if they were on a hayride. All were in good spirits.

At some point, Tommy noticed the squalor: the collapsing shanties, the naked brown kids with weird sores and swollen bellies, the dead dogs rotting where they fell. The trenches of scummy water. The stench. The mosquitoes whining in his ears. The landscape didn't jibe with the slide shows Pastor Jones had shown at church, which made Guyana look like a lush resort.

Tommy didn't point out these aberrations, but turned to listen to Pastor Jones, who raised his voice above the tractor's thrumming diesel engine. He was boasting, again, about how everything thrived at the mission. About the ice cream tree, whose fruit tasted like vanilla ice cream. About the protective aura surrounding the Church's property: There was no sickness there, no malaria or typhoid, no snakes or jungle cats ventured onto it. Not one mishap whatsoever. The adults nodded and smiled as they listened. Tommy turned toward the jungle again. The bush was so dense he couldn't see but a yard in before it fell away into darkness.

The tractor veered down a narrow road and passed through a tight stand of trees. The canopy rose two hundred feet above them. The light dimmed as they drove through this tree tunnel, as if they'd entered a candle-lit hallway and someone was blowing out the candles one by one. The air was so still it bordered on stagnant. Tommy glanced behind them at the receding brightness, then ahead, to where his father waited.

They drove into a large clearing. Here were a few rustic buildings, and beyond them, rows and rows of plants. A dozen or so settlers stood along the entry road, and the two groups shouted joyfully to each other. Tommy didn't immediately see his dad. He was disappointed, but unsurprised; his old man was probably nose to the grindstone, as always. He lifted his duffle bag onto his shoulder and jumped onto the red earth, happy to have arrived, at long last, in Jonestown.

CHAPTER 2

CHURCH

The power of the church seized Jim Jones from a young age. Like many, he found an acceptance in the church that otherwise eluded him.

James Warren Jones was born on May 13, 1931, in tiny Crete, Indiana, the only child of an unhappy couple. He later described his father, a disabled WWI vet, as a bitter, cynical person. His mother, who supported the family as a factory worker, was a scandalous figure about town: She drank, smoked, cursed, and was a vocal member of the local union.

Not only was the family untraditional, it was guilty of a notable transgression in a midwestern town—the Joneses were churchless. The young Jim Jones, who spent much time alone and unsupervised, felt like an outcast on many levels.

When Jones was a small boy, the family moved to the slightly larger town of Lynn, five miles away. There, a neighbor brought Jim to the local Nazarene church, where he was transfixed by the preacher. Everything about the man behind the pulpit awed him, from his regal satin robe to the deferential treatment given him by the congregation. Here was a role model for Jim Jones, something to aspire to.

He sampled other denominations—the pacifist Quakers, the somber Methodists—before finding his way into the Gospel Tabernacle at the edge of town.

Pentecostalism has always belonged to the marginalized. Its adherents practice a very physical devotion to God that is reflected in *glossolalia* (speaking in tongues), ecstatic dance, and faith healing. A conservative

Christian would view the sheer exuberance of a Pentecostal worship service as unsophisticated, perhaps even unbiblical. Pentecostalism is warmth and catharsis, a fizzy soda to Calvinism's sour water.

"Because I was never accepted, or didn't feel accepted, I joined a Pentecostal Church," Jones would tell his followers in Jonestown. "The most extreme Pentecostal Church, the Oneness, because they were the most despised. They were the rejects of the community. I found immediate acceptance, and I must say, in all honesty, about as much love as I could interpret love."

While other children liked to role-play teacher-student or doctor-patient scenarios with their friends, Jones chose preacher-congregant games. By age ten, he was holding pretend services in the loft of the barn behind his house, a white sheet draped over his shoulders for a robe as he read from the Bible or pretended to heal chickens. A woman who belonged to the Gospel Tabernacle discovered Jones's gift for oratory and started grooming him as a child evangelist. But when he started having nightmares about supernatural phenomena, his mother, Lynetta, made him stop attending services.

But she couldn't stop him from preaching. By sixteen, he was shouting the gospel of equality under God in the black neighborhoods of Richmond, Indiana, where he moved with his mother after his parents separated. He slicked back his dark hair with the comb he kept in his back pocket, staked out a spot on a busy sidewalk, and quickly drew an audience.

Richmond, a city where almost half the adult male population had once belonged to the Ku Klux Klan, was still deeply segregated in 1948, and Jones's message of Christian inclusion fell sweetly on the ears of African American passersby. Here was a white teenager who was vociferously, publicly, arguing for equal rights in a place where blacks were pushed to the fringes of town. They couldn't believe it.

The experience was a turning point for Jim Jones: He'd discovered his platform.

At age twenty-one, while majoring in education at Indiana University, he became a student pastor at Somerset Methodist Church in Indianapolis. He attempted to integrate the church, but several families walked out when the first black visitors were ushered in. It was one thing for white believers to nod in passive agreement when their preacher said that all humans were created equal in the eyes of God; it was quite another to stand shoulder to shoulder with a black person, sharing a hymnal.

In 1954, Jones decided to open his own church. He chose a neighborhood forced by court order to desegregate, and went door-to-door inviting African Americans to his church, which he called Community Unity. He championed racial equality and began doing faith healings. His performances were so popular in Pentecostal circles that he was forced to buy a larger building in 1956 to accommodate the Sunday morning crush. He named the new church Peoples Temple Full Gospel Church.

The question of faith healing is a question of faith: Either you believe God has the power to cure you, or you don't. Most Christians believe God does have this power, and they deliver their petitions for relief to him as simple prayers: "Dear Lord, please heal me from x, y, or z." Most Christians also believe that if you enlist other believers to pray for you, your chances of being heard, and healed, increase. Get a preacher involved, and your chances at bending God's ear skyrocket. Who, after all, has a more direct line to the Almighty than God's intercessor on earth?

So, following this logic, it's not much of a stretch to believe that when a pastor lays his or her hands on a sick congregant, the chances of healing also increase. This instills a kind of magic in the preacher: God is touching the supplicant through the preacher's hands. The Bible supports this belief. In Matthew 10:8, Jesus commanded his twelve disciples to "Heal the sick, cleanse the lepers, raise the dead, cast out demons. Freely you have received, freely give." The New Testament states that the apostles Peter and Paul performed many miracles, including raising the dead. Even today, some Christians believe mainstream ministers such as Pat Robertson possess a healing gift.

Skeptics dismiss faith healing as psychological, not biological. They reduce such claims to the power of positive thinking. If, say, a woman who suffers from chronic chest pain due to a heart condition or stress believes in faith healing, she *will* feel the pain dissolve when a healer lays hands on her. Science may attribute her sudden relief to a rush of endorphins, but for her, the experience has a self-authenticating power that defies logic: God healed her, and that was the beginning and end of it.

Hyacinth Thrash believed Jim Jones had the gift.

She first heard about Jones in 1955, when she was fifty.

At the time she was childless, twice divorced, and living with her younger sister, Zipporah Edwards, in Indianapolis. They women were raised Baptist, and had later converted to Pentecostalism, but in 1955, they were between churches, having quit their last church after a new preacher arrived and immediately demanded a larger salary from his working class congregation.

The sisters watched church television instead. Televangelism was brand new, and although some people criticized it as a poor substitute for indolent believers, it was the perfect solution for Hy and Zippy, who revered God but couldn't say the same for his pitchmen. If a TV pastor offended them, they could just turn him off.

When Zip saw Jones preaching on a local television channel, she thought Jones was a fine speaker, but what excited her more, that Sunday, was his choir. There they stood in matching satin robes, blacks and whites side by side like keys on a piano, singing her favorite hymns. Zippy had never seen the likes of it.

"I found my church!" she shouted. She got up and pulled Hyacinth into the room. As they watched the service, a longing bloomed in them.

Born in a whistle-stop town deep in Alabama, the sisters had grown up in a close-knit family. Their father had steady work as a train cook, and their mother cleaned houses for white people. (Hyacinth was named by one of her mother's employers.) Although they wore flour-sack dresses, they never went hungry.

Their household was harmonious, but Hyacinth noticed from a young age how things shifted the moment she stepped off their yard. The sign outside a neighboring town read: "We don't allow no niggers in this town. You better get out before the sun goes down and if you can't read, better get out anyhow." Only landholders could vote, perpetuating white power.

She sometimes ran into former slaves who bore the name of their erstwhile master branded on their backs.

When she was in grade school, a family friend was lynched. A group of white men followed him through town, taunting and trying to incite him. When they kicked him in the buttocks, he could stand it no longer and lunged at his assailants. They strung him up from a tree as a warning to other so-called insolent blacks.

"Papa, isn't there a better place?" Hyacinth kept asking her father. He was reluctant to leave their farm and heritage, but the lynching persuaded him that no African American was safe in the South. In 1918, the family boarded a train to join the Great Migration of two million blacks who left the Jim Crow South searching for better lives. As Hyacinth later wrote, "After the Civil War, we was freed but we wasn't free." Their train was segregated all the way to Kentucky. Among the family's possessions was a cherished biography of President Abraham Lincoln.

They settled in Indianapolis with the help of relatives who'd gone before. Although Hyacinth, thirteen, was eager to reap the North's promise, her subpar education held her back. In her Alabama town, black children only attended school in the winter, so that they could work the fields during the growing season. She was ashamed of her learning deficit, and rather than be stuck in a class with younger kids, she dropped out of school altogether after ninth grade. She held a series of unskilled jobs: baby-sitting, cleaning, operating the elevator at the Indiana State House, and married twice, to unfaithful men. She was heartbroken to learn she couldn't have children.

In 1951, when Hy was forty-six, and Zip, who'd never married, was forty-two, they'd saved enough money to buy a modest two-family home in the Butler-Tarkington neighborhood, an area recently forced to integrate, and took in boarders to make their mortgage payments.

Indianapolis was less overtly racist than the South, but it was by no means an egalitarian city. As soon as black families started moving into the neighborhood, for-sale signs lined the streets. By the time the sisters arrived, the lone white holdouts lived next door. The middle-aged couple refused to talk to the sisters. If they happened to be sitting on their porch when Hy or Zippy came out to sit on theirs, they'd abruptly go back inside.

So, on that Sunday morning when Zipporah turned on the television and saw a white man inviting believers of any color to visit his church, she was both astonished and thrilled. Reverend Jones described Peoples Temple as a church whose "door is open so wide that all races, creeds, and colors find a hearty welcome to come in, relax, meditate, and worship God." Soon afterward, the sisters donned their finest dresses and white cotton gloves, and took a street car to Jones's church.

They discovered the television had not lied. Not only was the choir integrated, but the pews were, too. The usher marched them up the center aisle to the front, where the white congregants greeted them warmly. It felt like a homecoming. The joyfully serene atmosphere was redolent of their girlhoods: Here were the same tidy pews, the soulful organ voluntary, the wafts of perfume and hair pomade, the children dolled up and peering over the seat backs. Here were the hymns they knew by heart. Here was a handsome young white minister preaching the word in a gospel cadence, afire with the Lord.

The scene from the pulpit was no less thrilling. It must have been slightly intimidating for Jones, a callow twenty-four-year-old, to look down at the rows of faces before him, each expecting a private miracle. His early sermons, which were rambling, disjointed, and filled with stilted King Jamesian English, such as "verily" and "doeth," reflected his inexperience. Perhaps he thought the affectation gave him an air of sophistication. After all, his college degree was in education, not divinity. A line lifted from a church newsletter printed in April 1956, two months after he was ordained by Assemblies of God, is exemplary of his strained composition: "The fullness of him that filleth all in all who is in you all and through you all and above you all."

During his sermons, the young Jim Jones mimicked the Pentecostal flourishes that mesmerized him as a kid: the dramatic pauses, shouted words, the pulpit fist bangs for emphasis. His dramatic healings moved the room to wonderment and reverence.

After the service ended, Jones strode up the aisle to stand at the entrance to the sanctuary, shaking hands and sharing a few words with worshippers as they filed out. He grasped each sister's hand in his own and looked them in the eye, according them a dignity and respect that few whites had for them.

Despite being impressed with Peoples Temple, the sisters got lazy. It took effort to dress up, catch that street car. They reverted to TV church. After a few weeks, they found a flier on their doorstep. It said that Pastor Jones and twelve of his members would be on their block that Wednesday evening and planned to stop by. He'd not forgotten them. The sisters, excited, tidied up and prepared refreshments. As promised, Jones arrived with his disciples and sat in their immaculate parlor, listening wholly to them as the sisters spoke of their history, aspirations, and heartbreaks. Then, he laid soft hands on their shoulders and prayed for them. By the time he left that night, Jim Jones had gained two more followers.

The sisters would become part of the church's largest demographic: black women. They spent most of their Sundays at the peak-roofed church at 1502 N. New Jersey Street. After the morning service, they helped run the soup kitchen in the church basement before attending vespers. They also volunteered in the Temple pantry, which distributed kitchen staples and used clothing to needy families. The outreach programs fostered relationships between Temple members as they drove through Indy together looking for donations of stale, expired, or overripe food. Hy and Zippy were equal partners with their white counterparts in a common cause; race was beside the point.

Jones kept pushing boundaries. The subject of his sermons—improved rights for women, blacks, and the poor—was heady stuff back in the 1950s. He didn't use ambiguous parables about mustard seeds and lost sheep to instruct his congregation, but became a living example of his message. He integrated his household as he did his church, adopting several nonwhite children, including, in 1960, a black son who became his namesake: James Warren Jones, Jr. At the pulpit, he could now relate his personal experiences with racism and thus gain credibility with his increasingly dark-skinned flock. When his adopted Korean daughter died in a car accident in 1959, he was forced to bury her in a segregated graveyard. As his wife, Marceline, walked down the street holding Jimmy Jr.'s hand, a woman spat on her. He'd later even claim to be a minority himself—part Native American and part African American—although his blood relatives denied this after his death.

Jones offended some and convinced others. He took his message beyond the sanctuary. When he learned that several Indianapolis restaurants discouraged minority patrons by oversalting their food, or only serving them takeout, Jones announced on his television program that he was going to fast until they changed these racist practices, which they did. He also forced the Methodist Hospital to integrate. He chose a black personal physician, and when he was hospitalized for an ulcer, the hospital administrators assumed he was black as well and assigned him to a negro ward. They tried to move him to a white ward when they discovered their mistake, but Jones refused to leave, and took the opportunity to grandstand by giving patients sponge baths and emptying their bedpans.

In the late 1950s, Jones appeared to be at the forefront of the civil rights movement, but scholars would someday cast doubt on almost every aspect of Jones's ministry, even suggesting that his adopted children were mere props that he acquired to generate headlines and attract followers.

Nevertheless, in 1961, his renown prompted Mayor Charles Boswell to name Jones head of the city's fledgling Human Rights Commission. In an *Indianapolis Times* story announcing the appointment, Jones addressed miscegenation fears raised by his church. "The Negro wants to be our brother in privilege, not our brother-in-law," he said. In his first weeks as commission head, Jones convinced three local restaurants to accept black patrons and offset owners' fears that this would hurt business by bringing carloads of Temple members to fill empty seats.

His prime targets, however, were Indy's churches.

"The most segregated hour in America is the Sunday morning worship hour," Jones liked to say. After concluding morning services at the Temple, he'd drive a group of black members to a white neighborhood. Led by their fearless pastor, the visitors would walk into a church, politely greet the ushers, and wait to be seated. Jones called this "witnessing to integration."

It took individuals to overthrow the system. A middle-aged seamstress from Alabama named Rosa Parks. Four college students in North Carolina who camped out at a whites-only lunch counter for days, enduring hatred and spittle, until they were served.

Jones recruited Hyacinth and Zipporah to be part of his integrationist efforts. At one church, the pastor started singing "Old Black Joe," a song idealizing slavery, to offend them. At another, a man opened the windows next to them on a snowy day, attempting to freeze them out. One church leader said he would have roped off an area, had he known they were coming. Hyacinth began to dread these confrontations. Jones told the media he received death threats for his actions, as well as slashed tires and rocks launched through the Temple's windows.

For Hy, the last straw came when a white man stood up and said they'd be bombed if they didn't leave. Jones led his flock into the field next door and preached to them there. The experience terrified Hyacinth; she'd seen what happened to blacks who overstepped boundaries in the South. She had second thoughts about Jim Jones, and told him God should take care of integrating churches himself.

Her misgivings fell by the wayside, however, when she learned she had breast cancer. Her doctor diagnosed it, and when she pressed her fingers to her chest, she could feel the hard tumor herself. The following Sunday, Jones laid his hands on her and prayed. The lump was gone by Wednesday. Seven doctors examined her and confirmed that the mass had disappeared. One doctor told her it was a miracle, and a nurse danced with her in the hospital corridor. Misdiagnosis, spontaneous remission, or miracle? It didn't matter. Hyacinth was convinced that Jim Jones healed her.

She'd follow him anywhere after that.

CHAPTER 3
REDWOOD VALLEY

I n the early 1960s, the prospect of World War III loomed large. In the Soviet Union, Nikita Khrushchev repeatedly threatened to annihilate the West while, in the United States, the Kennedy administration warned citizens to avoid looking at bright flashes in the sky and suggested aspirin to treat radiation-induced headaches. American schoolkids practiced duck-and-cover drills that were pointless against nuclear fission but made adults feel better, and families built fallout shelters in their backyards.

In churches across the nation, preachers used the mounting tension to pressure their flocks to get right with God before the coming armageddon.

Jim Jones did something far more practical: He made plans to move his congregation to a safer place. He claimed to have had a vision of a mushroom cloud exploding over Chicago and predicted that Indianapolis would also be wiped out. After reading an *Esquire* article in 1962, titled "Nine Places in the World to Hide" (from a nuclear attack), he moved his family to one of the locations on the top of the list—Belo Horizonte, Brazil—with the idea that he would establish himself there before sending for his church members.

But he didn't speak Portuguese and struggled to find work and feed his family. During his nearly two-year absence, his associate ministers managed the church but, without Jones's showy performances, Temple membership dwindled. Where services once attracted more than two thousand people, they now drew less than one hundred. Hy and Zippy started church shopping again. Faced with the Temple's extinction, Jones returned to Indiana, and his presence at the pulpit again filled the pews.

But his nuclear paranoia did not subside. He predicted Russia would launch missiles at the United States on July 16, 1967, and again warned his congregation of the need to find a safe haven. This time, he picked northern California, which was also named in the *Esquire* piece, and was more palatable to his flock; he wasn't pressuring them to leave the cozy Midwest for a politically unstable third-world nation, he was just asking them to take a two-day drive across the country.

As schools let out for summer vacation in 1965, dozens of families piled their possessions onto their cars and rode westward in a long caravan, with Jones in the lead vehicle. The migration split families. For some, church was a Sunday affair, more social club than a lifestyle. They'd rather take their chances with the bomb than forsake everything to follow an eccentric preacher into the unknown. He'd failed in Brazil; there was no guarantee California would be a success. Relatives of the migrating members wondered how their loved ones could fall for Jones, whom many saw as a crackpot, while those who left Indiana worried about their kin's safety.

The move was an acid test: Only those who believed Jones was a seer—endowed with a paranormal ability to predict the future—would uproot themselves from all that was familiar and follow him. All told, about one hundred fifty people followed him to California that summer; these would become his core membership. Most of these original Hoosiers would also follow him to Guyana, and die there.

The move also divided Hyacinth and Zipporah. Zippy wanted to go, but Hy was reluctant. She enjoyed the life they'd forged in Indianapolis, and took great pride in their hard-won home. She'd finally found that better place she'd asked of her dad fifty years earlier.

Then she became lame. What started as a strange numbness in her leg turned into trouble walking. X-rays revealed a spinal cord tumor. She had it surgically removed, but was left with permanent nerve damage that forced her to walk with a cane and made it impossible for her to keep her cleaning job. Meanwhile, Zip kept bugging her to move to California. Morning, noon, and night, she pleaded. She worried Hy with the impending nuclear holocaust one minute, and reassured her that Jones would cure her leg—just as he'd cured her breast—the next.

Jones also called members who didn't join the caravan. He used different ploys to goad his old congregants to join him. He told Jerry Parks, who was ill, that he'd die if he didn't move to California, so Parks went, bringing his mother, wife, and three children. For Hyacinth, he painted an idyllic picture of the small town where the group settled. He told the sisters he'd find them employment; the local mental hospital was closing, and many Temple members had set up government-subsidized care homes to take in displaced patients. It was easy money: Care-home operators didn't need experience; they just needed room for boarders. The offer appealed to Hy, especially given her limited mobility. For the past ten years, she and Zip had volunteered at a psychiatric hospital, helping organize picnics and clothing drives; she found caring for the patients rewarding. Toward the middle of 1967, after much late-night contemplation, Hy told her sister she was ready to go.

They packed up their memories: age-curled photographs from Alabama, mildewed books, treasured mementos from their deceased parents, and left Indianapolis in high spirits on an early summer morning. That year had heralded several victories for civil rights. The Supreme Court overturned state laws banning interracial marriage, and President Johnson appointed Thurgood Marshall to be the first black justice in the high court. Nonetheless, the sisters were wary about running into local bigots and whites-only cafes as they drove cross country for the first time, so they planned accordingly, packing a cooler with enough sandwiches and tea cakes to last the entire trip. They drove most of the way on Route 66, through seas of grain, over narrow steel truss bridges, through ghost towns and deserts. They were sightseeing America. The feeling of movement rejuvenated them. There was still excitement left in them. There was still life.

The Temple's arrival in rural Mendocino County, California, was impossible to miss. Word got around that an entire Indiana church relocated to town, and the local paper ran a flattering feature on the group headlined "Ukiah Welcomes New Citizens to Community."

But the welcome was not universally warm. Ukiah's population numbered less than 10,000 and included few African Americans before the Temple moved in. Some black Temple members were turned away when they tried to rent apartments. During an outing to swim in Lake

Mendocino, local bigots baited the group, calling them "niggers" and "nigger lovers."

The harassment made the Hoosiers leery of outsiders and protective of their black members. It also made them feel persecuted, and therefore special; they were fighting for their dream of racial harmony.

Jones did his best to smooth the transition. With his education degree, he landed various teaching jobs to support his family, and spent his free time driving from one member's home to the next, listening to their complaints, giving advice, reassuring them that their noble cause would eventually triumph. He held services in borrowed quarters or even on front lawns, keeping members loyal with his boundless concern and energy.

Hyacinth's faith in a better place only grew in Ukiah. She and Zippy found a two-bedroom apartment and became close to a white, middle-aged couple they'd known only superficially in Indianapolis. Mary and Alfred Tschetter would stop by the sisters' home for supper, to watch television, or simply relax on the porch and catch the evening breeze. Hy and Zippy had never spent so much time in a companionable setting with white folks, and they marveled at the ease of it. After such an evening, Hy found herself forgetting about the color of her skin altogether until she looked in a mirror. Jones's good works reverberated in each of his followers.

After the harassment at Lake Mendocino, Temple members built a pool in Jones's front yard at 7700 East Road in Redwood Valley so they could swim in peace. Youngsters learned the backstroke in it; the elderly stayed limber in it. The experience of working together to build the pool was so empowering that the group decided to build their own church as well, directly over the pool. They hired a construction company for the heavy labor, but members cheerfully pitched in to complete smaller jobs, such as installing windows and tile. Inside the simple redwood building, the space was equally divided between the pool and a large open area for meetings; members shared a pride of ownership as they attended services. They'd built a sanctuary of their own making.

The bonds uniting them grew stronger as they became an ad hoc family, sharing encouragement and sustenance, pitching in to paint or remodel each other's homes. As Jones promised, Hy and Zip were able to open a care home. They purchased a ranch house in Redwood Valley, ten miles north of Ukiah, and took in patients discharged from the local mental hospital as part of Governor Ronald Reagan's deinstitutionalization drive. The state paid them $270 per month per patient, and Zip learned to drive so she could ferry their charges to medical appointments.

In their spare time, they folded and stamped bulletins and letters soliciting donations for Jones's ministry, and baked pastries to sell at a table in the church parking lot after services. Zip's original cranberry sauce cake, a cranberry-and-nut cake smothered in pink icing, always sold out early, despite the six-dollar price tag. Across from their home was a pear orchard and, after the harvest, the owner let the sisters comb the trees for leftovers. They spent many pleasant afternoons peeling and slicing the fragrant white fruit at church canning parties, putting up hundreds of quarts of pears, peaches, corn, zucchini, and string beans culled from backyard gardens. The jarred preserves were distributed among church care homes and the community's poor.

The Temple was now the center of their lives.

The group's influence and numbers kept expanding. The editor of the *Ukiah Journal*, George Hunter, became a friend, as did county supervisor Al Barbero and Sheriff Reno Bartolomie, who noticed that local hoodlums seemed magically transformed after joining the Temple ranks. To reinforce this good will, Jones donated money to the sheriff's department to buy much-needed equipment.

Meanwhile, Jones's message was quietly evolving. The more he studied the Bible, the more he noticed the number of errors, contradictions, and inconsistencies it contained. More alarming were the loathsome acts God condoned: slavery, mass murder, rape, and an astounding amount of violence. He began to doubt the authenticity of the Bible—and of God himself.

Jones spelled out his concerns in a self-published booklet titled "The Letter Killeth, but the Spirit Giveth LIFE," a phrase plucked from 2 Corinthians 3:6: "Who also hath made us able ministers of the new testament; not of the letter, but of the spirit: for the letter killeth, but the spirit giveth life." Jones interpreted the verse this way: "The Bible kills, but love makes alive. People are not saved through the reading of the Bible."

The tract would become the cornerstone of his ministry, and was handed out to visiting worshippers to explain Jones's creed. Later, he'd use stronger words: The Bible murders.

The booklet, which the Federal Bureau of Investigation found in Jonestown after the massacre, represents important early evidence of Jones's break with Christianity. He didn't dismiss the Bible completely, but used it to legitimize his paranormal power: "There is a prophet in our day who unquestioningly proves that he is <u>sent</u> from God," he wrote in "The Letter Killeth." "He has all the gifts of the spirit as given in the Bible: Word of wisdom, word of knowledge, faith, gifts of healing, working of miracles, prophecy, discerning of spirits, tongues and interpretation of tongues (See 1 Corinthians 12:8–10). We must have a prophet who is living the Christ life to direct us in this hour."

That prophet, of course, was Jim Jones. Some members of his congregation balked at this bold claim. Others saw a certain logic in it: You can twist almost any verse of the Bible to your meaning. Over the years, Jones would continue to chip away at his followers' faith until they had nothing left to believe in but Jim Jones.

Once the church's growth peaked in Mendocino County, the Temple bought thirteen used Greyhound buses, and Jones took his show on the road in a much-hyped miracle crusade. The Temple public relations crew placed ads in newspapers across the country advertising "the greatest healing ministry through Christ on earth today." Jones filled local auditoriums in Los Angeles, Philadelphia, Chicago, Detroit, Cleveland, and Brooklyn, New York. He'd astound locals with his healings and apparent clairvoyance, then invite them to come home with him: "I've got acres of fields of greens and potatoes and strawberries and pears and tomatoes, I've got grapes, I've got the harvest on a hundred hills," he'd boast. "Take me up on my offer and come to California . . . come out there in those beautiful fields of Eden. See what we're doing out there for freedom. And I'll tell you, you won't want to come back."

The raven-haired preacher vowed to care for them, deeply, individually. All they had to do was get on the bus.

Many did. Usually these new proselytes were park-bench winos, prostitutes, junkies, and impoverished single mothers—those who most needed the protective overcoat of a church. "The dregs of fascist USA," Jones called them.

In bucolic Redwood Valley, Temple members put a roof over their heads and food in their mouths. They cured heroin addicts, sitting with them around the clock until their tremors and vomiting subsided. They helped single mothers pay for schoolbooks and clothes. They brought destitute seniors to doctors for checkups. They offered the newcomers a place in their home, a cup of warmth, a listening ear. Jones's ministry was based on kindness. In return, the new acolytes pledged him their unswerving loyalty.

Some locals resented the large influx of urban outsiders, most of whom were black. Malicious rumors spread about strange goings-on at the church and in the growing number of Temple communes around town. By 1970, however, it became clear that Peoples Temple, and Jones's ambition, had outgrown Redwood Valley, and Jones started holding services in a high school auditorium in San Francisco's Fillmore District. The move was a huge jump for a man who'd started out as a sidewalk screecher in a minor Indiana town.

And so, one Sunday morning about a year later, as churchgoers streamed into Benjamin Franklin Junior High, a wayward teenager named Stanley Clayton joined them, eager to hear the preacher that had set the black community abuzz. Dressed in a Sears wide-lapel three-piece suit and accompanied by his foster mother, the seventeen-year-old had arrived on a Temple bus that regularly transported worshippers from the East Bay to San Francisco. As he wove through the crowd looking for a seat, he was surprised to see so many people in jeans and T-shirts. Where he came from, folks "suited down" for church.

The service began with a rousing performance by the Temple's integrated choir, the women dressed in light blue robes, the men in matching blue shirts and black pants. Blacks and whites, side by side, singing gospel standards. This was as much a revelation to Stanley Clayton on that day as it had been to Hy and Zippy fifteen years earlier. It was that first exposure to the Temple, that first insight into how the world could and should be, that would sustain Stanley for years to come.

If you could sum up the seventeen-year-old Stanley with one word it would be *rage*. With his dark-as-ebony skin, he drew attention wherever he went, usually of the unwelcome sort. Despite the "black is beautiful" ethos of the day, for Stanley, a white complexion was the standard for all things good—intelligence, attractiveness, power—and he was acutely aware of his place at the opposite end of the color spectrum. His skin was so dark that even other African American kids teased him. "Smudge," they called him, or "Bosco," after the chocolate syrup.

Stanley seemed doomed to a life of hard luck from the moment his mother, an alcoholic who had seven kids with seven different fathers, pushed him into the world. The family lived in the slums of West Oakland, where they subsisted on welfare and the mother's meager factory wages. Any extra money went to replenishing her booze cabinet, not the refrigerator. While Stanley's little brother cried from hunger, Stanley, when he was old enough, helped himself to the neighborhood grocery store, pushing around a shopping cart while slyly eating a package of bologna. He went to school in rags, and spent evenings closed in a back bedroom with his siblings, watching television and trying to avoid drunken strangers in the hall. His home was a renowned party pad, and after too many bottles of Night Train wine, with its 17.5 percent alcohol content, fights invariably broke out. The boyfriends beat up his mother, and if he or his siblings tried to intervene, the boyfriends beat them as well.

The rage spilled over. When he was nine, he hit a girl in his class for calling him "darkie," and was sent to juvenile hall. It was the first entry in what would become an extensive rap sheet of crimes committed in his fury of have-notness.

By the time he started middle school, he was running a black market in coffee and cigarettes. He'd steal the merchandise from local stores, then sell it to his neighbors. It kept him in food and clothes until he tried to rob a shop in an upscale Berkeley neighborhood. The suspicious owner saw him slip a can of Folgers beneath his jacket, and locked the front door before calling the police. When Stanley found he was trapped inside, he went nuts. He kicked the door and hit the woman, and when the officers arrived, he swung at them, too. A court convicted him of assault and battery as well as petty theft, and sentenced him to a year at the California Youth Authority prison in Stockton. He was twelve years old.

There were thousands of kids like Stanley Clayton in the East Bay. In Oakland, there was a hair-trigger relationship between the large, destitute black population and the predominantly white police force. Shoot first, ask questions later, seemed to be the Oakland PD's motto. The Black Panther Party was born from this brutal atmosphere, pledging to defend the community from police violence. And it happened that Stanley's foster mom was the aunt of Huey Newton, cofounder of the Black Panthers.

Whenever the dashing, eloquent Newton stopped by Miss Jessie's for a visit, Stanley hung at his elbow, absorbing his every word. The gospel of the Panther leader was radically different from Miss Jessie's. Rather than abiding injustice in hopes of some distant heavenly reward, Brother Newton called on black men to arm themselves against racist oppression. When Stanley was released from the youth authority, he came home to find Newton and his comrades tailing squad cars with loaded shotguns, policing the police. Black is powerful was the message Newton broadcast to the brothers on the block.

Peoples Temple seemed a happy medium between Newton's militancy and Miss Jessie's pray-about-it passivity. On that first Sunday, Stanley was wooed by the choir, wowed by Jones's healings, and won over by his call to create a brotherhood based on equality and respect.

Being surrounded by that huge, musical, magical, integrated fellowship was like being engulfed in a giant embrace. It was everything Stanley longed for. He felt caught up in greatness, freed.

"I want to be part of this," he told his foster mother.

A few months later, after he turned eighteen, he moved to Ukiah to be closer to Jim Jones.

CHAPTER 4

"DAD"

S ome people link Jones's self-aggrandizement to a trip he took in the mid-1950s to meet Father Divine. He was just your average "holy ghost man," they say, until he went to Philadelphia and met a black preacher who claimed to be the reincarnation of Jesus Christ.

Father Divine's charisma and message of racial and gender equality drew thousands of followers. He controlled virtually every aspect of their lives, requiring them to remain celibate, live communally, and sign their wages and property over to him. They hung his photograph on the walls of their homes and called him Father.

After his first visit to Philadelphia, Jones wrote that he felt revulsion upon hearing Divine's followers call him Father, and nauseated by their leader worship.

But envy lurked below his aversion: Over the years, Jones would copy most of Divine's ideas and techniques. He'd even call his Guyanese agricultural project The Promised Land, the name Divine used for his communal farm in upstate New York. Jones's self-proclaimed "miracle crusade" would stop at Divine's Peace Mission repeatedly over the next decades as he tried, sometimes successfully, to steal sheep from his rival's flock.

In the spring of 1973, Jones began a sermon in San Francisco with these words: "For some unexplained set of reasons, I happen to be selected to be God." He described the miracles he'd supposedly performed around the world, and even claimed he could raise the dead. "You may not believe, but I'll tell you, there was never a miracle done in the world, 'less I did it.

I am God the Messiah," he said. He paused dramatically and stepped away from the pulpit to throw a Bible to the ground, then surveyed his shocked audience. "See that? I'm still alive," he gloated. Several newcomers walked out in protest. Others waited uneasily for Jones to finish formulating what would become his predominant message: God had done nothing to help humanity; Jim Jones had done everything.

At first, he merely extolled the Golden Rule of do unto others as you would have them do unto you, by emphasizing traditional church outreach: bringing casseroles to shut-ins, helping frazzled new mothers, organizing field trips for urban youth. He combined the Apostle Paul's mandate for Christians to pool their resources and Karl Marx's directive "From each according to his ability, to each according to his need," and called it *apostolic socialism*, or *divine socialism*.

During services, he championed his new religion by reading from newspapers. The world seemed to be imploding in the late 1960s and early 1970s, and his message struck a nerve. The headlines were saturated with death: Vietnam, nuclear war, murdered civil rights leaders and student protestors. Americans of every stripe were angry, insecure, afraid. Gone was the *Leave It to Beaver* complacency. The establishment fissured along with its enabler—mainstream religion—and people turned to alternative sources for guidance—including gurus, spiritualism, astrology, and self-help groups.

The time was ripe for Jim Jones. As he stood before his growing congregation in his baby-blue robe and slicked-back hair, he felt the crowd's adoring gaze radiating over him. As he spoke, they punctuated his sentences with "Hallelujah!" and "Yes, Lord!" It was more love and respect than he'd ever known. When he claimed to be their savior, many believed it. He'd saved them from the street, fed, clothed, sheltered, and empowered them. They worshipped him for it. He dangled hope in front of the despondent, and built a ministry around it.

They used to call him Jimba. Now they called him Father.

Despite his desire to convert people to divine socialism, most visitors still came to the Temple for the spectacle of Jones's healings. In Guyana, he'd tell top aides that he learned to perform miracles by studying itinerant preachers at tent revivals as a young man. His motivation was primarily financial; "I thought that there must be a way that you could do this for good, that you can get the crowd, get some money, and do some good with it," he said.

When he started doing his own so-called miracles, he initially did the grunge work himself, jotting down details of overheard conversations to use in discernments. "There's a woman here tonight who is sick with worry about her little girl . . ." he'd tell the crowd. Or "There is a man here whose right leg is lame due to a farming accident . . ." It was easy to fool people into thinking he was a clairvoyant. He was so secretive about the fraud that his own wife believed it. Later, he recruited a few confidants to perpetuate the deceit. Known as Jones's staff, some disguised themselves as invalids who rose from their wheelchairs and walked. Others dug through trash bins collecting personal data for his supposed revelations. They were crafty and brazen. One would pretend to be a pregnant woman and knock on a target's front door, desperate to use the bathroom. Inside, she'd take an inventory of the residence, including the photos on the living room wall, the drugs in the medicine cabinet, even the preferred brand of cat food, and pass the information along to Jones.

Over the years, the deceit grew more streamlined. In San Francisco, greeters would write down the names of visitors and pass the information along to staffers, who'd rush upstairs to call the person's home, acting as a pollster. The data from the subsequent survey they conducted was then brought to Jones, who'd read it from scraps of paper during the calling-out portion of the service. His sunglasses, which he rarely took off in public, served a key function: They hid his eyes while he read from his crib notes.

At the same time, he sought to inspire trust in visitors by using the crude language of the street and stating his economic status on signs hanging behind the pulpit: "Pastor Jones wears a used choir robe to cover his modest clothing. . . . His robe is not symbolic of any special glory or honor."

Few knew the darker side of his ministry: he started drugging people surreptitiously to "prove" his paranormal abilities. His aides who worked in hospitals stole tranquilizers for him; others feigned insomnia to get sleeping pills. Jones was especially anxious to obtain Methaqualone, better known by the brand name Quaalude, which was widely prescribed at the time as a hypnotic and sedative.

His staff slipped the drug to old women under the guise of offering them vitamin C. The potent sedative would disorient them or knock them out entirely, and when they came to, they'd find a cast on their leg and a concerned staff member telling them they'd fallen and broken their tibia. At the next service, Jones would cut off the cast with much fanfare, and command them to walk. The audience would go wild as they witnessed yet another of Father's "healings."

Jones also drugged people to punish them. He made troublemakers "drop dead" during services as a general warning not to defy him, then "resurrected" them as the drugs wore off. He warned a man caught cheating on his wife that he would feel the effects of "touching God" in his body. A short time later, as Jones ordered him to have his picture taken with the three women he was sleeping with, the man collapsed and was carried out of the sanctuary. "His blood pressure and pulse revealed he was dead," a witness later wrote. "Jim eventually went back to revive him. Anyone who doubted that he had died was urged to go back and look at him."

Another man mocked Jones's "miracle" of multiplying fried chicken at a potluck; he'd seen another member drive up with buckets stamped KFC. That man was given a slice of poisoned cake, and the ensuing diarrhea and vomiting brought him to his knees. Still weak, he was led to the front of the church to apologize for questioning Jones's powers.

At the same time that he was privately toying with his followers' health and well-being, Jones's church swelled into a movement. As the number of Temple members rose into the thousands, he formed a governing board called the planning commission, comprised of his one hundred most faithful followers.

His energy seemed boundless. He opened a satellite church in Los Angeles, and every other weekend led a bus caravan of members on a six-hour drive south to preach there. Every Wednesday, he chaired a disciplinary meeting. In between, he hobnobbed with politicians, managed church business, and counseled individual members. He could preach for hours and not flag. He boasted that he only needed a few hours of sleep a night, so dedicated was he to the cause, and demanded the same of his top aides.

While his assistants swilled coffee or chomped on hot peppers to stay awake, Jones availed himself of stronger stuff: Dextroamphetamine, sold on the street as *dexies*. An associate pastor, David Wise, who was curious about Jones's supernatural energy, discovered a prescription bottle for the drug in Jones's toiletry bag. Wise was furious: Jones berated his aides for not keeping up with him, but he was secretly hooked on speed. Dextroamphetamine is prescribed to treat attention deficit disorders, and while the drug does enhance users' focus and alertness, prolonged and heavy consumption can make the user paranoid—which is exactly what happened to Jim Jones.

He began warning his Redwood Valley congregation that unnamed enemies were "after" him and on a Sunday afternoon in the summer of 1972, his words seemingly came true. After a potluck in the church parking lot, as folks milled about socializing and a group of teenage boys played basketball, shots rang out. Jones fell, clutching his chest as a red stain spread across his gold shirt. Women screamed. His aides rushed him to the parsonage. A half hour later, the Temple leader strode back into the sunshine. Miracle of miracles, Father healed himself.

"Jim was shot but they couldn't kill him!" people cried.

The incident served as "proof" of his godhood, as well as "verification" that his life was in jeopardy. In truth, Jones had staged the whole thing. Outspoken progressives were being gunned down across America: Malcolm X, Medgar Evers, Martin Luther King, Jr., the Kennedy brothers. To be assassinated was to be important, and Jim Jones longed, more than anything, to be important.

The shirt he was wearing was displayed in the sanctuary so everyone could marvel at the bullet hole. Jones told his congregation that he'd "neutralized" the bullet, and then he made an ominous statement: "Lenin died with a bullet in his body, and someday, so will I."

One can only imagine the cynicism necessary to plan such a drama. Which aides did he trust enough to help him pull it off? What did he use for the fake blood? How long would he wait, while his followers suffered, before miraculously reappearing? How would he explain the absence of a bullet?

Jones had a history of staging such attacks. Once, while visiting friends in Indiana, Jones was alone in a room when a rock shattered the window. As the family ran in, he shouted that racists were trying to get him. But they discovered the rock had been thrown from inside the room; the glass lay below in the yard. Jones vehemently denied breaking the window himself, and his wife, Marceline, backed him up, costing her the friendship.

In California, the Temple and its leader were supposedly attacked on a regular basis: Molotov cocktails were thrown at Temple properties, dead animals flung into yards, glass shards hidden in Jones's food. In one bizarre instance, he announced during a service that a hypodermic needle filled with poison had been concealed in his underwear. He wondered aloud whether he should wear a helmet to protect his head from snipers. In August 1973, the new San Francisco church was gutted by arson. Jones, who arrived at the scene while the building was still ablaze, told investigators that he intuited something was wrong. As "luck" had it, his staff had moved important files to Redwood Valley the weekend before. In March 1974, a security guard found an alleged bomb underneath the fuel tank of Jones's bus, number seven. The Temple leader removed the device himself, before anyone else could get a close look at it.

These staged attacks helped Jones close ranks. By creating a siege mentality, he spread the message that their movement was in danger, and that it was time to forget petty differences and dedicate themselves fully to the cause—and to him. The phantom enemy ruse worked well to keep members in line; Jones would employ it to even greater effect in Jonestown.

Shortly after the bomb scare, the Temple issued a press release saying visitors would be checked as they entered the Sunday morning service. But they weren't merely checked, they were downright frisked. Women were subjected to a seventeen-step procedure by female guards, who ran their fingers through visitors' hair, felt along their underwear lines, and peeked inside their shoes. Babies were unwrapped, old women prodded. Rake combs, umbrellas, and other sharp objects were confiscated, as were cameras and tape recorders.

Coming to Jim Jones's church was now akin to entering a high-security prison.

CHAPTER 5

EDITH

O n February 5, 1976, a squat, middle-aged woman stood begging in San Francisco's Financial District. The city had awoken to an inch of rare snow, and on California Street, businessmen turned up the lapels of their overcoats and rushed between glass towers, servants to capitalism's amoral bidding.

Few of them noticed Edith Roller as she braced herself against the chill, timidly holding aloft a flyer for her church. With her outmoded cat's-eye glasses and dowdy clothes, she was easy to overlook.

Edith stood only a few blocks away from Bechtel, the nation's largest engineering and construction company, where she worked as a secretary. She felt awkward and somewhat embarrassed, and hoped none of her coworkers would see her panhandling, but Reverend Jones's orders were clear: The entire congregation was to pamphlet for the next six days to raise money for the mission in Guyana. Edith only had time to do so on her lunch break.

The leaflet Edith held was harder to ignore. On the cover was the photograph of a starving mother and baby in war-torn Biafra. As the woman gazed at the camera with fierce dignity, her child gripped the withered sack of her breast in both hands, trying to extract milk that had dried up long before. Below the image was a Bible verse: "For I was hungry and you gave me something to eat, I was thirsty and you gave me something to drink, I was a stranger and you invited me in, I needed clothes and you clothed me, I was sick and you looked after me, I was in prison and you came to visit me." Matthew 25, verses 35–36. Striking and confrontational, the flyer summed up the mission of Peoples Temple: to offer succor in a world where, as Jones repeatedly told his flock, "Two out of three babies go to bed hungry every night."

Out of the twenty-five well-fed passersby that Edith approached, only one stopped to drop a quarter into her palm. When the lunch crowds thinned, she turned her wrist to glance at her watch before stuffing the flyer back into her purse, feeling both dejected and eager to return to the warmth of her office. Tomorrow, she'd try a different spot.

An opinionated loner of sixty-one, Edith Frances Roller had a finely honed sense of justice. She was born in a Colorado coal town where she witnessed the struggle of miners, including her father, to obtain living wages and safe labor conditions. Her father died, after years of backbreaking work, from silicosis, a painful, incurable respiratory disease caused by inhaling silica dust in the mines.

She graduated from Colorado State Teacher's College with degrees in history and political science, and when World War II broke out, went to work in Greece for the United Nations Relief and Rehabilitation Administration, where she helped refugees displaced by the fighting. After the war, the Office of Strategic Services, the precursor to the CIA, hired her, deploying her in Asia.

When she returned to the States, eight years later, she settled in San Francisco, where she got an MA in creative writing from San Francisco State College in 1966. She stayed on at the school after she graduated to work as an academic secretary.

Her life was more or less placid—books, opera, quiet dinners with a good friend—until a student strike broke out at the college in 1968. At first, students protested the administration's collaboration with the Vietnam draft by providing records to the Selective Service, but their list of grievances grew. They demanded the creation of an Ethnic Studies Department, and the employment of more nonwhite teachers. The strike lasted a record five months. Every day as Edith walked across campus, she passed battalions of police in riot gear, ready to disperse the protesters by any means necessary. She saw police beat kids bloody with their batons and drag them, screaming, to police wagons. More than four hundred students were arrested. A rock shattered a window of the administration building where she worked. The violence rattled her. The plight of the striking students echoed all the other injustices she'd witnessed in her life; they seemed to be yet another dispensable minority. She rankled her bosses and coworkers by arguing vociferously on their behalf. One day, she found herself stranded in a hallway clogged with students holding a sit-in. As a photographer for the campus paper snapped a picture, she just stood there in a polka-dot dress, her shoulders slumped in mute sympathy. She'd worked for the college for seven years, but now felt like a cog in the wheel of oppression.

In July 1969, she decided to speak out publicly. She held a press conference to announce she was resigning in protest of the school's "outright fascist trends." Her coworkers scoffed when they heard about it—who cared what a lowly secretary had to say?—but Edith foresaw this reaction, and addressed it in the eleven-page press release she sent to local media. "I have already been informed what the acting president is to reply when asked about my statement. Two words: 'Edith who?'"

But reporters did come. And although the *San Francisco Chronicle* buried its brief mention of Edith Roller, the item caught the eye of Jim Jones. He told his aides to find her and invite her to his church.

Peoples Temple was a natural fit for Edith. Although she described herself as a "square, conservative old lady," she had the soul of a freedom fighter, and Jones recognized this. She longed for a way to foster social justice in the world, and the Temple provided it.

Jim Jones also enthralled her. On her third visit to the Temple, Jones called her onstage and clasped her hands, which were inflamed with arthritis, in his. "It will be all right," he said, peering into her eyes. And so it was. The stiffness that made her typing work an exercise in pain disappeared. Edith was bowled over by this apparent miracle and moved to Ukiah to be closer to Jones. She taught high school equivalency classes at the town's evening college, and an apostolic socialism class at the church, which Jones made mandatory for all Temple members living in Redwood Valley.

Edith Roller appeared to have found her calling.

The Temple's move to San Francisco in 1972 marked a parallel rise in power for Jim Jones. The new building at 1859 Geary Boulevard, once a Masonic Temple, was a three-story structure with ornate brickwork. It was flanked on one side by the former Fillmore auditorium, where legendary psychedelic rock stars such as Jimi Hendrix and Jefferson Airplane cut their teeth, and on the other by a Kentucky Fried Chicken.

With the move to the Fillmore, African Americans became the Temple's largest demographic, and Jones tapped into several conspiracy theories swirling through the black community to increase his draw.

One was the so-called King Alfred plan, which posited that the federal government would place blacks in internment camps during a national emergency, as was done with Japanese Americans during World War II. The plan was pure fiction, created by a novelist who photocopied portions of his manuscript and distributed them on a Manhattan subway, where they worked their way into popular hysteria. But Jones noted that fences being constructed around vacant lots in San Francisco were "proof" that the plan was underway, and instructed members to write hundreds of letters to Congress in protest. He also latched onto a scaremongering tract called "The Choice," which combined real incidents of government abuse with imagined future horrors to suggest the existence of a massive, systemic plan to exterminate African Americans.

Jones didn't need to resort to fiction; he could have drawn examples from real life. During a two-year period beginning in January 1968, for example, police killed twenty-eight Black Panthers in what the group said was a concerted effort to destroy them. And in 1972, a new horror came to light: Federal scientists in Tuskegee, Alabama, had allowed hundreds of poor black men to endure syphilis for forty years while they pretended to treat them, just so they could study the effects of the disease.

One of the most cherished narratives in the black church is that of the exodus, in which Moses led the enslaved Israelites out of Egypt to freedom. There are clear parallels between the Israelites and the Africans who came to America in chains. Jones appropriated the exodus narrative for himself, painting himself as a modern Moses who would save his people from the depredations of the US government.

He was preparing them for his ultimate goal, moving them to the "promised land" of Jonestown.

While Jones's miracle services attracted religious folks who believed in faith healing, mostly poor whites and blacks, his apostolic socialism appealed to anyone who was unhappy with the status quo. San Francisco has always been a haven for fugitives from the straitjacket of middle America. Hippies, queers, black militants, feminists, vegetarians, anarchists: Most everyone in the city felt passionate about something, and the Temple was a natural church for this counterculture. In 1974, Jones established his third California church in South Central Los Angeles and quickly filled it.

He called himself the "spokesman for the people." He was charismatic, intense, and warm when he needed to be, but just unpolished enough to be viewed as authentic. In his polyester leisure suits and thick comb-over, he came off as earnest, if a bit rustic. He initiated friendships with local progressive leaders, including American Indian activist Dennis Banks and radical feminist and Black Panther member Angela Davis. He trotted out his multiracial family for the cameras. His churches in San Francisco and Los Angeles were planted smack dab in the middle of the ghetto, where they became a mecca for the urban poor, offering free health care, child care, career counseling, drug rehabilitation, legal aid, and food. What wasn't to like? The veneer was spotless.

Soon, the politicians came calling. With a throng of followers who voted en bloc and were available, at a moment's notice, to canvass neighborhoods and fill rallies, aspiring public officeholders longed for Jones's blessing. In 1975, at the height of Jones's power in San Francisco, the Temple helped elect Mayor George Moscone, City Supervisor Harvey Milk, and District Attorney Joseph Freitas. Former members would later say Jones broke the law by bussing in out-of-district followers to cast their ballots for his favored San Francisco slate.

Moscone acknowledged his debt to the Temple in several conversations that were surreptitiously recorded by Jones's lieutenants, and showed his gratitude by giving several Temple members city jobs. He named Jones head of the San Francisco Housing Authority. Crucially, when the church was later accused of being involved in criminal activities, neither Moscone, Milk, nor Freitas would heed calls to investigate the charges.

At the same time that Jones was courting the city's power brokers, the Temple was becoming enshrouded in secrecy. With his popularity growing, Jones worried that the Temple's inner workings would be exposed. He began to bar the public from some services, and required members to carry identity cards. Guy Young, a white parole officer who'd attended the church in Redwood Valley in 1968, was shocked at the change when he returned five years later. He'd become disenchanted with the stodgy Presbyterian denomination of his youth and longed for a church that was more engaged with the times. Although he dismissed Jones's supposed powers as a tool to draw people into the cause, he was impressed with Jones's street-level ministry. During his first visit to the Geary Boulevard church, however, he was stunned. The gentle, all-embracing vibe that had drawn him to the community in Redwood Valley had been replaced by a suspicious militarism. He noted some of the Temple guards were carrying guns, and when he walked in, a group of women interrogated him: "Why are you here?" "How did you hear about the Temple?" "What do you think about Jim Jones?"

Young was a good friend and former housemate of Temple attorney Tim Stoen, who the women called over to vouch for him. Guy stayed, convinced the church's good works and prestige outweighed its strange secrecy, and he eventually became one of Jones's associate pastors.

He also collaborated with Temple attorneys to get members' jail sentences reduced by convincing court officials to release offenders to the Temple's care. One of the people Young sprung from jail was Stanley Clayton.

In Ukiah, Stanley had moved in with a white couple from the Temple and attended South Valley High continuation school. As he completed his high school degree, he was able to tap into a large pool of adults who were eager to proofread his term papers or walk him through quadratic equations. He'd fallen several grades behind due to dyslexia, an ear deformity that left him partially deaf, and his chaotic childhood. Temple counselors kept him on task; if he cut class or flunked a test, he would be called before the entire congregation to answer for himself.

The tough-love approach worked. When he received his diploma, Jones pressured him to stay in Redwood Valley, but Stanley politely declined. He was done with country living, done with watching the same two channels on television, done with listening to white-boy music on the radio. He wanted to go back to the East Bay. He wanted to show his mother his diploma and hear her say that she was proud of him.

But without the stabilizing effect of the church, Stanley soon found trouble. His mother barely glanced at him or his diploma. Local police arrested him for public intoxication and for breaking into a warehouse to steal a charity donation jar. In 1975, when he was twenty-three, Berkeley police caught him red-handed carrying a typewriter out of an elementary school. He was sentenced to three years in county jail.

Four months into his term, he was working on the yard crew picking up trash when his release was announced over the loudspeaker. He thought someone was trying to trick him and ignored it. Finally, a guard came over demanding to know what was wrong with him that he didn't want to leave.

Guy Young had intervened on Stanley's behalf and was waiting for him outside. He drove Stanley straight to 1859 Geary Boulevard in San Francisco, an hour away, and led him into a small room. A few minutes later, Jim Jones walked in.

"You don't have to stay if you don't want to," the Temple leader said.

"If you got me out of there, I'm staying," Stanley emphatically replied.

Jones laid down the rules: no cigarettes, booze, or drugs. Such vices were the bane of the black community, Jones lectured, and kept otherwise bright young men like Stanley mired in poverty and crime. He needed a clear mind to participate in the social revolution.

Stanley agreed to the terms, and joined the growing number of people living inside the Temple building. By night, he spread out a sleeping bag in the balcony, which was reserved for children during services; by day he cleaned the church. He showed his gratitude to Jones by keeping the place spic and span. He wanted Jones to be proud of him, and it worked. Jones named him head janitor.

The Temple upheld Stanley. He fell in love with a seventeen-year-old girl, Janice Johnson, who had a megawatt smile and kept him honest. For the first time in his life, he felt like he belonged.

Edith Roller did, too. Although not part of the planning commission, Edith was revered for her dedication and erudition; Jones flattered her by calling her *Professor* Roller. But her three sisters had reservations about the Temple. When the miracle crusade stopped in Detroit, her sister Dorothy tried to get into the service. Because she was a white, well-spoken older woman, she raised red flags. Although she gave "correct" answers to the political questions the greeters asked (she was an atheist who worked for Madalyn Murray O'Hair), they grew suspicious when she said, enigmatically, that she'd been in touch with "one of the Temple's principal enemies." She didn't elaborate, but it was clear she wasn't friendly to the cause. They refused to let her in. She stood by the door for eight hours before giving up.

The episode widened the rift between Edith and her sisters. They demanded to know what kind of church screened its visitors, and didn't buy it when Edith told them of Jones's assassination fears. After one testy phone call that ended with her sister Mabs hanging up on her, Edith summarized her convictions in a letter to her: "True love is doing something about the condition of minorities and other disadvantaged people." Jones recruited Edith to write for a short-lived magazine he launched to promote the church, and assigned her the lead article, introducing the reader to Jim Jones. As an intellectual and atheist, she couldn't relate to Jones's religious appeal, however, and portrayed him solely as a great socialist leader. Jones rejected the article as too political; he was still, in 1972, reluctant to openly advertise himself as a socialist, fearing it would turn potential converts away.

He encouraged her to find work at the Bechtel Corporation, the engineering services giant that was rumored to provide cover for the CIA. She quickly landed a job as a secretary. Among her bosses were George P. Shultz and Caspar Weinberger, who, respectively, would become President Reagan's secretary of state and secretary of defense. When Edith wasn't transcribing the men's speeches or straining to operate the primitive ATS computer that replaced her typewriter, she was copying internal memos for Jones, who liked to collect the private documents of influential people and companies for potential blackmail.

Risking her job was one of the many sacrifices Edith made for Jim Jones. She did her best to practice the self-denial he insisted was necessary to live a life of principle. For example, Jones said that true followers should be equally tolerant of hot and cold, pleasure and pain, and should treat everyone—friend or foe—equally. Edith obediently bathed in cold water and told the dentist to hold the novocaine. She signed her paychecks over to the Temple, so that the money could finance charity work; bought clothes at consignment stores; and, harkening to Jones's chronic pleas for money, even sold several prized personal items, including a statue from her travels in India and her late mother's bedspread.

When Jones warned the congregation that the government planned to round up blacks and intern them, she believed him. She knew from her history studies that governments had oppressed minorities throughout history, and she'd seen the wretched plight of the Jews in Europe with her own eyes.

Jones recognized Edith as a dedicated foot soldier, and in 1975, he asked her to keep a daily journal of her life in the church. This would not be a mere diary, he assured her: It would be the historical record of the Temple movement. She kept it for almost four years. Her entries, for the most part, were dry and reportorial: the time she woke, what she ate, highlights of the Temple services. She took notes by hand throughout the day that she periodically typed up and gave to Jones's aides for safekeeping.

She believed Jones possessed a remarkable gift of insight: Once, after a service, he grasped her hands in his and gazed into her eyes without saying a word. While others might have found this gesture unnerving, Edith interpreted it as Jones's acknowledgment of some problems she was having at work. She stood up during a service one Sunday to say that Jones reminded her of another great leader, Vladimir Lenin. She was reading Edmund Wilson's *To the Finland Station* at the time, which included a sympathetic portrait of the Russian leader. Jones was deeply flattered.

Nevertheless, when Jones pressured members to live communally as part of his divine socialism philosophy, she balked. She liked her solitude, and her cozy Victorian apartment near Golden Gate Park, where she enjoyed walking after work. In the evenings, she listened to opera on her radio, or read books of poetry or political theory. Crowds made her nervous; she could only take them in small doses during Temple services or bus trips.

But Temple aides kept pressuring Edith to move into a commune. The Temple leased apartments across San Francisco and Los Angeles for common dwellings, and even subdivided the upper floors of the Geary Street church into a warren of claustrophobic sleeping spaces. The Jones family lived in an apartment on the third floor.

Everyone was expected to move into a commune sooner or later. It was the first step toward the mass migration to Guyana—although members didn't know this at the time.

When a church secretary continued to press Edith to go communal, she told the woman to mark her file as "not ready." She had too much stress at work, she said, and no time to sell off her belongings.

But she knew she couldn't delay the move forever; after several years in the church, she'd learned it was folly to defy Jim Jones.

CHAPTER 6

TRAITORS

E ven in Indiana, Jones showed a pathological fear of abandonment. When a man named Earl Jackson stopped attending his services in Indianapolis, Jones sent him a fevered note: "I am going to speak sincerely and frankly! God sent you to the Peoples Temple and you must not release yourself! I know there are things about the *Message* that you may not see but it is *God* . . . you will be making a serious mistake if you leave our Temple that God has ordained and declared you to be a part of. Don't go out to see the proof of what I just said . . . Please hear my counsel which I give with a heart full of love for you!"

The jarring blend of affection and threat would become Jones's standard response to members who tried to part ways with him. The subtext is striking: If you leave me, bad things will happen to you.

He constantly devised new ways to bind people to him. Every church member older than eleven routinely signed the bottom of a blank piece of paper referred to as an "attendance" or "meditation" sheet. Anything could be typed over their signature: an incriminating statement, a false confession, a healing affidavit, a power of attorney. This was proof of their loyalty to the cause, they were told; the sheets would only be used if they turned against the church. Then, Jones pressed further. On Wednesday nights, during members-only meetings, his aides passed out papers and pens and told everyone to admit to imaginary crimes en masse: What would they do if someone harmed the cause? What would they do if someone hurt Father? They were encouraged to be explicit and violent.

39

When one of Jones's secretaries instructed the congregation to write a statement to the effect that they would kill anyone who harmed the movement, Guy Young balked. He carried a gun for his probation job, and if the statement was ever turned over to authorities, his threat would be taken very seriously. He decided to write *waste* instead of *kill*, but one of Jones's aides told him to be more specific. He refused. Jones was called over, and he asked Young to define *waste*. Young said it meant *kill*. They left it at that.

Jones was hiding more than the drugging of his congregants and his own growing addiction. In California, he shed Midwestern conventions and embraced the Golden State's emphasis on sensation. In 1968, while the hippies celebrated free love in the Haight-Ashbury, Jones embarked on an affair in Redwood Valley with a married congregant named Carolyn Layton. At the time, Marcie was in traction for chronic back pain. When she found out about the romance, she threatened to divorce him, but he turned their children against her, and vowed to prevent her from seeing them if she left him. This gave her pause. She knew how devious he was, and didn't doubt for a minute that he'd do it. His threat kept her in the church, playing the role of devoted wife, until the bitter end.

In line with his principles of divine socialism, and the burgeoning women's liberation movement, he denounced marriage and family as bourgeois inventions and initiated numerous, secret affairs with both male and female followers. "My love will not reach you if you put a piece of flesh between you and me," he told his congregation. He did his best to dismantle families by splitting them into different communes. He expected his followers to call him father and Marceline mother.

He impregnated several of his lovers. Carolyn Layton had a son with him in 1975; others he pressured to abort. Jones bragged about his dalliances in crude language to his long-time associates, and dismissed them to his inner circle as unimportant. He said he only had sex with members to help them "relate to the cause," and that it was a sacrifice he did not enjoy making. He only made it, however, with thin, small-breasted white women and handsome young men. The rank and file knew nothing of his predations; he kept up his image of ministerial rectitude for their benefit.

* * *

Congregations naturally defer to their leader because they believe he or she has their best interests in mind. This relationship lends itself to a lack of critical thinking in adherents, as well as a passive acceptance of the leader's decisions. So, when Jones decided that members should be physically punished for their trespasses, no one challenged him. At first, the Wednesday night "family meetings" in Redwood Valley were normal counseling sessions; members were called to account for bad behavior and gently rebuked. Jones gradually made them violent. Typically, the meetings began with Jones calling a member on stage to start the dressing down: "So-and-so is such a nice person, a really special man," he'd tell the assembly, "but what he did is unacceptable." Then the harangue would start. Audience members would take turns pointing out the person's transgressions: past, present, real, or suspected. An offhand quip, money withheld from the church, skipped meetings, a refusal to pamphlet: The slightest trespass could be perceived as waning dedication, and thus a cause for discipline. The verbal attacks became more virulent and menacing, until one day, Jones ordered the first member to be spanked with a belt. Once that line was crossed, beatings became de rigueur. Adults caught smoking or drinking were lined up and spanked en masse.

Children, however, bore the brunt of the abuse. As families were broken up and kids farmed out to different communes, parental authority weakened and discipline fell to church leaders. If, during a catharsis session, the children's parents were present, they were expected to whip their own kids to show their support for Jones's edicts. Likewise, their criticism of their child was supposed to be the harshest. If they balked, Jones accused them of disloyalty.

Sometime in 1972, the belt was replaced by a wooden plank dubbed the "board of education." Jones acted as judge and jury, dictating the number of blows, and a microphone was held to the child's mouth to amplify his or her cries. Often, a large black woman named Ruby Carroll wielded the board, and if the child couldn't or wouldn't stand still, two adults would hold the child in place. Sometimes, children would collapse after being battered and had to be carried offstage.

Jones's cruel streak did not end there. The youngest kids were subjected to special terror called the "blue-eyed monster." This consisted of leading them into a dark room where a creepy voice announced: "I am the blue-eyed monster and I am going to get you," before the paddles of an electroshock therapy machine were held to their chest, delivering a jolt of electricity.

As Jones sat high on the rostrum like King Solomon on his throne, meting out outrageous punishment for infractions such as stealing, lying, or cheating, Edith Roller duly noted his judgments in her journal:

John Gardener, 15: 120 whacks with the board of education for calling someone a "crippled bitch." "John screamed as he took 70 whacks; at that point Jim commuted his sentence."

Clarence Klingman, 12: seven rounds boxing Mark Sly, 15, for stealing. "Mark gave him some severe punches while Jack Beam stayed behind him with paddle to make him stand up. He kept saying he didn't feel well, had the flu . . . for complaining he was made to take several hits while being held."

Little Ronald Campbell, 3: "Even after being up all night with the toothbrush (scrubbing floors), he bit a little girl today. Jim assigned him to work all night. Jim had Dave Garrison bite him so that he knows what it feels like."

After being disciplined, the offender was required to say "Thank you, Father" into the microphone. The next week, Jones would tell the congregation that the member's behavior had improved, thereby justifying the discipline.

At a certain point, Jones decided no one could leave his church.

Those who did were called traitors or defectors and, in San Francisco, Jones ordered them to move five hundred miles away from the church and never speak ill of it, lest harm befall them. One family moved all the way to the East Coast, but not necessarily out of lingering respect for Jones's supposed powers. He held their false confessions over their heads.

"No one has a right to leave, and if you do, even if you come back, I'll never forget it," he told his congregation. He likened them to the spokes and hub of a wheel; each part was integral to the whole.

Not only were they not allowed to leave, they were not allowed to question. Jones grew furious if anyone challenged him, especially in public.

"We won't allow any dissidence," he stated on July 25, 1976. "We're interested in instilling respect and reverence for the center of this movement."

It was harder to quit the church after you went communal. Jones promised members lifetime care in exchange for their complete financial commitment. Members sold everything they had—homes, stocks, and jewelry—and gave the proceeds to the church before moving into a Temple apartment so they had nothing to fall back on if they left.

Still, some did dare leave, and they were endlessly harassed for doing so. Jones's aides cut words and letters from magazines and assembled them into threatening missives, then smeared the pages with poison oak. Temple attorney Tim Stoen reviewed threats to make sure they were vague enough not to break any laws: "We know where you live," read one. "We're watching you all the time, we know where you work, we know your home number, we know your trashy life, honkey. You drive your dead mama's car. Keep your ass clean and your mouth clamped up. No pigs." Jones's staff would leave the notes on defectors' porches in the middle of the night. They also called in threats from pay phones in outlying San Francisco neighborhoods, wearing gloves and terminating the conversation quickly so the call couldn't be traced. Other intimidation tactics included publishing a newspaper obituary in the defector's name or renting a hearse and letting it idle in front of the person's house.

Over the years, Jones's warnings became more dire: Leave and you will die. The day before Edith Roller begged on her lunch hour, Jones announced that a member who joined another church had fallen ill and died for doing so. Another woman who left had "just given herself the death sentence," he said on another occasion. On yet another, he claimed to see the ghost of a defector who'd been killed in a work accident sitting in the pews. "You cannot escape this movement!" he warned his congregation.

David Wise took his chance anyway. As an associate pastor in Los Angeles, he was privy to Jones's smoke and mirrors. The last straw came when Jones asked him to install security bars over the windows of the pastor's quarters in the LA Temple, then publicly chastised him for doing so, saying they were a fire hazard. He quit the post, but Temple henchmen found him and drove him to the San Francisco church for a confrontation with Jones. He managed to escape from the building, and was waiting for the bus when Jones's security men caught up to him again. When he refused to come with them to talk to Jones from a pay phone, they left and returned with a large group of backups. Wise slipped by them wearing a long-haired wig and a poncho. He went into hiding for twenty-five years.

The defection that angered Jones the most, however, was that of eight college students in 1973. The "Gang of Eight," as they came to be called, represented the Temple's best and brightest. In a letter they wrote explaining their decision to leave, they pointed out Jones' double standards: Jones had sex with his staff while everyone else was supposed to remain celibate and rechannel their sexual energy into the cause. Jones advocated racial equality, yet the church leadership was almost exclusively white. Jones claimed to be mounting a socialist revolution, yet, they alleged, 99.5 percent of the members knew nothing about socialism.

Their searing criticism infuriated Jones. No one had dared be so blunt with him before. And these weren't average members, but included the children of families who'd followed him from Indiana. And although they promised not to badmouth Peoples Temple, Jones worried that their defection would trigger others to follow suit.

Not long after the "Gang of Eight" left, Jones proposed a radical idea to his planning commission. Black Panther leader Huey Newton had recently published a memoir called *Revolutionary Suicide*, and Jones asked the commission if they'd be willing to kill themselves to keep the Temple from being discredited.

This was something completely different from Newton's conceit, which he explained in his book's introduction: "Revolutionary suicide does not mean that I and my comrades have a death wish; it means just the opposite. We have such a strong desire to live with hope and human dignity that existence without them is impossible. When reactionary forces crush us, we move against these forces, even at the risk of death." Newton didn't have far to look for examples of this coinage. The Oakland police gunned down an unarmed Panther member, Bobby Hutton, seventeen, on April 6, 1968, two days after Martin Luther King was killed. Police threw tear gas into the house where Hutton was staying, and when the teen emerged with his hands lifted in surrender, they shot him twelve times. Newton considered Hutton's death a "revolutionary suicide" because he was killed while he was involved in a movement to overthrow the white racist establishment.

But Jones twisted Newton's idea into something else entirely. He asked the commission members what they thought about jumping off the Golden Gate Bridge together. Such an extravagant act would generate news coverage for their cause, he explained. After a brief silence, Jack Beam, who had followed Jones from Indiana with his wife and children, leaped out of his chair. "Go ahead and kill yourself if you want, but leave the rest of us out of this!" he shouted. Emboldened by Beam's defiance, several others also told Jones they had no desire to kill themselves, cause or no cause.

But Jones wouldn't let go of the notion.

At a planning commission meeting held on New Year's Day, 1976, he treated the thirty-odd members present to a glass of wine. The Temple forbade alcohol consumption, but Jones said the wine was a token of his love, and passed out small cups of a purple liquid. He waited until everyone had drained their cup before stating that drink was actually poison. They would all be dead within an hour, he added. Some members thought he was just being theatrical, and sat stoically, waiting to see what Jones would say next. Patty Cartmell, a rotund Hoosier who assisted Jones with his healings, tried to run out, and was restrained by guards.

"Are there any other traitors in here who want to try to get to a doctor?" Jones asked the astonished group.

After a tense forty-five minutes passed, Jones admitted the drill was "only a test."

"I had my staff watching each of your faces to determine if you were indeed ready to die," Jones said. "I know now which of you can be trusted and which of you cannot." He chided Cartmell for clinging to life, insisting that it was a privilege to die for your beliefs. The drill forced them to do some deep thinking about their level of dedication, he explained.

Afterward, some of those present felt proud at being included in the hazing ritual, which Jones told them to keep secret. A few learned the hazing wasn't over yet: After the meeting, Jones called several aides aside to tell them he really was thinking about killing off the planning commission. Several commission members had defected, and he feared more would follow. By his reasoning, it was better for them to die than to "spread lies" about him. He was debating two options, he said: loading the entire commission onto Temple buses and driving them off the Golden Gate Bridge, or loading them onto a plane and having someone shoot the pilot.

He, of course, would live. He'd need to explain to the world why they had chosen to commit suicide. Although he hadn't yet decided on the reason he'd give for such a startling act, his list of possibilities included: to protest racism, to protest capitalism, or to protest people who bad-mouthed the Temple.

He pursued the suicide-by-plane idea and sent one of his regular paramours, a long-nosed twenty-one-year-old named Maria Katsaris, to flight school in Redwood Valley.

Jones told the congregation that the Temple needed pilots to ferry people and supplies to the agricultural mission in Guyana, but four people knew the true reason for her lessons: Jones, Katsaris, Carolyn Layton, and another top associate named Teri Buford. After Maria got her private pilot's license in July 1975, Guy Young went for a ride with her one bright, crisp morning, completely unaware of the dark undertones of the flight. Maria claimed that she was putting in hours toward her commercial pilot's license. Soon after, however, she abruptly dropped out of the flight school, telling her roommate that she didn't enjoy flying.

At that point, Jones had a grander plan in the works: Jonestown. He told members he was going to create a new society in the middle of the virgin jungle, a utopia that would be free of sexism, racism, elitism, and all other evil -isms. He referred to it as "the promised land" or "freedom land." He purchased a remote tract of land in Guyana and sent pioneers down to start clearing it in 1974. Over the next few years, they gave regular updates to the excited congregation over a ham-radio set, and their letters were eagerly passed around. They described the mission's water as "better than any water you ever tasted," the weather as "never too cold or too hot," and said they lived in a continual state of bliss where "women deliver babies with no pain whatsoever." All this was untrue, of course: Jones commanded the settlers to only relay upbeat news about the mission; he wanted to lure as many of his followers to Guyana as possible.

He had no desire to see his followers flourish in South America. He was already fantasizing about their deaths.

Would his people die for him if he asked them to? The question of how far he could push his followers had long fascinated Jones. After the massacre, a man who attended Jones's church in Indianapolis would tell the FBI an eerie story that paralleled Jonestown's final hours. During a routine meeting, Jones halted the proceeding to ask those present if they would lie down on the floor if he asked them to do so. There was a quizzical pause, and then a few people said, yes, they would. Jones asked them to do so. Some slid from their seats faster than others, but soon the entire group was stretched out on the ground. Jones remained seated, silently considering the bodies at his feet. After several seconds, he stated that he was no better than they were and slipped to the floor to lie among them.

Did Jones harbor a death wish for himself and his flock? If you paid close attention to his message, which Edith Roller did, a foreboding subtext starkly emerges:

"I love socialism," Jones told his congregation on September 6, 1975, "and I'd be willing to die to bring it about, but if I did, I'd take a thousand with me."

In February 1976, he stated: "The last orgasm I'd like to have is death, if I could take you all with me."

"A good socialist does not fear death," he said several months later. "It would be the greatest reward he could receive."

Edith didn't have a chance to discover this dark thread herself. She turned in her journal pages as quickly as she typed them up, and Jones interspersed his chilling statements among thousands of other words he uttered, about racial injustice, about peace, about feeding the hungry, where they were harder to find, and hear.

Reading through her journal in its entirety, however, it is clear that he was already scheming to kill his followers long before he cloistered them in Guayana. He made his most direct reference to his ghastly plan on May 9, 1976: "The day is coming when I'm going to issue an order that will shock you."

CHAPTER 7

EXODUS

After several years of resistance, Edith finally buckled and moved into a Temple commune. Her new apartment was located in the seedy Tenderloin district, at 1029 Geary Street, apartment 47, a mile from the church.

Her heart sank when she walked into it for the first time. Whereas her Haight apartment overlooked lush backyard gardens, the windows of her commune faced a narrow light well that separated her building from the shabby hotel next door. Across the street, Frenchy's Adult Superstore and a massage parlor advertised their services in garish neon. The neighborhood bars churned out drunks whose fistfights woke her up, and prostitutes teetered by on platform heels at noon.

She'd tried to negotiate the terms of her move. Not quite comprehending the nature of group living, she asked Temple secretaries if she could live in a commune alone, and when they told her that was impossible, she asked not to be paired with a chatty senior. They disregarded her request, moving her in with a talkative seventy-one-year-old black woman named Christine Bates, whom everyone simply called "Bates."

More unpleasant surprises were in the offing: The building's long, dark hallways reeked of urine, and cockroaches lurked beneath the furniture. And then there was the food. Edith was mindful of eating healthy fare; her diet consisted of fresh produce, whole grains, and tofu. The first meal she was served as a communard consisted of macaroni salad, a hot dog, and pudding. She noted her disappointment in her journal. On another day, residents were given bologna sandwiches for both lunch and dinner. Her complaints were met with shrugged shoulders. The budget was tight, she was told; others were grateful just to have a roof over their heads. There was no time for her petit bourgeois concerns.

She knew better than to press the issue: During her first month in the commune, Jones mentioned several instances of members who were harmed for disobeying him. One woman had a stroke because she questioned Jones's actions. Another was in a coma for refusing to move into a commune. And a man was killed a few hours after he defected.

Edith experienced a slew of stress-related problems after the move. One morning, a colleague noticed half her face was drooping; her doctor diagnosed Bell's Palsy. The paralysis disappeared after a few days, but was followed by an irritating twitch below her left eye. Next came a painful bout of hemorrhoids. In her distress, she looked at a photo of Jones that she kept on her living room table and called out his name; her discomfort receded, but flared up a few days later.

Edith missed her solitary evening strolls through Golden Gate Park, which stretched over forty-five emerald blocks through the west side of the city to end at the Pacific Ocean. Now, as she spent evenings typing up her handwritten notes at the kitchen table, Bates wanted to talk. The relationship quickly soured. When Bates interrupted her, Edith turned up the opera show on the radio, or simply ignored her. In retaliation, Bates took to slamming doors while Edith was asleep.

Like all Temple communards, Edith was given a monthly allowance of eight dollars. To afford what were now indulgences, like an ice cream cone, a cheap steak dinner, or a bottle of Emeraude perfume, she asked her sisters for money. One sent twenty-five dollars, the other, in what Edith took as a reproach, sent two one-dollar bills. Despite everything, Edith was still a firm believer in Jim Jones and his cause. Given her writing skills, she was often summoned to the church office to type public-relations materials, including op-eds and letters to the editor supporting the Temple, and she felt valued for her efforts.

Hyacinth Thrash and Zipporah Edwards lived one floor below Edith, in apartment 38. They shared their two-bedroom unit with the Mercers, a blind couple in their seventies who were living in Philadelphia when they heard Jones speak on a local radio station and boarded a bus to California to find him. Hy and Zip were as divided on their decision to move into a commune as they'd been on their decision to move out West. Hy didn't want to leave Redwood Valley; she enjoyed the peaceful vibe of the countryside and taking care of the women who lived in their care home. Several times she started to tell Jones she didn't want to move to San Francisco, but cut herself short. Noting her hesitation, Jones told her he'd bought some land in Redwood Valley for communal senior housing. The sisters would be attended by on-site medical staff as they aged; they wouldn't have to worry about a thing. Hy was swayed by his argument: The sisters had no children to look after them; their nieces and nephews lived far away and had families of their own. She certainly didn't want to spend her last days in a nursing home. Temple attorney Tim Stoen drew up the paperwork deeding their care home to the Temple and by the time she learned the commune was actually located in San Francisco, not Redwood Valley, it was too late to back out.

The deception was the last of many discouraging turns Hy had witnessed Jones take over the years. She had many quibbles with his ministry, chief among them his disrespect for the scriptures. It wasn't until she moved to San Francisco that Hyacinth heard Jones talk of throwing away the Bible. He said he didn't believe the stories she cherished of the virgin birth, Christ's resurrection, or Noah's ark. Hyacinth was shocked to hear this. She believed God was all-powerful, capable of anything.

She was also upset that Jones hadn't healed her leg. She began visiting an acupuncturist, and the sessions improved her gait, but Jones made her cancel them. Evidently, he didn't want her to think anyone else could help her. And yet, Sunday after Sunday, as he performed miracles on complete strangers, he passed her over. She sat near the front of the sanctuary with her cane resting against the pew, waiting for him to call out her name, but he never did, and every Sunday she limped out of the church trying to mask her hurt feelings.

Other things bothered her. Most of the congregation was now black, but the leadership remained white. A little schism opened inside her, a secret rebellion. When Jones told members that they should consider the Temple their sole family and to throw away photos of deceased relatives, she refused. She loved her parents too much to forget them. When Jones ordered everyone to pamphlet to raise money, Zip stood on a street corner jingling a donation cup but Hy excused herself; it hurt to put all her weight on her good leg for long periods. Jones tried to pressure her by showing her a photograph of a crippled girl begging from a car, but she stood firm. "Hyacinth will never make a revolutionary," he told her sister.

Zipporah was completely sold on Jones, to the point that Hy felt she couldn't discuss her misgivings with her anymore. Zip praised Jim, and Jim praised Zip. On the cross-country bus trips, Zip rode on Jones's bus, while Hy stayed behind to care for their boarders. One of Zip's jobs was to screen potential members to see if they'd be a good fit for the Temple. After returning home from a miracle crusade, she bubbled with adulation for Jones's supposed powers, and chided Hy when she said she missed their family in Indiana. Hy learned to bite her tongue. Once, when she questioned Jones's fairness on a matter, Zippy threatened to tell him, and Hy felt her blood run cold. She recalled one of her papa's favorite sayings: "Trust no live thing and walk careful 'round the dead." She wondered what her father would say of Jim Jones. She'd forfeited two homes, twenty years' worth of tithes, and now her Social Security income to him. She lived in a commune full of people who believed he was God. She felt increasingly alone.

While Hyacinth was entertaining private doubts about Jim Jones at 1029 Geary Street, one mile to the east, a young reporter at the *San Francisco Chronicle* was doing the same thing at 901 Mission Street. Marshall Kilduff's beat was City Hall, and he'd started to notice odd things at the Housing Authority meetings. Usually, the proceedings were tedious exercises in low-level bureaucracy. Tenants complained about landlords, contractors bid on maintenance projects, the commission reviewed Section 8 applicants. When Moscone named Jim Jones chairman of the authority in late 1976, the tenor of the meetings changed entirely. Reverend Jones swept through the door surrounded by an entourage: a coterie of white aides carrying paperwork, a group of imposing black male bodyguards, and a busload of senior citizens who filled the public seating area. As Jones sat on the dais wearing sunglasses, his guards—also wearing sunglasses—stood glowering behind him, while his aides crouched at his side, whispering and passing him notes. Meanwhile, the old folks erupted in applause whenever Jones spoke, sometimes delaying the proceedings for several minutes. The whole spectacle was absurd. A few months earlier, Kilduff had noticed the same weird display at a fundraiser for Jimmy Carter's presidential bid. While the candidate's wife, Rosalynn, drew only tepid applause, Jones received a thunderous ovation. Who was this man? Kilduff decided to sniff around.

He visited the Temple on a Sunday in January 1977, and received a canned tour: Here was the whirlpool for arthritic seniors, the day care for working parents, the kitchen which prepared free meals for low-income families, the legal-aid office that helped them navigate city services. He was shown a teen sleeping off a heroin overdose, a man getting physical therapy for a bum knee. A display case filled with plaques and commendations from the city board of supervisors, the state legislature, the National Association for the Advancement of Colored People, and other important groups. The only thing that appeared suspect to Kilduff was the entry hall decor of leopard-skin sofas and smoked mirrors, which made the place look more like a bordello than a house of God. When the worship service began, he was ushered to a front pew in the crowded auditorium, and was dismayed to see his editor, Steve Gavin, sitting there, along with another *Chronicle* reporter. His colleages weren't there in a professional capacity, but were attending the service with everyone else. Kilduff exchanged an awkward greeting with them.

Despite the polish, Kilduff had a hunch that something was amiss. The carefully integrated pews, the sound bites of his handlers: It all seemed a little too wonderful. When he pitched a story on Jones's political clout and the Temple's secretive nature to Gavin, his editor rejected it outright. The *Chronicle* had run several flattering stories on Peoples Temple, Gavin argued, and it would look schizophrenic to be aggressive now.

Undeterred, Kilduff approached a fledgling bimonthly magazine called *New West*, which was interested. But word got back to Jones about the piece, and his hackles went up. He convinced *New West* to cancel the assignment, saying it would jeopardize the church's outreach programs. Next, *San Francisco* magazine accepted the pitch, but as Kilduff was revising the article, the editor who accepted it left and the new editor killed it. The expose seemed destined for the dumpster, but then *New West* hired a new editor, Rosalie Wright, who agreed with Kilduff that something strange lurked behind the Temple façade, and encouraged Kilduff to dig deep.

The magazine sent a photographer to a housing authority meeting to take pictures of Jones and his entourage, and a few hours later, Wright was barraged with phone calls. They were friendly enough at first: Was she aware of all the good work Pastor Jones had done in the community? As the days passed the calls became more menacing, impugning Kilduff's credibility and demanding Wright cancel the story. In the following weeks, the magazine's offices, both in northern and southern California, were besieged by phone calls, sometimes more than fifty per day. Prominent businessmen, social activists and politicians, including Lieutenant Governor Mervyn Dymally, joined the refrain: "Don't criticize Jim Jones." Temple allies even pressured *New West*'s advertisers to stop buying space in the magazine.

Jones refused to let Kilduff interview him, saying he was too biased; he also denied having anything to do with the campaign to stop the article. The threatening calls and letters, one warning of "militant action" should the article be published, prompted Wright to move her family into a safe house. Kilduff also got his share of calls. Sometimes they'd be from people claiming Jones cured their drug addiction. Other times, in the middle of the night, they'd be from people who didn't say a word. He got the message anyway: They knew where he lived.

It wasn't the first time the Temple unleashed hellfire over an impending news story.

In October 1971, when Jones's miracle crusade stopped in his home state, *Indianapolis Star* reporter Brian Wells attended two services in one day. He noticed that the folks healed in the morning session bore an uncanny resemblance to those healed in the evening session. When he published this observation, Temple supporters inundated the *Star* with angry calls and letters, including a five-page missive from attorney Tim Stoen, demanding a retraction. It was a tactic the Temple would refine over the years: Write something negative about Jim Jones, prepare for an onslaught of outraged readers and menacing lawyers. The ploy was enough to intimidate the most seasoned newshound.

In 1972, a religion writer for the *San Francisco Examiner* picked up the mantle. In a series of four articles, Lester Kinsolving ridiculed Jones's claims that he could raise the dead, and questioned the Temple's business transactions. When the third installment appeared, a group of 150 Temple members picketed the sidewalk outside the paper from morning to night. Meanwhile, the editor working on the series was besieged by threatening phone calls and moved his family to a motel for good measure. When the Temple threatened to sue the paper for libel, it killed the last four articles of the series, which charged the group with welfare fraud and child abuse, and depicted Jones as a sex-obsessed fraud.

The *Examiner* was nervous for good reason: At the same time that Temple lawyers were pressuring it to drop the series on the church, it was being sued for libel by Synanon, another controversial local group that helped rehabilitated drug addicts—and it was losing. The Synanon lawsuit would end up costing the paper's publisher, Hearst, a record six hundred thousand dollars.

The press seemed to have backed off Jones's case, until Kilduff came along.

The impending story created such paranoia at 1859 Geary that Jones started rehearsing members as to the "correct" answers to reporters' questions, a practice that would become routine in Jonestown.

Jones himself called friendly *Chronicle* reporters and asked them if they knew what Kilduff was writing about or whom he'd interviewed. The Temple's PR man, Mike Prokes, spent hours working his Rolodex. Prokes was once a reporter for a Modesto television station; his boss sent him to Redwood Valley to do a follow-up on the Kinsolving series, but he was seduced by Jones's message and stayed.

The Temple's best efforts failed to derail Kilduff's *New West* piece. The story was too juicy, the reporting too solid. After an *Examiner* columnist wrote about Kilduff's travails placing the article, he started getting a different sort of phone call, from former Temple members who wanted to talk. At Kilduff's insistence, they bravely agreed to publish their names, and he corroborated their accounts with an extensive paper trail.

The article, which appeared on newsstands across the Bay Area on August 1, 1977, blew the cover off Jones's charade and set the city abuzz. It was more damning than Jones could have imagined.

"Inside Peoples Temple" began with these words: "Jim Jones is one of the state's most politically potent leaders. But who is he? And what's going on behind his church's locked doors?"

The defectors shared a similar tale: Jim Jones was once a loving preacher who wooed them with compassion, but he became a cruel and paranoid tyrant. Two men who once guarded Jones's "cancer bag" revealed the mechanics of his healings, including their instructions to eat the chicken gizzards, if necessary, to protect the hoax. A father described how his sixteen-year-old daughter was paddled so severely that her butt looked like hamburger. Yet another former member divulged how the church profited from operating care homes that received government subsidies. Still others spoke of Jones's constant demand for money, paychecks, homes, and jewelry.

The Temple denied everything. Temple aides burned compromising files, then tried to make the article disappear by buying entire stacks of *New West* from vendors. But the cat was out of the bag; other reporters started following the story and more defectors surfaced, triggering an avalanche of local and national news coverage. The media that once hailed Jim Jones as Gandhilike was now calling him a charlatan. Thousands of miles away, he fumed in his eponymous village.

Before the article appeared in print, Rosalie Wright had called Jones to read it to him. He left that same night for Guyana. At the settlement, he alternately sedated himself into indifference and cursed a blue streak over Jonestown's ham radio. One amateur radio operator who helped patch calls between the jungle outpost and San Francisco was so offended by his vulgar screed that he doubted Jones was the "bona fide minister" he said he was, he later told the FBI, and stopped relaying calls from Jonestown altogether.

Jones's powerful friends helped him mitigate the damage. His old friend California Lieutenant Governor Mervyn Dymally wrote the Guyanese prime minister to reassure him that Jones was an upstanding citizen, and the men he helped elect—Mayor Moscone, City Supervisor Harvey Milk, and District Attorney Joseph Freitas—rallied behind him as well, refusing to heed calls to investigate the Temple. Moscone told reporters that there was no proof of criminal activity, only allegations of wrongdoing.

On August 21, 1977, the Temple issued an official response to the growing media uproar. The press release began with a blanket denial of misconduct, then blamed the smear attacks on a "well-coordinated conspiracy," several years in the making, to destroy the church for its socialist beliefs.

While Jones paced in Guyana, Temple aides in San Francisco began a massive effort to bring his followers to him. The exodus was planned down to the last detail. A fleet of some seventy "special aides" departed the Temple well after midnight and drove to the communes, where they knocked on apartment doors and cheerfully inform the disoriented residents that Father had called them to the promised land. As the aides helped members pack, "coordinators" guarded the phones to prevent anyone from making calls, "reassurers" comforted those staying behind, and "troubleshooters" dealt with anyone who was hesitant to leave. They were told they could go to Jonestown another time, but they'd have to pay their own way. Although members were told they could visit the project for a few weeks or months and return home, this was clearly not the case from internal staff memos, which refer to the trip as being final for those taking it.

Once the communards were packed, they were driven to the Temple and loaded directly into buses, where Marceline Jones gave them a pep talk before their trip. A "freak-out table" was designated for those who made it to the Temple but then panicked or didn't want to leave behind pets. Aides promised their animals would be shipped down later and gently guided them toward the waiting buses.

To dispel suspicions of an evacuation, members left from different airports. Some departed from San Francisco, others from Oakland, others were bused to Miami.

The local press kept a close eye on the Geary Street headquarters, and noted the plywood shipping crates being nailed together in the back parking lot and the late-night departures of Temple buses. All signs pointed to a mass exodus, but the Temple decried this depiction as biased and sensationalistic reporting and stated the church was "absolutely not pulling out of San Francisco or California." San Francisco, nevertheless, felt the move in hundreds of empty classroom chairs and unpunched time cards, as entire communes were emptied in a matter of days. Members just vanished, without informing their relatives or settling their accounts. Collection notices piled up.

Fred Lewis, who was not a Temple member, returned home from his job as a butcher one evening to find his apartment stripped and his wife of seventeen years and his seven children missing. He later discovered that church staff had taken his furniture to sell in the Temple's secondhand store. His wife left him a mattress, but no goodbye note. At first, Lewis worried his family had been kidnapped. Upon learning the truth, he went to Geary Boulevard to demand an explanation, but no one answered the door.

In some cases, children were taken to Guyana by noncustodial parents, or without permission of their legal guardians.

Temple aides forged letters to members' relatives, which only raised more alarms. "I am still quite puzzled as to just why all of a sudden you gathered the kids up and went to (South America) on the spur of the moment without telling anyone," responded one member's brother. "This does not seem like the sister I know. I noticed you typed your letter, were you in the church office or something?"

Many of Jones's followers were thrilled to be going. Stanley Clayton certainly was one of them.

On August 13, 1977, he was buffing the wood floor in the Temple sanctuary when a counselor called to him.

"Boy, this is your lucky day!" Lee Ingram told him. "You're going to Guyana!"

Ingram told him that his girlfriend Janice was on her way down, too, before counting four twenty-dollar bills into Stanley's palm. He told him to buy some summer clothes; he was leaving that night.

Stanley bought new jeans and boots at J. C. Penney and Woolworth, then stopped by a liquor store. The allure of so much cash in his hands was irresistible. He got drunk, and in his inebriated state decided there was one person he must see before he left: his mother.

He took a bus to Berkeley, and knocked at her door wearing his new duds.

As always, she looked dismayed at the sight of him.

"I just wanted to tell you that you won't be seeing me no more," Stanley said.

"Where you going, boy?" she asked in a scornful voice.

"I'm going to South America."

"Boy, you ain't going nowhere!"

He tried to put his arms around her to hug her, but she squirmed away.

"Get outta here, talking crazy to me," she said.

Stanley wasn't surprised at her reaction; he'd told her many lies in the past. But this time, he was telling the truth. He was going to make something of himself, be part of something important.

When he returned to the Temple, everyone was in a panic looking for him. His plane was departing in an hour. A counselor sped him to the airport and marched him up to the security checkpoint before handing him his passport and ticket.

At JFK, Janice saw Stanley walking toward the boarding gate, and her face lit up. She squealed and ran to him, leaping into his arms.

"I told them I wasn't leaving without you!" she cried.

It turned out that Janice got all the way to New York before she balked. She refused to go to Jonestown without Stanley. She wanted them to experience every thing together.

CHAPTER 8

PIONEERS

I n July 1974, Jim Bogue boarded the *Cudjoe* in Miami and set sail for Guyana with fifteen other church members. Their designated captain was an Indiana native who was unlicensed, and had never before piloted anything as large as the sixty-eight-foot shrimp trawler. The ten-day journey was harrowing. The group tailed a homeward-bound Guyanese vessel across the Caribbean, and crowded into the wheelhouse when rough seas cracked the windshield and washed loose cargo overboard.

After registering in Georgetown, the Americans followed the country's coastline north, and crossed into Venezuelan waters before realizing they'd overshot the Waini River, their entry point to the jungle. By the time they navigated the river mouth, the tide had gone out, and the *Cudjoe's* rudder snapped on the bottom. They clamped it together as best they could, then waited for the water to rise high enough to carry the ninety-ton vessel onward.

Such fits and starts characterized the early days of Jonestown. What the pioneers lacked in skill, they made up for in dogged persistence.

The draw of that lonely outpost, some four thousand miles away from California, was different for everyone. Some wanted to escape the ghetto. Others wanted to be part of a bold social experiment. They were going to give a big thumbs-down to AmeriKKKa. Everyone they knew was going. They planned to volunteer at the mission for a few months. In the beginning, Temple members referred to the settlement as the promised land or freedom land. In the end, it would only be known as Jonestown, a place of misery and mass death.

Guyana seemed tailor-made for the Temple project. It was English speaking, socialist, and dark skinned, a rough reflection of the Temple membership. The former colony of British Guiana was liberated in 1966 and its first prime minister, a black man named Forbes Burnham, declared the newly christened Guyana a socialist state.

But while most Caribbean nations owed a large chunk of their national income to tourism, Guyana didn't have the natural resources that travelers demanded of such latitudes. It had the heat, but not the white beaches. By a cruel trick of nature, the Amazon's tremendous effluent flows north from Brazil, washing away Guyana's sand and dumping a thick layer of mud on its coast.

Under Burnham's reign, Guyana suffered worse problems than being snubbed by tourists: It didn't produce enough food. Large sectors of the population suffered from disease and malnutrition. One of Burnham's revolutionary ideas was a campaign he called, simply, "Grow More Food." It proposed that the country attain agricultural self-sufficiency by farming its vast hinterland, an area that comprised 75 percent of Guyana's landmass and was only accessible, for the most part, by boat or light aircraft. When the coastal dwellers balked at moving to the rain forest, Burnham extended the invitation internationally, and Peoples Temple accepted it.

The Burnham government offered the Temple 3,800 acres along its Venezuelan border, and in February 1976, the Temple signed a twenty-five-year lease at 25 cents per acre, roughly one thousand dollars per year to rent its earthly paradise. Burnham was eager to use the settlement as a model to convince his countrymen that farm cooperatives could be sustainable and profitable, and encouraged the group to hire locals who'd lost their jobs after the closure of a neighboring manganese mine.

But the government also had a slightly sinister reason for directing Jones to its rainy northwestern corner. Guyana and Venezuela were embroiled in a long-simmering territorial dispute, with Venezuela claiming more than half of Guyana's territory. A few years earlier, Venezuelan militants attacked a Guyanese border town, leaving six people dead. By placing a large community of Americans along its border, Guyanese officials hoped to deter future incursions, and intimated that the settlers could use any means necessary to protect themselves.

Jones appointed a loyal Indiana family, the Touchettes, to run the pioneering effort. Unlike most Temple families, Jones hadn't split up the Touchettes. Charlie and Joyce arrived in Guyana on the same boat as Jim Bogue, and oversaw the project's development with the help of their sons Albert and Mike, both in their early twenties. The settlers lived in a Port Kaituma boardinghouse and drove seven miles down a potholed road to the site each morning. They were afire with missionary zeal, determined to make their paradise a reality. One amateur agronomist insisted on collecting all the pits and seeds from every piece of produce the pioneers ate, and cultivated plants in jars. Others memorized pages of agricultural texts.

The task of razing the soaring jungle, with its massive hardwood trees and tangled undergrowth, was immense. The settlers hired a crew of local Amerindians, who, armed only with axes and cutlasses, cleared fifty acres of bush in three weeks.

After the pioneers spent a year laboring mostly by hand, a government ferry arrived in Port Kaituma in July 1975 bearing a much-anticipated shipment of a DC6 Caterpillar bulldozer, and shortly afterward, a backhoe. The enterprise then kicked into high gear, as the settlers widened the entrance to the property and razed more land. As the settlement grew, stretching out between giant walls of jungle, the pioneers started marking off spaces for the cottages and dormitories that would eventually house one thousand people.

Unlike other members, Jim Bogue's reasons for joining Peoples Temple were not lofty. A father's heartbreak drove him to Jim Jones.

In the summer of 1962, he took his family on a camping trip to a beach in Northern California. As dusk fell on the first night, Jim gathered his three oldest kids, his daughters Teena, Juanita, and Marilee, to watch the fishermen catch night smelt. Tommy, a few months shy of one, and his brother Jonathon, two, stayed behind with their mother, Edith.

Bogue and his daughters watched men haul nets of the eel-like fish from the thundering surf until the cold Pacific wind drove them back to the tent. It was only then that Jonathon's absence was noted. The toddler had simply wandered off, perhaps trying to catch up to his dad and big sisters. Edith assumed her husband had the boy, and he assumed the same of her. The beach was dark, the waves surging with the rising tide. Word of the missing child raced down the beach, and strangers ran over the sand shouting Jonathon's name, their flashlights raking the night. A few hours later, his tiny body washed ashore a few miles south of the campsite.

The devastating loss propelled Jim Bogue on a spiritual quest.

He'd been raised Mormon, but left the sect when he left his parents' home. He had no interest in pacing the streets for two years on the obligatory mission; he liked his smokes and beer. But Jonathon's death made him long for the same sense of cosmic order he'd had as a boy. He wanted to know what happened to the souls of children, and if there was any way he could see his beloved son again. He visited a clairvoyant, consulted a Buddhist priest, and devoured books on parapsychology, ESP, and paranormal activity.

He couldn't discuss his pursuit with Edith. Each of them blamed the other for their son's death, and this precluded all discussion of the tragedy. They'd had problems communicating long before Jonathon died. Edith was a quiet woman whom Jim found difficult to read, even after fourteen years of marriage and five children.

The pair had met when he was twenty-two, and she was fifteen. He owned a gas station in Fairfield, California, and she walked past it on her way to high school. In those days, he thought she was "as cute as a bug's ear." He was awkward with women, and was therefore surprised when she returned his smile. When their sidewalk flirtation became physical, Edith's mother drove them to Reno to get married. Edith bore her first child at seventeen. But she never settled into the marriage, and continued to flirt, and more, with other men. Jim heard about her escapades from his in-laws, and sometimes from the men themselves. He tried to excuse her behavior; she was just a child when they met, and he figured she felt robbed of her youth. He hoped she'd ease into domesticity, but the affairs continued. After Jonathon died, they retreated into separate corners to grieve and the chasm between them widened.

In the middle of Bogue's questing, he moved his family to Ukiah, California, to be closer to his parents. It was there that he heard about a preacher, just up the road, who claimed to be a seer.

And so, on a Sunday in February 1968, he drove his family thirteen minutes up Highway 101, past miles of denuded grape trellises, to

Redwood Valley to see if Jim Jones had the answers to his questions. As he entered the building where Jones was holding services, Bogue noticed that the crowd's adoration for the preacher was almost palpable. He watched closely as Jones called out private details about the people in the pews, and ordered a wheelchair-bound woman to rise and walk, then dance, up the aisles. He did indeed seem to possess some kind of extraordinary power. When Reverend Jones laid his hands on bent supplicants, they rose up with renewed hope, a hope and renewal Bogue wanted for himself.

At the urging of several members, the Bogues stayed for a potluck after the service. Jones sat down next to Bogue and told him of his dream of founding a community based on equality and love, where no one would be hungry, marginalized, or lonely. The pastor exuded serenity. In his warm brown eyes and boyish smile, Bogue found compassion. The family spent the better part of that Sunday at the church, together in a pleasant environment, and on the drive home, Jim Bogue felt a little less hollow inside. Perhaps this church represented the healing their family needed.

They returned the next Sunday, and the next, and were quickly drawn into Temple life. They attended picnics and dances, helped paint other members' homes and organize food drives. Their children played with Temple kids. Edith volunteered for secretarial work, and helped with the church's "telephone tree." The Temple helped the couple focus on something larger than themselves.

The Bogues didn't need Temple charity. They operated a care home for mentally disabled adults out of one side of their duplex, and Jim did occasional massage work—a family trade—on the side. Like other members, the Bogues agreed to donate 15 percent of their income to further Jones's ministry, and when Jones raised members' contributions to 25 percent, they didn't object. There was so much need in the world. Neither did they balk when Jones asked if they could house a couple of Temple members who were down on their luck.

But the glow faded for Jim Bogue after a few months. Reverend Jones had a doomsday obsession that didn't resonate with him. He'd learned that the primary reason why the church moved to California from the midwest was to avoid a nuclear attack. The attack never happened, and the whole thing sounded a bit absurd to him. And then there were the false affidavits.

He'd sat in a room with a large group of members as a church secretary told them to incriminate themselves on paper. The statements were merely a loyalty test, she said; they'd be filed away for safekeeping and only made public if a member tried to betray the cause. There'd been attempts on Father's life, she said, and he needed assurances that his followers were willing to put their reputations on the line to guarantee his safety.

Parents were told specifically to confess to molesting their children. Bogue blanched at this, but saw other parents that he respected write without hesitating. Still he paused, pen in hand. Most Temple members would have a moment like this at one point or another, a moment when they ignored what their gut instinct said was wrong or unfair and followed the crowd. Some members crossed that line and forgot about it. Others were nagged by a sense of wrongness. Jim Bogue dashed off a sentence claiming to have abused his three daughters and handed his paper to the secretary, eager to get rid of the repugnant words. His "confession" was collected with everyone else's and filed away in the church office, but it lingered in his mind like an insult.

When he told Edith he was quitting the church, she appeared to take the news calmly. But Edith was smitten with Jim Jones, and the first thing she did after her husband's announcement was to consult her pastor. Jones gave her detailed instructions on how to proceed.

The next afternoon, as Bogue refurbished a secondhand trailer that he'd bought for a family trip to see his brother in Alaska, a patrol car from the Mendocino County Sheriff's Department nosed up his driveway. A deputy walked over and handed him an eviction order and a separation petition. Stunned, he left to spend the night at his parents' house.

The next morning, he marched back into his house and told Edith he wasn't going anywhere. It was his home, too. She threatened to divorce him and take the kids unless he returned to Peoples Temple. She also let him know that, with Jones's encouragement, she'd drained their joint bank account and taken his name off the care-home license.

Her actions left Bogue penniless and homeless. He refused to leave the house. A few hours later, one of Jones's associate pastors, a thin black man named Archie Ijames, showed up. Ijames reminded Bogue about the statement he'd signed saying he molested his daughters. Bogue started to protest, but Ijames cut him off. The false confessions were meant for situations like these, where members tried to betray the church by leaving.

Bogue was numb with anger. When he called Jones to complain, the preacher was too busy to talk to him. Bogue was at a loss. Jones was esteemed in the community, friendly with local power brokers. Bogue's first job after moving to Ukiah was as a janitor at the courthouse, where he developed a healthy fear of authority. Who was he to defy Jim Jones?

Confronted with Jones's brazen interference in his private life, he felt like the country mouse: timid, feeble, and tongue-tied. He gave the situation more thought. Despite everything, he loved Edith. And what was church once a week, compared to losing his family, his home, and his financial security?

And so he did what he'd always done, he shut his mouth and gritted it out.

When Edith struck up a relationship with family friend and Temple member Harold Cordell, he pretended it wasn't happening. Harold Cordell was also married, a father of five kids. Bogue rebuilt Harold's electric stove when it broke and lent him money to buy a car. But a few months before he left for South America, Bogue returned from his second job working the late shift at the Masonite company as a machine operator, and found Harold sleeping on top of his bed, while Edith slept under the covers. Edith swore nothing untoward had happened. She gave him some drawn-out, convoluted reason that seemed perfectly logical to the two of them, and Bogue didn't know what to believe. As he turned on his heel, he briefly entertained the notion of shooting them both and stuffing their bodies into the septic tank in the backyard.

He tamped down these violent emotions. He'd trained himself, by then, not to do the normal thing. Since Jones forced him to rejoin his church, he'd signed more false statements and confessed to being a violent revolutionary who would kill for "the cause." He'd watched children, including his own, beaten, and struggled to override his human and paternal instincts to protect them. He'd transported food that was stolen from a San Francisco warehouse and distributed it to the church communes. He'd sunk deeper and deeper.

Bogue needed to believe that the scene on his marital bed was innocent. He considered Harold a good friend, but more importantly, Harold was

Jones's bus driver, and a planning commission member. He was in a position of power, Bogue was not.

So when Jones pulled Bogue aside several years later, during which time the church had slowly yet inexorably come to dominate his life, to ask him if he'd be willing to help establish the Temple's overseas mission, he immediately said yes. Jones flattered him, saying Bogue's inventiveness and experience working at a hay farm would make him an ideal pioneer.

He knew the appointment would make Edith proud; here was the man she most admired in the world choosing her husband for a crucial task. He knew he was expected to assent, but he also felt oddly honored that Jones asked him.

"Don't worry, Jim," Jones assured him. "As soon as you get settled in, I'll send Edith and the kids down to you."

Jim Bogue cast his hopes and dreams on the project. It represented, for him, a clean start for his family; a place where he'd regain his rightful place in the household. A place where his children would look up to him, and his wife would again cherish him. When he first arrived at the jungle plot, he thought of his wife and kids with each stroke of his cutlass, each chop of his garden hoe. They were his motivation as he labored in the searing equatorial heat and brushed away malarial mosquitoes. He was preparing a new home for his family. He imagined giving them a tour, his kids bubbling with excitement, Edith's heart defrosted at last as she saw the utopia he'd built her. Twenty years after they met, he was still inspired by her schoolgirl smile, so full of hidden Edens. He wanted her to feel the calloused pads on his hands, his bronzed and muscled arms. They were proof of his love.

He built Jonestown's first structure, a dock for offloading cargo from trucks, fashioning the floor from wooden poles and the walls from tree bark. It later became the banana shed. He laid the foundation for the kitchen using a garden hose as a level. He fixed the Caterpillar and the backhoe when they broke down and work came to a standstill. He solved the water problem: The barrels they used to collect rainwater runoff from the roofs were infested with mosquito larvae, so Jim went out with a posthole digger one morning and, after probing several depressions in the earth, struck the water table. He eventually dug three wells for the settlement, providing the entire community with fresh water for drinking and bathing.

The greatest challenge for Jim Bogue, who was quickly named farm manager, was the soil. The rain forest dirt surprised him; it was completely different than the abundant, soft loam in California. The topsoil was acidic and only a few inches thick; underneath lay impenetrable red clay. If he scooped up a handful in his fist, squeezed it and let it dry, it turned into a rock-hard ball. The United Nations classified the jungle soil as "non-productive."

Nevertheless, he threw himself at the challenge. He spent all day, every day, learning the rhythms of tropical agriculture from the natives, resorting to hand gestures when their broken English failed. The Amerindians used slash-and-burn agriculture. The ash from the burned vegetation added another layer of nutrients to the thin soil, but the method forced them to move their crop locations every few years as they depleted nutrients and weeds outpaced the harvest. Bogue hoped that by sweetening the soil with enough crushed seashell and wood ash, and by staying on top of the weeds, he could beat the odds and keep the Temple farm operating permanently.

The first crop he planted was a hundred acres of corn. Each of his crew of barefoot natives, including men, women, kids, and seniors, carried a stick, and would poke a hole in the ground, drop in a few kernels, then cover them with a swipe of the foot before walking a few paces and poking another hole. It took seventy-five workers several weeks to plant the field.

But as soon as the corn started silking, brown moths appeared. They fluttered about the emerald leaves like flecks of mud, each female depositing thousands of eggs on the green stigmas. When the larva hatched, they followed the silk into the ear, where they burrowed into the tender kernels. Pesticides couldn't penetrate the cornhusks, so the Guyanese crew walked the field picking off the worms by hand. They'd quickly fill two-gallon buckets with the writhing pests. Bogue lost half the crop, and learned a valuable lesson: The jungle, with its constant warmth and humidity, was the perfect petri dish for anything that swarmed, slithered, infested, or infected.

There were other missteps. The climate veered between droughts and downpours. During the wet season, monsoonlike rains washed away precious topsoil and seedlings, something the pioneers learned to counteract by plowing along the contour of the hills instead of up and down them and by protecting tender sprouts in a covered plant nursery. During the dry season, they formed bucket brigades to transport water from nearby creeks.

At first, they planted the same food they were used to eating: temperate crops such as carrots, celery, and asparagus. But these never grew longer than a man's pinkie; the soil chemistry simply wasn't right. They started over with local greens: starchy tubers such as eddoes, sweet potatoes, and cassava, legumes such as pigeon peas and cutlass beans, as well as bananas, pineapple, and citrus fruits. They learned to adapt and experiment, forever preoccupied with their urgent task: finding a way to feed the hundreds of Temple members who would join them in the promised land. The mission's success depended on their efforts. They planted thousands of orange trees, and these were just starting to bear fruit when the farm came to its violent end, four years later.

Despite all his hard work, Jim Bogue remained the low man on the totem pole. Everyone knew that he'd tried to leave the church, and the community had a long and unforgiving memory. Jones certainly never let anyone forget his trespass. As soon as he assembled the shortwave radio and got it working, for example, the Touchettes banned him from using it, saying the order came from Jones himself. In the evenings, he smoldered as he heard the Touchettes laughing with their children or the folks back home. To appease him, they allowed him two short calls back to California. Both left him disheartened. The connection was poor, Edith sounded aloof, and the Touchettes sat at his elbow listening in to make sure he didn't say anything negative about the project.

He was a born tinkerer, and his inventiveness was a boon to the settlement. He engineered a quicker method of sowing seeds by converting the farm's spring-tooth tiller, which was dragged behind the tractor to break up soil, into a planter. Using discarded boards, he built a platform on top of the tiller upon which four workers sat and dropped seeds into funnels made from bleach bottles connected to pieces of cut-up hose. The seeds dropped into the furrows made by the tiller's tines and were covered by a chain dragging behind the mechanism. Bogue's invention allowed the settlers to plant five acres in one day, a job that previously took forty workers four days to complete.

But even this breakthrough didn't raise his status.

Night after night, as he lay on a thin cot in a roomful of men in the Port Kaituma boardinghouse, he remembered Jones's promise of sending his family down to him. Weeks turned to months. Whenever he asked the Touchettes about it, the curt answer was always "soon." After a while, he stopped asking. Birthdays passed. Anniversaries passed. Christmas. New Year's. He stopped watching the calendar, forgot what day it was. He was caught in a time continuum; the same steam rose from the tangled vegetation each day, the same loneliness filled his heart each night. He tried to stop thinking about Edith, his daughters, about Tommy, and focused on his daily chores. The quicker the village was built, he led himself to believe, the quicker his family would be sent to him.

He withdrew emotionally, then physically, from the others, and began spending nights alone in Jonestown. Their sycophantic praise of Jones irritated him, and he worried his resentment would make his tongue slip. He invented excuses for his nightly absence: He had to guard the beans he was drying so animals wouldn't get into them. He needed to maintain the tractor that evening so it wouldn't stall production the next day. As dusk fell, he unrolled his sleeping bag on the dock he'd built and lit a wiki torch fashioned from a rag dipped in a jar of diesel oil to ward off the vampire bats. He felt unmoored. It was eerie to be alone in the dimming jungle as the howler monkeys started bellowing at each other across the clearing. It felt as if he were the only, the last, man on earth. The glittering tapestry of stars seemed closer than his family.

But his solitary idyll did not last long. The other settlers decided to join him, believing they'd finish the project faster by living on site. Jim watched in dismay as they carried their bedrolls into the newly built senior citizens' dormitory, and with resentment as the Touchettes moved into a private cottage with their two sons.

Two years passed.

On the day Tommy arrived at Jonestown, in July 1976, Jim Bogue's biggest concern was purple nutsedge and pigweed. The weeds produced seeds before the cultivated plants, thus assuring their survival, and now that Northern Guyana was in the middle of its first rainy season, the jungle was quickly reclaiming the fields. His Amerindian crew spent entire days bent over in the drizzle, plucking weeds by hand. As soon as they finished one plot, they doubled back to reweed another.

He heard the tractor laboring up the muddy road into Jonestown before he saw it, and reluctantly stopped working. Jones was expected. He came periodically to check on their progress and filmed videos to show the folks back home. Everyone but Bogue was aflush with excitement. As farm manager, it was his job to debrief their leader on food production, and as he walked down a pathway toward the central area in his rubber boots, he ticked over the points he wanted to make. He lined up beside the road with the others, cheering with them as the tractor lumbered into view. Jones climbed out of the trailer bed and strode down the line shaking hands, looking, with his trademark dark glasses, khaki shirt, and greased-back hair, like a third-world dictator. Bogue composed his face into flat lines, hoping Jones wouldn't detect his low-simmering anger. He could hardly bear to glance at the newcomers jumping down from the trailer behind Jones, but the bubble of hope he knew would only hurt him rose in his chest anyway.

His eyes were drawn to a slight figure balancing a duffle bag on his shoulder. A boy. A teenaged boy. He looked away at his weed-choked fields and felt the pull of interrupted work. He knew better. But the kid was staring at him, a wide grin spreading over his face. It was Tommy. His son. Filled out and grown some, a scraggle of fuzz on his upper lip. Fifteen now, almost a man. Two years! Two years Jones had stolen from them. He rushed forward to fill his arms with his boy, eyes streaming.

Jones and the others stood back and watched the father-son reunion in smug unison. They'd kept Tommy's arrival a secret from him, like so many other things. But it didn't matter now. His family was being returned to him.

CHAPTER 9

THE PROMISED LAND

Tommy had never seen his father cry before. They weren't a family of criers, especially not his dad, who seemed to be a pillar of stoicism. The embrace was awkward for Tommy; the others were looking at them and laughing. He pulled away before his dad was ready to let him go.

Things had been bad for Tommy back in California after his father left. He kept finding trouble. He missed his dad. His mother couldn't control him, so Temple counselors placed him in the care of an African American woman who beat him regularly for minor infractions, such as getting home from school fifteen minutes late. His dad spanked him in the usual fashion, on the butt with a belt, but this woman grabbed his wrist and beat him with a section of rubber hose as he ran in circles, leaving welts all over his body. When another church member saw his bruises, Tommy moved into the Geary Boulevard church.

There were people living in every nook and cranny of the upper floors. A counselor led Tommy to a windowless supply closet and opened the door. Inside, a red-haired kid was sprawled out on the floor in front of a tiny television, watching *Creature Features*. It was Tommy's favorite show. He plunked down next to the kid, introduced himself. The boy's name was Brian Davis. Brian noticed a saxophone among Tommy's stuff and said he played, too. They had more things in common: They were both fourteen, and both came from families that were ripped apart by Jim Jones. Brian's father was a member, but his mother defected. His two younger brothers lived with her in a suburb south of San Francisco; Brian and his dad crashed at the Temple.

Both boys, after moving into the church, became wards of the Temple. They rarely saw their families, except at church services. They became comrades in mischief. They cut classes at Presidio Junior High School and skateboarded down to Ocean Beach to smoke and gawk at girls. Together they could pretend to be normal teens. Together, they were free.

They got caught smoking weed and spent two nights working on their hands and knees, first picking lint off the sanctuary carpet, then scraping linoleum off the kitchen floor. It didn't matter that they had school the next day; counselors prodded them when they started to fall asleep. There were worse punishments: when Tommy failed a class, Jones sentenced him to fifty whacks with the board of education, and Brian got fifty whacks for refusing to attend services in Los Angeles. It was humiliating, as a macho-posturing teenager, to be spanked in front of the entire congregation, to have a whimper of pain escape your mouth and be amplified by the microphone. It was difficult to keep your voice from breaking when you said "Thank you, Father" afterward, and it hurt to sit down for days.

After Tommy broke a Temple rule by associating with outsiders—an aunt and uncle who lived in San Francisco—and bringing Brian with him, the boys were moved into separate rooms and forbidden to speak to each other.

It was the last straw for Tommy. On the bus ride home from the Los Angeles Temple the next weekend, he got off at the Buttonwillow rest stop and walked into the darkness, hiding until the fleet of Greyhounds pulled back onto Interstate 5. He climbed onto the bathroom roof. It was the middle of the night. He had no plan. He just wanted out. He camped up there for several days. A transportation worker felt sorry for him and brought him food, but the man also notified the cops. Tommy told the police his church group had left him behind. When the police returned him to his aunt and uncle, Tommy divulged everything: the beatings, the fear, the control. They were appalled. They called his mother, but she said Tommy was exaggerating and insisted he return to the church building. His relatives were powerless to intervene. At the Temple, he told Jones the same lie he fed the cops: He'd been left at the rest stop.

Jones was dubious, but gave him a choice: He could go live with the uncle he hardly knew in Alaska, or he could join his dad in Guyana. The answer was obvious.

In Jonestown, Tommy found the work hard, but not unbearable. His dad taught him agriculture and carpentry: He got so good at hammering that he could pound nails with either hand. He had no idea that his dad was so knowledgeable in so many areas and Tommy's admiration for him grew. He relished spending time alone with him, reestablishing their bond. He'd missed him more than he realized, and felt centered again in his presence. He knew his father loved him deeply, and strived to please him. He was only fifteen, and he was building a town. He felt proud of his accomplishments.

There was an Amerindian boy there about his age there named David George, whom the Touchettes took in because his mother was too destitute to care for him. In Tommy's free time, he and David palled around the jungle together. Sometimes they'd stalk bizarre creatures, such as the giant horned rhinoceros beetle that sounded like a helicopter as it flew through the underbrush, a giant toad that the locals called "mountain chicken," because it supposedly tasted like chicken, or fish that crawled out of the streams and lived on land. They regularly ran across anteaters, sloths, snakes, armadillos, monkeys, and parrots. It was like living in a zoo. One day Tommy saw a fat earthworm sticking out of a hole and started pulling on it; its body kept unspooling until it was nearly as long as he was.

Sometimes the boys raced each other through the bush as if they were on a giant obstacle course, ducking under vines, bounding over logs. At first, David, running barefoot, always beat Tommy. "Come on, Yankee boy!" he'd call over his shoulder. David was a practical joker, and liked to hide from Tommy, ducking behind the broad trunk of a rubber tree, or into a ravine. There'd be a disconcerting silence where, just moments earlier, their laughter rang. Tommy would scan the shadows yelling David's name, hoping the elusive twenty-foot-long green anaconda would not choose this moment to appear. The jungle was disorienting. The same jumbled greenery spread in every direction; there was no path out. Just as he started to feel desperate, David would pop out, calling, and the race would continue.

* * *

In the early days, there was a real sense of camaraderie in Jonestown. Everyone did their part to make it a success. The old people sorted rice and cleaned vegetables, the able-bodied planted, weeded, sawed, and hammered. Very few Jonestown residents had ever gotten down and dirty on a farm; many referred to rows of cultivated plants as "aisles." But these urbanites were soon baptized with mud and sweat into rural life. They had a vested interest in making the farm productive; its success was their success.

During the rainy season, their afternoon labors paused when dark clouds rolled over the clearing, trailing gray curtains of water. The workers dashed for cover, squealing with laughter. Calculating the time you needed to outrun the rain was a game. Fifteen minutes after the downpour began, the sun would blaze overhead again as steam rose from the fields. The air would be filled with the clean mineral scent of washed earth, and the settlers picked up their machetes and hoes and hammers in high spirits. They were proud of their handiwork. It was fascinating to watch a seed you'd patted into the dirt sprout up and stretch toward the sky, branch out and flower into fruit, into vegetables. Parents knew their efforts would feed their children. Older members felt useful again.

In the evenings, the settlers washed off the mud caking their bodies in the communal showers and gathered for dinner together, a multihued family, to discuss the day's trials and triumphs. When Tommy arrived, there were only two dozen people living in Jonestown. In the early days, residents ate well: eggs and biscuits with coffee for breakfast, sandwiches for lunch, fried chicken or fish with local greens for dinner. Cans of Pepsi were shipped up from Georgetown, and the kitchen handed out peanut butter fudge as treats.

After dinner, they socialized in the large, open pavilion at the settlement's center. The seniors visited with each other, fanned by the evening breeze, and played dominoes or cards. Parents doted on their children. Sometimes the group watched movies or television shows sent from the States. Other times teens brought out a boom box and blasted funk music, doing the electric boogaloo while a few spry seniors danced the jitterbug. Couples snuck off to have sex.

There was a real sense, before Jones arrived, that they were creating a new world. Jonestown was a clean slate for everyone. You could shed your old self and become someone better there.

Shortly before the *New West* scandal broke, the Temple released a progress report on Jonestown. Hundreds of acres of land were now cleared, the document boasted, and the sawmill operated around the clock churning out frames for cottages that the settlers erected at the rate of one a day. The furniture department built beds, cabinets, and cribs. Jonestown was already a functioning village, with a medical clinic and a long tent that served as the school.

But the community was a long way from being ready to feed the hundreds of Temple members who inundated it in the summer of 1977, a fact acknowledged in the progress report itself: "Realistically, we can now expect that the farm will become self-sufficient within three to five years." Citrus trees need five years to bear fruit. The pioneers had also failed to produce enough meat: The chickens and pigs kept dying, and Jim Bogue couldn't figure out why. In May 1977, there were roughly one hundred people living in Jonestown, but by that fall there'd be seven hundred, five times more than the land could support. As Bogue watched groups of newcomers arrive on the tractor-trailer, he wondered how he was going to feed them all.

True to his nature, Tommy managed to find trouble even in Jonestown's halcyon days. As he thrilled at some small trespass, he was perpetually optimistic that, *this* time, he'd get away it. He rarely did.

One day an Amerindian offered him a cigarette during a work break, and he didn't think twice about taking it. They were in freedom land, after all. The Wednesday night catharsis meetings were gone, the board of education was gone, Jones was gone. When he was caught, he argued that it would be rude, in the local culture, to turn down a cigarette that was offered in friendship. The Touchettes didn't buy it, and ordered Jim Bogue to punish his son. Bogue whipped his son with a bamboo switch as the assembled residents watched, his hand strong, his heart crushed.

The Amerindians showed Tommy how to make a simple press to extract sugar cane juice, and he built his own in the plant nursery. He didn't even think to hide it. He was more interested in the mechanics of the contraption than in the rum it produced. His explanation didn't wash with the Touchettes: The Temple forbade alcohol. Period. Again, he got swats.

Things got worse whenever Jones came for a visit. The adults grew tense and snippy, and inevitably, there'd be an angry meeting in the pavilion featuring Tommy Bogue front and center.

Jones invented new punishments for him. After eating a slice of watermelon, Tommy planted some of the seeds and grew them into fruit. He wanted something for himself, something he didn't have to share with the entire community. The plants were discovered and Jones called him before the assembly to denounce him as an elitist. Everything was shared in a socialist society, Jones lectured; there was no mine or "yours"; there was only ours. Jones called for a plate of chopped hot pepper—Guyana grew many fearsome varieties, with names like Tiger Teeth, Ball o' Fire, and Bullnose—and as his father sat in dejected helplessness, and others looked on with interest, ordered Tommy to start eating. Here was something the boy could consume all by himself, he joked sourly.

"Keep chewing until I say 'swallow,'" Jones commanded. The first piece wasn't so bad, but by the fifth, the capsaicin scorched Tommy's nasal passages, and knifed tears from his eyes. He tried to maintain his dignity, to be calm and stoic like his father, but everything in him wanted to spit out the pepper and yell "Hell, no!" But then what? The punishment for directly defying Jones would be much worse.

Fed up, he began building a cottage of his own outside the settlement. It would be half fort, half refuge. He had it all framed up when it was discovered. He was accused of stealing from the cooperative, and ordered to dismantle the structure piece by piece and carry it back to the compound as Jones's son, Stephan, guarded him. When one of the fifteen-foot poles slipped off Tommy's shoulders, Stephan, a martial arts aficionado, slugged him behind the ear hard enough to make him stagger.

The next morning, Tommy was handed a shovel and a pickaxe and told to dig, which he did for sixteen-hour days for the next several weeks. He dug two pits for outhouses, one nine by nine feet, the other thirteen by thirteen, working alone as the sun burnt his skin off in layers. Worse punishments were yet to come.

* * *

After Jones moved to Guyana permanently, Temple leaders kept the exodus apace by showing members idyllic films of the colony. Jones had lost his PR battle with the news media but was now waging a new one to lure his followers to Jonestown. After showing the home movies, Jones's aides told him which scenes the congregation responded most favorably to, and he directed Temple PR man Mike Prokes to use his Super 8 camera to shoot more of the same. The resulting images were spliced together to portray Jonestown as a land of plenty. The camera panned over fields of pineapple, cassava, banana, over cute pastel cottages, over pink hibiscus and purple bougainvillea blooming along the walkways. A dog rolling lazily in the grass. A pink-walled nursery with workers coddling babies. Children holding monkeys, an anteater, an armadillo. A teacher writing on a blackboard. Smiling seniors stretching to Motown on the lawn.

In one segment Jones gave a tour of the grounds. At the eight chicken coops, which Jones said housed "thousands and thousands" of chickens, he claimed, "We've lost no chickens whatsoever, a miracle of miracles." Both statements were lies.

Another long segment featured food: Close-ups of bacon being sliced, a heaping platter of barbecued ribs, sausages dangling from the smoke-house rafters. In the pantry, Jones opened a trunk containing packets of Kool-Aid, and a cheaper knockoff, Flavor-Aid. A big deal was made of a chicken dinner: The camera zoomed in on a woman eating a large piece of fried chicken as Prokes admonished her several times to move her hands so he can film the meat. He shifted to a table of self-conscious children before returning to the woman, now holding an even larger piece of chicken.

Prokes interviewed several residents about their new digs. Back in California, Edith Roller must have smiled when her former roommate, Christine Bates, appeared on the projection screen wearing a blue sunhat and standing next to a big bush of white flowers.

"Grandma Bates, how do you like it here?" Prokes asked.

"I love it, I love it better than any place I've been in my life, and I've been many a place. . . . I've never loved a place, and been so healthy, and been so free, in my life as I am now," she said in breathless enthusiasm.

"When I came to this place I'd had arthritis in my knees for twenty long years. I couldn't stoop. When I came here I was on a cane. And I threw my cane away the second day I came here. I can stoop, I can sit down with my legs under me now, and I don't have a pain in my body. I thank you, Jim!"

In her journal, Edith noted that the residents "were probably told to dress up, as many were in their best clothes and jewelry."

Jim Bogue appeared in a segment featuring a group of men dressed in matching orange and yellow dashikis who sat on rows of chairs facing Jones. "We're a happy family, yes, we are," the men sang, before recounting how Jones spared them from various construction mishaps.

"I really appreciate being here, being able to work under father's direction," Bogue said softly when he was passed the microphone. "And I'm waiting for the whole family to be here as soon as possible."

Newcomers arrived faster than the workers could house them. In California, Jones had indicated that each family would have its own home, and parents were dismayed to learn this wasn't true. Sometimes parents were allowed to sleep with their kids on the first night, but this was an exception. Babies slept in the nursery, and small children slept in Dorm 3. Sometimes couples were assigned to the same cottage, and sometimes they were split up. Lucky couples got lofts, which had double beds. Others slept in bunks, one over the other. Room assignments depended entirely on the whims of the powers that be, and residents had no say in the matter.

Eventually, fifty-two cottages were built in the general housing area, not nearly enough for private family residences. Each dwelling measured fifteen by thirty feet—about the size of a typical living room—and housed an average of twelve people. Some had up to nineteen. The cottages were crude, but they had electricity, windows, and a deck with an overhanging roof.

A daily schedule evolved. Each morning at six, guards walked around pounding the cottage walls with their fists and shouting as a wakeup call. Residents emerged onto the walkways in bathrobes and flip-flops and made their way to the communal toilets, which consisted of long benches with rows of holes cut into them. For many it was strange, and difficult, at first, to have a bowel movement with an audience. Eventually residents let go of their modesty, and even conversed with their neighbors as if it were the most natural thing in the world. The showers were also locker-room style, a row of spigots sprouting from the wall. There was only cold water, which although shocking at first spray, was not entirely unpleasant after a long day of heat.

Jones and his inner circle lived better, of course. Jones was the king of his town, and his sons were the princes. Jones's secluded, two-room cottage was built on a small hill and was twice as large as the other dwellings. He kept up the illusion of a happy marriage; but Marceline lived alone, and his top two concubines, Maria Katsaris and Carolyn Layton, took turns in his queen-sized bed. His cottage was furnished with a small refrigerator to store his Diet Pepsis, food, and drugs, and had both an air conditioner and a screened-in porch to keep out the heat and bugs.

After their arrival, many folks grumbled that Jonestown was not like the movies they'd been shown in San Francisco. The chicken dinners were sporadic at best, the local swimming hole was enjoyed by a privileged few. The astute ones kept their observations to themselves. They'd forfeited their passports and money for "safekeeping" upon their arrival. They couldn't call a relative to retrieve them or hail a cab or a bus. They were in the middle of a wilderness, 4,000 miles from home.

At the end of July 1977, a group of thirty-nine Temple members flew to Guyana in a single day. Among them was Edith Bogue. Jim hadn't seen his wife in three years. He rushed toward her, but drew back when he noticed the coolness in her face. She managed a brittle smile, then informed him that she was still involved with Harold Cordell. They'd lived as man and wife in California during his absence and planned to continue doing so in Jonestown. The news struck Jim like a kick in the chest. The happily-ever-after fantasy that fueled him for years evaporated, and the old fury burbled up.

Still, as he saw Edith standing in the heat and mud in her clean city clothes with her soft, pale skin, he pitied her. He was bruised by remorse when it came to her: about getting her pregnant when she was fifteen, about the death of their son Jonathon, about driving with her to meet Jim Jones that fateful Sunday, nine years earlier. He leaned toward her: "Be careful about those Touchettes," he whispered. "They'll carry everything you say right to the top." And so did Edith, who marched over to Jones to tattle on her estranged husband. That night, he was called before the community and berated for his insolence. There seemed to be no end to his bad dream.

CHAPTER 10

GEORGETOWN

I n Guyana, Jim Jones was no longer the kingmaker he'd been in San Francisco, where he won powerful alliances by offering politicians hundreds of foot soldiers willing to canvass precincts, people demonstrations, and cross voting districts to cast their ballots.

But now he had something else to offer men in power: a bevy of attractive women willing to do *anything* for the cause. He'd used this tactic to a lesser degree in California, but found it far more successful in Guyana. In an insular country of black and brown people, where there was no television and little tourism, white skin was exotic, and to the *machista* men in power, the fair-haired Temple women were alluring objects. Jones soon realized he could use their crude fascination to his advantage. He selected a group of comely young women to live in Georgetown, and sent out these "PR girls" to bedazzle influential men at their offices and their homes.

The Temple purchased a spacious two-story yellow stucco home in an upscale neighborhood for its headquarters. Located at the end of a quiet street, 41 Lamaha Gardens was the base for the PR crew, which equipped a downstairs bedroom with a ham radio, three phone lines, typewriters, and equipment to record phone calls.

It was well known, in certain circles, that the Temple women used provocative means to promote their cause. A coy look, a short skirt, a shimmy: They worked their charm on everyone from customs agents to cabinet members. Some men were swayed by mere suggestion. Wives grew suspicious; when a group of four PR girls showed up at the home of the Minister of Health, Labor and Housing, Hamilton Green, his wife took one look at them and told her husband to let his secretary deal with them from then on. Jones's envoys spent most of their time on Georgetown's principal boulevard, Main Street, which was lined with government offices, foreign consulates, and private businesses. They sashayed past secretaries bearing booze and greetings from their leader, who'd given himself the pretentious title of Bishop in Guyana. The designation certainly wasn't used by the denomination that ordained him, the Disciples of Christ, but he thought it lent him more gravitas than mere Reverend. The women came off as pushy and confrontational, and their unstinting praise of Jones irritated some officials. "Don't give me your California hard sell," the Minister of Foreign Affairs, Fred Wills, chastised them. Wills did, however, concede to give them inside scoops in exchange for food. He asked the team to bring him a pint of milk a day, as well as soup, ice cream, oranges, and mangos.

Jones's star performer—his "political prostitute," as she once called herself—was a petite brunette named Paula Adams. She was constantly checking the tide of opinion toward the Temple, determining how much officials knew about the scandals back in the States before artfully leading them to believe Jones was under attack for his progressive views. The twenty-eight-year-old moved to Guyana in January 1974, and began dating the Guyanese ambassador to the United States, Laurence "Bonny" Mann, soon after. Mann was an easy target. He was a known playboy, and had no qualms about squiring his blue-eyed mistress around Georgetown's top restaurants and nightclubs, gossipers be damned. Mann was on his third marriage at the time, and Adams was wed to a Temple member in San Francisco.

The couple couldn't have made a stranger combination. Mann was an arrogant bon vivant, while Paula was quiet and down-to-earth, accustomed to the humble Temple lifestyle. She hailed from Ukiah, and entered the Temple a confused twenty-two-year-old who was wrestling with drinking, drugs, and manic-depression. In Georgetown, Adams played the part of long-suffering mistress to the hilt, complaining about Mann's all-night poker games, his possessiveness, his drunken rages. He, in turn, criticized the way she dressed, belittled her association with the Temple, and hit on her friends. Paula's ultimate allegiance was to Jones, which angered her lover. They moved into an apartment together, where she took dictation for him, had his Scotch ready when came home from work, and memorized which item he kept in each pocket of his guayaberas, so she could arrange them in his preferred order after his shirts were laundered.

Ambassador Mann was Jones's ace in the hole. Not only was he a high-ranking diplomat himself, he was also related to Prime Minister Forbes Burnham. Adams was a classic honey trap, exchanging sex for valuable information and influence. In the late summer of 1977, as the American media continued assailing his group, Jones was desperate for reassurances that the Guyanese government still supported him. Paula constantly queried Mann about the cabinet's position on Jones, and radioed the information to Jonestown nightly.

When Paula wasn't playing housemaid, she rifled through Mann's briefcase, taped his phone conversations, and jotted down any perfidious comments he made. She gave these materials to Jones, who underlined Mann's criticisms of Guyanese officials and indications that he was a less than ardent socialist, and periodically leaked them to his allies in the Guyanese cabinet.

Mann helped Paula ingratiate herself with local officials. "Most of Georgetown relates on a forum of drink," he told her. It was impossible to buy quality liquor in Guyana, so, on the basis of his recommendation, immigrating Temple members stopped at JFK's duty-free shop to buy bottles of single-malt whiskey for "the cause."

That summer, the most pressing issue on Paula's agenda was a fresh scandal: an unseemly custody battle involving so-called Bishop Jones. A five-year-old boy named John Victor Stoen, the son of Temple attorney Tim Stoen and Grace Stoen, was at the center of the case. Twelve days after "John John" was born, Tim Stoen signed a peculiar document:

"I, Timothy Oliver Stoen, hereby acknowledge that in April, 1971, I entreated my beloved pastor, James W. Jones, to sire a child by my wife, Grace Lucy (Grech) Stoen, who had previously, at my insistence, reluctantly but graciously consented thereto. James W. Jones agreed to do so, reluctantly, after I explained that I very much wished to raise a child, but was unable after extensive attempts, to sire one myself. My reason for requesting James W. Jones to do this is that I wanted my child to be fathered, if not by me, by the most compassionate, honest, and courageous human being the world contains."

Jones's wife, Marceline, signed the document as a witness.

Whether the document was just another loyalty test or an authentic declaration of paternity, no one will ever know. It's too late for DNA testing. Although Jones liked to brag that the boy's features reflected his own, John had a mop of thick dark hair that he could have inherited from either man, or from his mother.

Grace Stoen, who worked as a Temple counselor and accountant, defected in July 1976, after growing tired of Jones's relentless demands. But she was unable to retrieve her son, who was being raised communally and lived apart from her. Complicating the matter were two forms she signed before leaving. One gave the Temple parental authority over John and the other allowed him to travel to the promised land. A few months later, her estranged husband signed another power of attorney granting control of their son to church leaders, who whisked John to Guyana.

When the *New West* article appeared, Jones learned that Grace had initiated court proceedings to get John back. He quickly went on the offensive, ordering Jonestown residents to write affidavits claiming Grace was an unfit mother. They obliged him, portraying her as sexually depraved and emotionally unstable; they wrote similar statements about other former members who spoke to *New West*.

During the mass exodus, Marshall Kilduff called Ambassador Mann to get the Guyanese reaction to his investigation. Mann reported the conversation to Temple leader Jean Brown, who taped it for Jones. In it, Mann said:

"I said, 'Look . . . our embassy is three thousand miles away. Please look at it from my point of view. Please know that the bishop had a public office in San Francisco.' I said, 'If you are the chairman of a housing authority, if you are a public office holder in your own country and own city, would you expect us to believe you are a con man?' I said, 'Moreover, not a single allegation had been proved, not a single charge has been brought in San Francisco or anywhere else. . . . We have no quarrel with them.'"

Now, Jones wanted to make sure the Guyanese government would be on his side if Grace Stoen did, in fact, pursue the custody matter all the way to South America. In a rambling letter to Deputy Prime Minister Ptolemy Reid, Jones defended the affair. "Committing adultery with this woman was one of the more noble things of my life," he wrote. "I consulted with my wife and my entire church before I did it and I sure didn't want to have anything to do with her." On Main Street, Paula Adams assured cabinet ministers that it was "the only case of such a situation in our group."

Of course, these were lies. Jones never asked his congregation if he could have sex with an attractive devotee; he acted on impulse, not principle.

When a San Francisco court awarded Grace Stoen custody of her son in August 1977, the legal victory changed the entire tenor of Jonestown. Before the ruling, Jones had put on his best game face as he walked around his town, pausing to chat with seniors, visiting the newest litter of pigs with John John, and joking with the construction crew. After Grace got custody, he spent less time in the community, and more time secluded in his cottage raging over the ham radio to his San Francisco lieutenants about the custody case.

Then came another blow. Grace's estranged husband and Temple chief counsel Tim Stoen defected. A staff member who was rummaging through his briefcase learned he was withholding part of his paycheck from the Temple and had passbooks for various overseas bank accounts. After leaving, he joined forces with Grace to get John back.

This was a risky move for Stoen. He was privy to Jones's dirtiest secrets, from his lewd conduct arrest in 1973 for exposing himself to an undercover cop in a Los Angeles movie theater, to his shady real estate transactions, to the money smuggled into overseas banks, to the intimidation of defectors. Stoen himself had devised some of the scare tactics. He could blow down Jones's house of cards with a tiny puff of air, but by doing so, he would also implicate himself.

Temple aide Debbie Blakey would later report that before leaving, Tim Stoen returned to 1859 Geary Boulevard to try to purge compromising files containing his name. He'd later tell reporters that he left after realizing Jones's tyranny and paranoia were out of control.

For Jones, the stakes in the custody battle were extremely high. It wasn't just about who got physical possession of the boy. It was a matter of maintaining the respect of his people, who thought he was God, omniscient and all-powerful. If he was forced to return John John to his mother, he would lose his aura of inviolability, and there would be little incentive for his followers to obey, or fear, him.

CHAPTER 11

SIEGE

H yacinth Thrash and Zippy Edwards reached Jonestown a few weeks before the *New West* story broke. Jones himself drove the sisters to the passport office in San Francisco to fill out their forms, then pocketed the documents for "safekeeping." They left California believing they were going on a yearlong mission to help the Guyanese get on their feet.

In Jonestown, the sisters were assigned to smaller living quarters located behind the pharmacy that were reserved for longtime Temple members. There were only six cottages. Married couples occupied several, and Marceline Jones, who also had an air conditioner, lived in one. The sisters shared theirs with two other older women, one of whom had been Jones's housekeeper from Indiana. Each woman had a full-sized bed in a corner, and Zip crocheted bright rugs to cover the plank floor between them.

Every newcomer was expected to do fieldwork for their first weeks in Jonestown to partake as equals in the socialist endeavor, even seniors. But a group of elderly women, including seventy-two-year-old Zipporah, banded together after their first day and rebelled. "We didn't come here to work in the hot sun," they protested. Jones reassigned them to shaded jobs: plucking chickens, sorting rice, and making toys.

Jonestown seemed paradisiacal to Hyacinth at first. Its promise outshined the encroaching shadows. She enjoyed catching up with old friends, or sitting on her deck at sunset, watching the sky turn purple and orange and listening to the chorus of tropical songbirds. She delighted in the sprays of bougainvillea and hibiscus flowers that were planted throughout the settlement. They were living in a lush garden; everything seemed to thrive.

It was hard for Hyacinth to navigate the uneven wooden walkways on a cane, and especially difficult to carry a tray in the dining tent, so an aide started bringing meals to her cottage. After breakfast, she'd make her slow way to the field next to the pavilion, where she'd join other seniors in stretching exercises led by medical staff. Then she'd report for her job with the toy crew and spend a few hours in friendly company as she sanded wooden trains or stitched up dolls that were sold in Georgetown stores. Her days were largely unsupervised, and in the afternoon, she often stayed in her cottage to read and rest.

Her biggest complaints, when she first arrived, were the heat and bugs. Her cottage windows didn't have screens, and she spent hours stalking flies and mosquitoes with a swatter. And while the tin roof made a melodious sound during rainstorms, it turned the cottage into an oven as the sun curved overhead.

Still, she focused on the good things.

Right before Hy and Zip left California, word of the chicken gizzards spread through the communes. Rose Shelton, who handled the "passed cancers," admitted the sham to a few folks after the *New West* article appeared, and from there the news was whispered up and down hallways. Hy chose not to believe it. She was convinced that Jones was a true healer, and that he'd cured her breast cancer.

Jones obliquely addressed the *New West* charges. He was good at explaining things away. "We don't abuse children in this church," he'd tell his followers in a gentle voice. "You were all here as witnesses; you saw what happened. That child would have ended up in juvenile hall if we hadn't helped him. Our discipline is given in a loving manner, and it works. And he's doing so much better because of it."

True believers had an answer for everything. They excused Jones's peculiarities with the maxim, the end justifies the means. The beatings, the swats—it was all showmanship, they said. The discipline didn't *really* hurt. Jones's antics—like stomping on a Bible, saying "fuck" or "cunt" in the middle of a sermon—were all theater. He liked to get a rise out of people to force them to pay attention.

Those members who were offended by his increasingly bizarre and cruel behavior kept quiet, and in their silence, seemed to condone it.

When Jones said that John Victor Stoen was his biological son, Hyacinth Thrash refused to believe that, too. He made the announcement during a congregation-wide meeting in the pavilion. It was nighttime, and he sat in his usual place, in a light-green wooden chair on a stage at the front. He was holding John John on his lap and his children, biological and adopted, stood around him. As hundreds of his followers sat on hard benches facing him, Jones said he was forced to "relate" to Grace Stoen, despite his deep revulsion for her, to keep her in the fold. It hadn't worked, this they knew, as she was one of the former members who spoke with *New West*. He made a second announcement: Temple attorney Tim Stoen had also defected, and had joined forces with Grace to win custody of the child.

The conversation startled many, especially the seniors who were unaware that Jones was unfaithful to his wife. Jones continued, stating Maria Katsaris would now care for the boy. "His mother is Maria, and that's the way it is here. If anyone ever makes any other issue, then you'll have difficulty with me. John is my son."

Hy was dumbfounded. She turned on the bench to her sister and blurted: "That's Tim's boy up there!" Zip shushed her, but Hy continued to roil inside, remembering how in Indianapolis, Jones always preached marital fidelity. When had he changed?

In the late summer of 1977, Jones felt besieged on all sides. Apart from the media attack and the custody battle, a man named Leon Broussard had crept out of Jonestown early one August morning and walked to Port Kaituma, where he told police that Jonestown was a "slave colony" and complained that he was forced to haul lumber all day under the supervision of a club-wielding guard. When Broussard told Jones he wanted to go home, he said, several members jumped him before making him crawl to Jones's feet and beg for forgiveness.

Broussard happened to be in Port Kaituma when US Consul Richard McCoy flew up to visit Jonestown for the first time. Local authorities told him about the escapee, and McCoy interviewed Broussard before driving to the settlement. Jones told McCoy that Broussard was a liar and a drug addict, but agreed to pay his ticket back to the States. The conversation led McCoy to believe that Jones would send future malcontents home as well. In reality, Leon Broussard would be the last person to successfully escape Jonestown until its final day, although many others would try, and fail.

US embassy personnel had been making periodic checks on the American group since July 13, 1974, when a consular officer interviewed the nine pioneers living there at the time and reported to his higher-ups that they appeared "earnest, well-organized, and well-financed."

Shortly after the mass exodus began, McCoy flew to Port Kaituma to visit two residents whose relatives were concerned about them. In the wake of the bad press dogging the Temple, McCoy expected more such requests, and he wanted to establish a protocol for doing welfare-and-whereabouts checks on Americans living in the camp. He told Jones that he wanted everyone he interviewed to have their passports in hand so he could verify their identity, and he wanted to talk to them in an open space where they could speak without fear of being overheard.

The first person he interviewed was Carolyn Looman, a thirty-four-year-old Ohio native who called her parents from Georgetown saying she changed her mind about going to Jonestown. After they didn't hear anything more from her, they asked McCoy to check on her. McCoy spoke privately with Looman in the field outside the pavilion. He told her that her parents had sent a return plane ticket for her; if she wanted to leave, all she had to do was walk with him to his car, which was parked a few hundred feet away, and he would help her get home. Looman smiled and shook her head, saying her parents were mistaken; she was perfectly happy in Jonestown, where she taught seventh and eighth grades. What he didn't know was that the Temple had caught wind of Looman's phone call, and pressured her to change her tune.

The second resident McCoy wanted to see was John Victor Stoen. Grace and Tim Stoen wanted to know how the boy was faring. John John was trotted out, and seemed healthy enough, but it was tough to assess a beaming five-year-old.

McCoy returned to Georgetown satisfied with his findings, but the stench of Broussard's accusations lingered. Suddenly local officials were dropping by Jonestown unannounced. One pointedly referred to the *New West* charges and told Jones "the government does not approve of such tactics." A police investigator took pictures of the pit Tommy dug for punishment even as Jones's aides insisted it was excavated by backhoe. Yet other regional bureaucrats pressured Jones to send the settlement's kids to the Port Kaituma school, and allow Amerindians to live in Jonestown as unpaid apprentices.

Jones didn't want interference from outsiders, of course. He wanted to isolate his people so he could carry out his macabre plan. He argued that there was no room to house Guyanese on the project, and that the Temple children would be traumatized if they were separated from the group. He offered Regional Minister Fitz Carmichael, who was generating most of the pressure on the settlement, the services of his land-moving equipment, his doctor, his "water diviner" Jim Bogue, even a sizable donation to his political party, but Carmichael stuck to his guns.

Jones wrote Prime Minister Burnham complaining about the interference of these "low level, petty bureaucrats." He depicted his project as a noble charity, and expected deference, not interrogations. Several months later, Burnham himself handed down the order validating the Jonestown school.

American bureaucrats also had Jonestown in their sights. Based on a tip from former members, US customs agents did a spot check on ninety crates bound for the settlement, looking for smuggled guns. They found nothing, but passed along the tip to the International Police Agency, Interpol, which alerted Guyanese Police Chief C. A. "Skip" Roberts to be on the lookout for contraband. Roberts was a regular PR stop on Paula Adams's route, and when he showed her the Interpol report, she acted offended.

As it turned out, the customs agents just hadn't looked hard enough.

The Temple applied repeatedly for permits to import guns into Guyana, but when Guyanese authorities didn't respond to the requests, Jones resorted to gunrunning. Emigrating Temple members turned in their weapons before leaving the States, and these were broken down and hidden in false-bottomed crates marked "agricultural supplies." Because the Temple was permitted to import farm supplies duty-free, Georgetown customs officials routinely waved these shipments through without inspecting them. On the off chance that they did open a crate, the PR girls shimmied forth holding bottles of good whiskey.

The woman spearheading the Temple's gun-smuggling operation was a California probation officer named Sandy Bradshaw, who regularly sent Jones updates on her purchases:

"Tonight I got seven boxes (50 rounds each) for .38 bibles (hollow-point for defense) and 20 boxes (50 rounds each) of .22 bibles, both without signing for them," she wrote Jones in an undated memo. "Merry Xmas from the system! I will get more tomorrow since I got this break tonight."

The code name "bibles" was a nod to abolitionist preacher Henry Ward Beecher, who raised money for antislavery activists to arm themselves. The rifles the abolitionists accumulated were known as "Beecher's Bibles."

Jonestown's arsenal would grow to include more than thirty firearms, from .38 specials to a Ruger 30/.06 with a high-powered scope, to the Remington Model 700 .308 caliber bolt-action rifle used to kill Congressman Leo Ryan.

In one memo discussing Temple defectors, Bradshaw wrote Jones "there are enough bibles here to do a lot of praying if necessary." In another note, she dropped the code completely: "It is my understanding we can get as many rifles/shotguns as we wish." On Jonestown's last night, these weapons would be turned on residents when their leader commanded them to drink poison.

While the Interpol report exacerbated Jones's long-held paranoia that the US government was out to get him, a sharp turn in the custody battle would push him over the edge.

At the beginning of September, Grace Stoen's lawyer, Jeffrey Hass, flew to Georgetown with a copy of a California court order compelling Jones to return the boy to his mother. Paula Adams, informed of Hass's arrival by embassy officials, cozied up to him at his hotel, posing as a tourist along with Harriet Tropp, a Temple member with a law degree. Hass told the women that he had a court date on September 6, during which he planned to convince the Guyanese magistrate to honor the California order, and that he hoped to reunite mother and son by the end of the month. However, if his plan didn't work, he told the women that several former Temple members, including the Stoens, had consulted a private investigator about kidnapping children from Jonestown.

When the women reported the conversation to Jones, he was deeply rattled. He feared losing John John would open the door for other custody battles between Jonestown residents and their estranged spouses in the States.

His anxiety only skyrocketed when he learned that his closest ally in the Guyanese government, Deputy Prime Minister Ptolemy Reid, was traveling in the United States to witness the signing of the Panama Canal Treaty. Reid was Jones's go-to man. When Temple members started flooding the immigration office, Reid suspended protocol to allow them to be processed posthaste. He also transferred several pesky regional officials who voiced concerns about Jonestown, and refused to investigate their reports.

To Jones, it seemed too uncanny to be coincidence: His strongest ally was overseas while his enemy's agent, Hass, was in Guyana, trying to take John John away from him. His mind went wild with thoughts of conspiracy. What he engineered next would come be known as the *six-day siege*.

Shortly after eleven o'clock on the night of September 5—the day before the scheduled hearing—Jones called aside his adopted black son and namesake, Jimmy Junior. As a Jonestown guard, Jimmy, seventeen, carried a .38 on his hip and a carbine rifle in his hands. Now, at his father's bidding, he crept into the bush, then turned and aimed the .38 at Jones's cabin as his father pressed his body against a far wall. He squeezed the trigger and shots exploded in the darkness, striking terror into residents as they lay in their bunk beds. When Stephan Jones, who was also on the security force, and others rushed to the scene, they found Jones lying on the floor. He acted disoriented and told them he'd been standing at the window when he had a premonition and bent down, narrowly missing the bullet.

Thus began Jonestown's first, and longest, *white night*, a term Jones coined to denote any acute emergency, inverting the pejorative usage of black into white. It was the first of many fake assaults Jones would launch against the community to keep his followers fearful and obedient.

"Alert! Alert! We are under attack!" Jones shouted into the public address system, whose speakers were strung on poles throughout the camp and fields. He ordered everyone to convene at the pavilion. Panicked residents jammed on their rubber boots. In a few minutes, hundreds of people flooded up the dark walkways, many crying with fear, wearing their pajamas. Jones, standing on the stage at the front of the pavilion, was ranting and semicoherent. He told his followers that their government allies had deserted them, leaving fascists in control of the country. Mercenaries surrounded Jonestown at that very moment, he shouted, poised to invade and kidnap their children. Jones swore that he wouldn't let any of his people be captured: If they came for one, they came for all.

His aides passed out hoes, pitchforks, and cutlasses, and told residents to form a line facing the jungle. They stood shaking with fright and exhaustion all night and into the next day, when Jones permitted them to sleep in shifts. They were paired off; one slept on the ground while the other stood guard. No one was to surrender or be taken alive, he commanded; anyone who tried to desert would be hacked to death with a cutlass.

On September 6, as residents held imaginary invaders at bay with garden hoes in Jonestown, Hass won a crucial victory in Georgetown. Supreme Court Justice Aubrey Bishop ordered Jones to bring John Victor Stoen to his courtroom on September 8 to discuss the case and issued Hass a writ of habeas corpus compelling their appearance. The next day, Minister of Information Kit Nascimento offered Hass his plane, and the lawyer flew up to Port Kaituma to deliver the order to Jones accompanied by a Georgetown police inspector. When Hass reached Jonestown, now in the second day of its supposed siege, a throng of hostile residents watched him step out of his rented Land Cruiser. When he asked for Jones, Maria Katsaris told him the Temple leader had left two days earlier and was "on the river somewhere." She refused his request to look around. Dejected, he rode back to Port Kaituma, where two local officials told him they'd spoken to Jones at the camp forty-five minutes earlier. Clearly, this was not going to be an easy fight.

After Hass left, another wave of panic broke over Jonestown. When Jones returned from his hiding place and heard that Hass had flown up in the minister's plane, he was certain that the Guyanese government had turned on him.

He announced that he was moving the entire community to the nearest socialist country, Cuba, and started trucking seniors to the Port Kaituma river, where the *Cudjoe* was moored. The plan was to ferry groups of members to the island, 1,300 miles away. Jones told Jim Bogue to stay behind and sell off the farm equipment before joining them.

Hy was among the first group to reach the boat. It was the middle of the night, and she'd been up for hours listening to Jones howl about armed invaders. She was beside herself with anxiety. As a group of old women jostled down the narrow gangway, which only had a railing on one side, someone tripped, triggering a domino effect. Hy's cane slipped, and she was knocked down. An eighty-year-old woman fell into the water and broke her hip. But Jones pressed on. He passed out cutlasses and ordered the old women to defend the boat even as the injured resident moaned at their feet.

One of Jones's aides had thought to grab recording equipment before they left Jonestown and taped Jones as he addressed his geriatric corps. He denounced the Guyanese officials who helped Hass as "miserable sonabitches" who were "more interested of the approval of the special interest of the ruling class in United States than they are standing up for socialism." He suggested bribery was at work.

A few hours later, Jones announced that Cuba would only give asylum to him and his immediate family, but that the "rivers were blocked to the rest of my people. So, my God, if they won't let us all go, then none of us go." Hy was relieved. She'd been standing on the boat for hours, a heavy cutlass in one hand, her cane in the other. Her good leg ached. She just wanted to go to bed; she was too old and crippled for such maneuvers. When the truck returned the women to Jonestown at dawn, she found a stranger sleeping in her bed and shooed the person out before easing herself onto the thin mattress. She put her cane at arm's reach, in case Jones started hollering again.

Over the following days, Jones periodically allowed community life to return to normal for a few hours so people could shower, weed the crops, or prepare food. Then he'd call an alert again, and they'd drop their soap, trowel, or stirring spoon, and sprint back to the line. Aides gathered the older children in the school tent and younger ones in the nursery, giving sedatives to those who proved inconsolable. Teenage boys tried to prove their valor by charging to the front lines wielding cutlasses. When Jones wasn't ranting, he led his people in civil rights anthems, such as "We Shall Overcome." At one point, he walked down the line crying, bidding his followers farewell before the supposedly imminent invasion.

At the height of the six-day siege, the US Postal Service notified the Temple that the Social Security Administration had ordered it to stop forwarding Social Security checks to the Temple's address in Guyana. The move effectively cut off Jonestown's monthly income of $35,000, and was further proof, Jones said, of a systematic plot to destroy them.

On September 8, the lawyer Jones hired to replace Tim Stoen, Charles Garry, an avowed Marxist famous for defending the Black Panthers, held a press conference in San Francisco to announce the alleged conspiracy against the Temple. The meeting was dramatically interrupted by a second sniper attempt on Jones's life.

Jones kept up the scare.

In the pavilion, he held all-night rallies. He led his 700 followers in socialist anthems with a raised fist; parents cradled sleeping infants in one arm and raised their other. At Jones's cue, they turned toward the jungle to scream at the imaginary menace. "Come get us!" they yelled, and slapped their palms over their mouths in an Indian war whoop. There is a video of this: The pavilion is a blaze of lights against the dark jungle. Inside, as the camera pans over the crowd, some smile, other look serious, others bored. They're a snapshot of the 1970s: The men wear dashikis or bucket hats, the women's hair is styled into crowning afros or corn rows or worn long and center-parted. The old women wear scarves tied daintily beneath their chins. Their skin color runs the gamut from milk white to coal black, but the vast majority is dark-skinned. A handsome blond youth from Seattle named Michael Rozynko stands out, flapping his hand over his mouth with narrowed eyes, looking pointedly side to side as if to avoid the camera's gaze.

Jones upped the ante as his speech wore on: He would rather die than return to the United States. Wouldn't they?

He would rather die than surrender a single one of his people to the fascists. Wouldn't they?

He would rather die than endure more harassment. Wouldn't they?

He suggested they protest their treatment by committing revolutionary suicide, introducing the notion to rank-and-file members for the first time, and took a vote. Only two people raised their hands in favor of mass suicide, according to a survivor: Maria Katsaris and Harriet Tropp. Everyone else wanted to fight; they didn't come to the promised land to die—they came to thrive. They still believed Jones was sincere when he promised them a better life for themselves and their children.

On September 9, Jeffrey Hass returned to Jonestown. This time he flew up on a Guyana Defense Force plane, with several reinforcements: a court marshal, a superintendent of police, and a local constable. Justice Bishop told him the writ compelling Jones and John Victor Stoen to appear in Georgetown could be served by posting it at three locations in the community. When the party's Land Rover turned down the road into Jonestown, they noticed the security post, a small shed where guards radioed ahead to announce the arrival of guests, had been camouflaged with branches. It was the first sign of trouble. As they drove into the main area, again a menacing crowd gathered; here was the enemy Jones warned them about. Hass again asked to see Jones, and was again told he was gone. He was surprised to see Harriet Tropp there, no longer acting the friendly tourist. The court marshal read the writ aloud, then tried to hand it to Tropp. She let it fall to the ground, then kicked it away. The lawmen nailed copies on several buildings, but residents tore them down just as quickly. A group of brawny young men surrounded the party, arms crossed, biceps flexed. Some wore army fatigues. The officials told Hass to wait in the car. The superintendent of police, feeling the need to assert himself, asked residents to bring him all the weapons in the camp. They produced only two, a shotgun and a pistol, both of which were legally registered.

Back in Georgetown, a perturbed Justice Bishop issued his third, and most serious, order: "It is ordered that a bench warrant be issued for the arrest of the infant John Victor Stoen now in custody of the Respondent, and that the said child be made a ward of the court and that leave is hereby granted for contempt of Court on Jim Jones . . ."

When Paula Adams read the order to Jones over the radio, he took a second suicide vote. This time, the number of advocates rose to three: Maria, Harriet, and Carolyn Layton.

His followers overwhelming desire to live didn't faze Jones. On the next day, a Saturday, he radioed Marceline in San Francisco and told her the community was prepared to die unless the arrest order was cancelled or they were given shelter in another country. He gave her a list of nations to contact to request political asylum, including Uganda. "That chap [Idi Amin] seems to be able to stand up for what he believes," he said of the mass-murdering leader. Jones then gave his San Francisco aides a chilling ultimatum: They were to find Deputy Prime Minister Ptolemy Reid and tell him that the entire Jonestown community would commit mass suicide at five-thirty that afternoon unless he stopped the custody proceedings. In a taped message for Reid, Jones distorted the suicide vote, stating "all but two" residents were willing to die over the matter.

He gave his aides in the radio room at 1859 Geary Boulevard a little over two hours to find Reid. Teri Buford and Debbie Blakey frantically called FBI offices and police departments around the country asking if the politician was in town, but authorities refused to help them. Meanwhile, Dick Tropp, a former English instructor, drafted a final press release, sobbing as he composed it. Jones had assigned him the task of explaining to the world why they had committed so-called revolutionary suicide. Everyone in the room had loved ones in Jonestown—wives, babies, mothers. They popped tranquilizers to tamp down their emotions as they carried out Jones's agonizing dicta.

Finally, they tracked down Reid in Gary, Indiana, where he was visiting a friend. Marceline Jones, two aides, and Temple lawyer Charles Garry flew to Chicago, and drove to the house where Reid was staying. He wasn't there, but his wife assured the visitors that the Guyana Defense Force wouldn't attack Jonestown, and that Jones would not be arrested. Marceline relayed the information to Jonestown, and Jones called off the threatened mass suicide.

When Hass returned to the Georgetown court on Monday, September

12, he learned that the custody suit had mysteriously ground to a halt. "We tried to get an arrest warrant for Jones, but the court clerk refused to sign it," he later told a reporter.

After the six-day siege concluded, a gloom settled over the settlement. Instead of enjoying the freedom land that their pastor had spent years selling them, residents felt shell-shocked. The crisis had passed, but Jones warned them that someday there might be a white night that they wouldn't survive.

The siege was the first rehearsal for Jonestown's last night. Jones had presented his mass suicide idea to his top aides earlier—he called it the "last-stand plan." The scheme was a pointed reference to Custer's last stand of 1876, in which Lieutenant Colonel George Custer staged a final, suicidal attack on the Native American forces overwhelming his troops. Discussed in memos as if it were inevitable, the Temple's last-stand plan called for the mass suicide of church members in a moment of crisis as a form of protest. Jones gave various triggers for the plan: to show solidarity with Chilean socialists, to protest capitalism, to defy America.

For Jones's lieutenants, pledging to die for Jim Jones was just another loyalty test. The more loyal you were, the more you wanted to die. The last stand was discussed among the Temple's inner circle to the "point that it was boring," one of his top aides would later tell the press. After the mass suicide, Jones's appointed *angels*—aides he'd designated to survive—would kill the Temple's enemies, including defectors and certain public officials. The church had amassed millions of dollars in overseas accounts to finance the hit squad, and Teri Buford would later claim that Sandy Bradshaw, the probation officer and Temple gunrunner, was to be its head.

Jones had taken the initial major step in his last-stand plan by sequestering his group to a remote location where he had complete control over them. But now he faced another hurdle: He couldn't figure out how to kill them.

CHAPTER 12

BULLETS TO KILL
BUMBLEBEES

The rank and file were unaware of the last-stand plan, of course. The leadership knew Temple members would not willingly kill themselves or their children. But Jones wanted the historical record to indicate that his followers agreed to commit mass suicide, so he laid the groundwork for this bald-faced lie. "Should anything happen that would kill Jim or bring about a last stand on the part of the organization in Guyana—please try to put both his life and death in perspective to the people," Teri Buford wrote to Charles Garry's secretary during the September crisis. "I am sure that many will say that it was perhaps a 'crazy or hysterical act' and my answer to that is that it has been the collective decision of the group and Jim for a long time that if it is not possible for us to live the lifestyle which we believe is the only fair and just way to live, then we believe we maintain the right to choose the circumstances of our deaths. If we do make a last stand, it will not be as an act of giving up but rather as a demonstration in the hopes some people will wake up."

Garry's secretary, Pat Richartz, fired off a six-page response, upbraiding Jones for misinterpreting Newton's concept of revolutionary suicide. Newton urged revolutionaries to go down fighting, not to kill themselves, she wrote. Richartz also questioned Jones's brand of socialism, writing, "all roads lead to you—there doesn't seem to be any independent thinking . . . or collective element in the decision making."

Buford herself was conflicted about the last-stand plan. At the height of the September crisis, she disobeyed Jones's frantic demand to send down more guns and ammunition, fearing he would enact the mass extinction. As he raged over the airwaves from Guyana, she fiddled with the tuner knob on the shortwave radio in San Francisco, creating poor reception and distorting Jones's voice. Debbie Blakey, who was in the room, later informed Jones of her actions.

Jones's bizarre threat lowered his credibility in Georgetown. US Consul Richard McCoy dismissed the stunt as a "psychological ploy." Guyanese Ambassador Laurence Mann grew irritated at the letters flooding his office suggesting "people would die" if Jones didn't get custody of John Victor Stoen. Deputy Prime Minister Reid was particularly embarrassed by it; as the nation's second-in-command, he had his share of headaches, including a massive sugar strike that was crippling Guyana's fragile economy. After the crisis was averted, he told Jones's representatives to direct all communication to his inferior, Minister of Home Affairs and Immigration Vibert Mingo.

On the trip upriver to Jonestown, Stanley Clayton, who arrived shortly before the siege, was in fine spirits. "It feels so good to be free," he told another church member, a young woman. "It feels so good to be in a socialist land under black leadership."

The woman believed Stanley meant Temple members were finally free to do whatever they wanted. And what she wanted to do on that slow river journey was to have sex with a brawny Guyanese deckhand, so she did.

The next night, an angry Jones called her before the entire pavilion. She'd broken the Temple rule forbidding relationships with outsiders. "I did it because Stanley said I was free," she told the crowd. Jones then turned his fury on Stanley, and his guards followed suit, shoving and slapping him. His attempts to explain himself were futile.

The next day, when he complained about this treatment to his buddy Ed Crenshaw, Ed advised him to go with the flow.

Stanley now understood Stanley Gieg's cryptic remark to him on the ride into Jonestown. When Stanley told Gieg, who was driving the tractor-trailer, how excited he was to be in the promised land, Gieg cut him off. "It's not what you think," he'd said, refusing to elaborate.

As they bumped down the pitch-black road for nearly an hour, Stanley realized that Jonestown was even more remote than Redwood Valley. And when he arrived at the camp, eager to spend the night with Janice, a counselor told him there was a mandatory three-month separation for all newcomers who were in a relationship but not married to each other. It was the first he'd heard of it. He moved into a cottage full of strangers with disappointment.

During the six-day siege, he was shocked, like everyone else, when Jones started talking about suicide. He thought perhaps it was a loyalty test. He saw Jones's secretaries raise their hands to commit revolutionary suicide, but he voted against death with the rank and file. He held a cutlass against the jungle for six days because everyone else was doing it. He was going with the flow, as Eddie told him to do. At one point during the crisis, Angela Davis and Huey Newton called in to encourage the community, and Stanley's spirits were buoyed when he heard Newton's voice booming over the PA system: "I want the Guyanese government to know that you're not to be messed around with." A rumor had gone around that Newton was Stanley's uncle—a falsehood Stanley didn't bother correcting—and as Newton spoke, some residents turned to give him a thumbs-up. Janice, however, was terrified. He did his best to comfort her; Jim Jones would never let anything happen to them, he assured her, folding her against his sweat-drenched T-shirt.

For many, Jones's manic, at times incoherent, rantings during the crisis became background noise; they responded by rote with a cheer or a curse when everyone else did. Others secretly wondered why Jones, who maintained he was God, didn't use his paranormal powers to save them, or why the enemy would hike through the virtually impassable jungle when they could simply drive into the settlement. Yet others noticed a pattern: Jones waited until midafternoon to call the alerts, after workers had picked enough food for supper.

One man who did take Jones's threat seriously was Temple attorney Gene Chaikin.

Gene was a Los Angeles real-estate lawyer when he and his wife, Phyllis, met Jones in 1972. Both came from leftist backgrounds, and Jones's socialist message struck a chord in them. In short order, they moved from Los Angeles to Ukiah with their small children and became part of the planning commission. Gene was part of the leadership group that flew down to Guyana to scout out the area that would become Jonestown and negotiate the lease. By 1977, however, the Chaikin marriage, like that of many other church members, was strained by Jones's constant demands on their time. The family was further weakened when their children were moved into other members' homes to be raised communally.

During the September crisis, Gene flew to Guyana from San Francisco to calm Jones down. But once he was there, he realized Jones was ratcheting up the crisis as a strategy. Reid had always supported the Temple in indirect ways, Gene warned him; putting the politician on the spot would only antagonize him. Charles Garry told Chaikin that the mass suicide threat was "dumb, stupid shit," and the Temple's Guyanese attorneys concurred that Jones's behavior was unbecoming of a leader.

But Jones refused to listen to Gene, so the attorney grabbed his suitcase and stormed out of Lamaha Gardens to hail a cab to the airport. He'd reached his breaking point. He was leaving Peoples Temple and Jim Jones behind.

In a letter to Jones, Gene elaborated on his reasons for defecting: "A relatively modest and ultimately controllable incident was made, by you, into a catastrophe of major proportions involving the full expenditure of such goodwill and energies as we have available. . . . The whole thing was handled in a hysterical and destructive fashion." He conceded that Jones had won this round, but what would he do when Hass returned? "I have substantially lost confidence in your leadership," Gene continued. "You will ultimately alienate all of your friends and tear the organization and people apart.

"I left because I am no longer willing to live in a situation of weekly or biweekly crisis, and the atmosphere of anxiety, hysteria and depression that exist with it." His letter is remarkable for its bluntness. He stopped short of calling Jones insane, suggesting, instead, that he suffered a "lack of balance—both of perspective and behavior." Although Gene agreed that creating a "conspiratorial atmosphere" in California had encouraged members' devotion to the cause, the tactic had gotten out of hand in

Guyana, where Jones had become so uptight that he was using "bullets to kill bumblebees." The only way Gene could make himself heard above the "claque of 'yes people'" surrounding the Temple leader was by taking a dramatic action himself, by leaving.

Gene's move was audacious, but Jones had the upper hand: Gene's two children—Gail, sixteen, and David, fourteen—were in Jonestown. Gene asked Jones to send them out, and Jones initially agreed, but then sent Gene's estranged wife instead. "Phyllis will come in tonight and I suppose we will talk," Gene wrote when he heard about Jones's about-face. "But I think you and I now have very little to say to each other."

Jones began to employ this tactic to prevent other defections: Whenever a resident left Jonestown for a medical checkup or some other business, he made sure at least one of the person's relatives stayed behind as ransom in case the resident tried to flee. Gene Chaikin was forced to return to Jonestown when Jones withheld his children, and he soon started complaining of a host of mysterious ailments: muscle spasms, chills, sudden sleepiness, poor balance, blurred vision, and an acute desire to cry. Perhaps he suspected he was being drugged into submission, but he was never able to confirm it.

After Chaikin's marriage broke up in Jonestown, Jones assigned school secretary Inez Wagner to seduce and spy on him. Gene made the mistake of falling in love with her, even as she reported their private conversations to Jones, who no longer trusted him after his attempted defection. Jones feared Gene would mouth off and routinely sedated him whenever important visitors came to Jonestown. Teri Buford discovered this one day when Maria Katsaris brought a tray of grilled cheese sandwiches to the radio room, where she was working. Most were sliced diagonally, but one was cut straight across. Buford reached for it, but Katsaris stopped her, saying, "That one's for Gene." The implication was clear.

Garry flew to Guyana in October for a three-day visit. He wanted to meet Jones in person to see if the Temple leader was crazy, as Gene implied, or if he was just being theatrical, as other Temple aides assured him. When he got to Jonestown, he was impressed with the orderly village the pioneers had carved from the jungle. Jones seemed calm, and apologized for overreacting. "No one ever intended to die," he assured his counsel.

Although Garry admired Jones for his commitment to socialism, he quickly came to dislike him as a person. One night during the visit, Garry was sitting at a table with Jones, his wife, Marceline, and a group of Temple leaders, when Jones casually mentioned that he'd once had to "fuck" sixteen people in one day to keep them dedicated to the cause, and that two of those people were men. Although no one else flinched, Garry was mortified. He didn't think it was appropriate for a leader to use sex to control his followers. He sought out Gene but found him weirdly placid, considering the urgent conversations the men had only weeks earlier. Gene repeated the official story: The suicide threat was just a ploy—Jones would never follow through with it.

Garry's quibbles were small, it seemed, compared to the hundreds of smiling faces he'd observed. Everyone he'd spoken with had nothing but praise for Jones's socialist utopia.

When Garry returned to California, he, too, toed the line.

"I have seen paradise," he told reporters. "I saw a community where there is no such thing as racism . . . there is no such thing as ageism . . . From what I saw there, I'd say the society being built in Jonestown is a credit to humanity."

CHAPTER 13

RUNAWAYS

Tommy Bogue liked to perch at the edge of the pavilion and study the faces of newcomers.

They assumed Jonestown would have the same relaxed atmosphere of the Temple's headquarters in Georgetown, where they'd spent their first few days waiting for clearance from immigration and health authorities. At 41 Lamaha Gardens, jazz played on the stereo, sodas cooled in the refrigerator, and after a satisfying dinner, folks gathered to watch movies or play board games.

By the time they regretted coming to Jonestown, it was too late.

"No one leaves until all are here," Jones announced. "If you want to go home, you can swim. We won't pay your fucking way home."

The dismay and anxiety he read on the new people's faces served as an affirmation of his own unvoiced feelings. From his father he'd learned to master his facial expressions and vocal intonations, but these new faces didn't yet know to lie, and Tommy referred to them whenever he needed a sanity check.

His parents' marriage had completely dissolved in Guyana. Now his dad was in a relationship with a black woman from Mississippi named Luna Murral, who was there with her five young kids. They'd sat together in the trailer on an errand to Matthew's Ridge and talked the whole way, and in quick succession, Jones performed a marriage ceremony to seal their bond and assigned them to a loft. Jim Bogue changed his last name to Murral, and Harold Cordell changed his to Bogue. Just as Jones substituted white for black to indicate something pejorative—as in white nights—he also encouraged men to take the surnames of their common-law wives to signal a break with patriarchal tradition.

Tommy was thrilled to see Brian Davis among a group of new arrivals in May 1977. Brian came alone; his father wouldn't move down for eight more months. The boys shared a bond of trust that was a rare in an organization where members were expected to pledge allegiance to the cause above all else, and Tommy felt closer to Brian than he did his own mother or sisters. After all, his mother had narked on his dad the very day she arrived in Jonestown, and his sister Marilee had informed on him soon after: One day, as the siblings were standing outside the warehouse, Tommy told her how easy it would be to break into it and take a new pair of sneakers to replace the disintegrating pair on his feet. Marilee turned and walked inside the warehouse: "My brother's fixing to steal out of here, so I figure I'd best tell you," she told the attendant as Tommy listened in disbelief. The attendant told Marilee not to worry about it, and Tommy wheeled away, both relieved and angry. He resolved never to speak to his sister again.

Brian would never nark on him like that. In Jonestown, the boys drifted off together to roughhouse and blow off steam. After the September crisis, it felt like they were living in an episode of *Night Gallery*; a sense of doom pervaded their lives.

One evening as he walked by the warehouse, Tommy found a box containing two dark green hooded capes. He took them. At night the friends would don their "cloaks of darkness" to move invisibly through Jonestown, spying on people or sneaking food from the kitchen.

Brian, too, learned to bite his tongue around others. In the communal toilet when he casually remarked to another resident, "Well, Steve, I've been here seventy-two days," the man reported Brian to Jones, saying the teen sounded "hostile, or sad and sarcastic."

After the six-day siege, the boys began planning their escape. Neither had any intention of committing revolutionary suicide—they weren't even sure what the term meant. They were too young to die, for socialism or anything else. They were only sixteen, still virgins. They would not die virgins, *hell no*.

Although Tommy's first attempt to escape by building a shelter in the bush failed, he'd resolved to do better the next time. After the elitist watermelon incident, he was assigned to the banana crew, where he managed to stay out of trouble for several months. "I'm out of the woodwork now," he'd congratulate himself at the end of an arduous day. People stopped scrutinizing his every move, comment, and facial expression for signs of anarchy and started to trust him again.

When he was put in charge of an Amerindian crew tasked with cutting back the vines creeping into the fields, Tommy started plotting again. He'd lead the crew out of sight of the compound, then stop working and ask them to teach him how to survive in the jungle.

The Amerindians showed him to build snares for birds and small mammals, to identify edible plants, to differentiate between look-alike vines: One oozed a clear, drinkable tea-flavored sap, the other a milky poison. They showed him how to fish by smashing the bulb of an Indian soap plant and tossing it into a stream, where the mild toxins it secreted stunned fish long enough to scoop them out of the water by hand. They taught him how to treat a snake bite by spreading bitter cassava over the wound, and the importance of watching for cumulus clouds; the huge drifting cotton balls that appeared lethargic at noon often turned into violent thunderstorms by dusk. They taught him to squat and study the earth for signs of animals—tufts of fur, flattened brush, and scat—whose trails often led to water. To recognize the tall, slender manicole palm, which grew in swamps. To develop a jungle eye, in order to get his bearings by focusing *through* the trees at breaks in the foliage. To ditch trackers by walking up streams or in circles.

He shared this knowledge with Brian. They schemed in whispers, out of sight, in the dark. They wouldn't repeat Tommy's mistake of staying close to Jonestown this time, but planned to hike forty miles up the Kaituma river to the Barima river, which flowed into Venezuela. As they traveled, they'd fish and live off the land. It'd be *My Side of the Mountain*, set in Guyana instead of the Catskills. After they reached Venezuela they'd figure out, somehow, how to get back to the States. Getting out of Jonestown would be the hardest part, Tommy figured; the rest would follow. One night they broke into the warehouse, squeezing through the thatch leaves, and stole boxes of condoms to sell in Amerindian villages. They'd need money to buy provisions and to call home at some point. They waited patiently for the right moment to make a break for it.

That moment came on November 1, 1977.

Tommy got in trouble again, this time for falling asleep while Jones was speaking during a late-night meeting at the pavilion. He was sentenced to collect coals from piles of burned brush for use in the kitchen ovens. It was a hot, heavy, dirty job. Jones asked for a volunteer to watch him, and Brian raised his hand. The leadership was distracted and had forgotten about the duo's escapades in San Francisco. "You'd better make damn sure he works," Jones told Brian before moving on to the next order of business.

In the kitchen the next morning, the teenagers stuffed matches, flashlights, food, and the condoms into the gunny sacks used for hauling coals, and grabbed a pair of cutlasses. As they ran through camp, Brian hammed it up, shoving Tommy and shouting "Move it!" as they sprinted toward the tree line. They hit it and kept on running.

They made good headway until darkness fell. There was no jungle eye at night. When they raised their hands in front of their faces, they could feel the heat emanating from their palms, but couldn't see them. They kept tripping on vines, startling at weird noises. All the fanged and clawed creatures hunted at night: the jaguar and puma, the anaconda and emerald tree boa. The world's largest beasts. They decided to turn back to the road running between Matthew's Ridge and Port Kaituma. As it cut through a steep hill, a group of figures surrounded them. It was the Jonestown guards.

The boys raised their cutlasses, prepared to go down swinging. They were so close to freedom. "You raise those knives up, Stephan's back there with a rifle, ready to shoot you," one of the guards shouted, and Tommy didn't doubt he would. As the guards marched them toward the glowing pavilion, Tommy blazed with disappointment. They'd almost made it. The throng was waiting for them, angry at being hauled out of bed. Jones sat in his light-green chair on the platform at the front, and as the guards pushed the boys toward him, Tommy wondered what new torture he'd come up with this time.

The Temple leader had a mean look on his face. Tommy sensed the crowd behind him, seething like a giant, hungry animal, ready for the night's sport. Over Jones's head hung a large sign with its message printed in capital letters: "Those who do not remember the past are condemned to repeat it." Tommy believed it had something to do with reincarnation, but at that moment, it seemed like a personal reminder that, despite his eternal optimism, he could never outrun trouble. He was meant to repeat it.

In a low growl, Jones asked the boys how far they thought they'd get. Tommy took the brunt of the criticism because he'd been in Jonestown longer than Brian. Jones asked one of the guards for his version of their apprehension, then reached over to switch on the tape recorder resting on the table beside him. The tape, Q933, was one of 971 audiotapes that FBI agents recovered from Jonestown after the massacre.

It starts midsentence, as the guard berates Tommy:

> . . . I'd just like to say, this idiot . . . you've been in the bush, but you've only been around where people are always at . . . and there ain't going to be no animals there. You get out in the Venezuelan jungle, and you're going to run into every kind of fucking thing. They would've killed you, you're lucky we found you. You know what lives here, man, you know it. Don't say you don't.

> Jones: What lives there? You know about . . . You know about it? The puma? The leopard? The ocelot? 'Bout 50 different uh, breeds of uh, poisonous reptiles? Are you aware of this—any of this? How long you been around here?

> Tommy: Fourteen months, Father.

> Jones: The anaconda?

> Tommy: I'm not aware of all of this—

> Jones: Thirty-six-foot long? Can crush a horse in seconds?

> Tommy: Yes, Father.

> Jones: Didn't you think you should've told your brother this? Tripping out in jungles? Did you not think that this government is our ally?

Tommy: Yes, Father, I did.

Jones: Well, how did you manage to think you were going to get in
Venezuela with the government alerted? I've alerted every person
in this government. From the prime minister on down. The
border patrol said, if you try to cross, you'd be shot. How did
you think you were going to get out of here?

Tommy: I was—I was going to go down there by the uh, Barima
River and stay down there.

Jones: Well, they've all been alerted. No boat would dare pick you
up, it'd a been a violation of the law.

Guard 2: Coast Guard was already notified here to come up and
down the river looking for you already. So, you didn't have a
chance in the world.

Jones: You think I've located in this jungle, knowing all the scalawags
like you that've done this shit before, after we've been through
Leon (Broussard's) lies . . . We knew there'd be others. So we had
firm working alliances. We wanted Leon gone, 'cause we knew
he was a babbling idiot by the time they found him. Talking
about fighting in World War III. We didn't want his big fat ass
around . . . Anybody got any questions to ask these assholes?

This was the signal for the audience to join the verbal attack. The size
and sound of the crowd's fury is frightening even on a low-quality tape
recording. How much more so it must have been for the two sixteen-
year-old boys that night. Jones turned the microphone off and on as the
session grew more heated, editing on the fly. The recording shows Jones's
disturbing ability to switch from a gentle rebuke to an enraged bellow in
the space between two words as he whips the crowd into an angry frenzy.
A woman shrieked that the boys were "shameful bastards," and "goddamn
white fascist bigots." More insults followed, and violence was expected,
encouraged. "Vile filth," Jones called them, before spitting several times.

Tommy's mother, Edith, rushed forward to slap her son's face repeatedly until Jones told her "enough."

The conversation took a surreal turn when Edith proposed she cut both boys' heads off, then commit suicide, "to keep the church from getting in trouble." Reason had flown the coop.

Edith: Why do you think you deserve to live when neither of you want to serve anybody or care about anybody? Why do you think you deserve to live? To just do your own thing?

Tommy: I don't really deserve to live.

Edith: That's right. You don't.

Brian: I don't— I don't think I deserve to live either.

There was a long debate about whether the boys should die. Several people volunteered to kill them. Any time the teens interrupted to try to explain themselves, they were shouted down. At one point, a man tackled Brian from behind; Tommy saw his friend slammed to the dirt floor from the corner of his eye. The man wasn't Brian's father, who was still in California, but another member in the throes of devotion to Jones. The man straddled Brian's chest and started to choke him, sputtering insults as Brian's face turned red. After watching the display impassively for a few minutes, Jones called the man off.

He stopped the recording before determining the boys' punishment, but a slip of paper retrieved by the FBI picked up the thread. The typed release, signed by Jim and Edith Bogue and by Joyce Touchette, Brian's guardian in his dad's absence, permitted the boys to be physically restrained by chain to prevent them from running away again.

The following day, leg irons were welded onto the boys' ankles. The hot metal singed their skin before their feet were plunged into buckets of water. Next, a three-foot chain was welded onto their shackles, connecting them. To further humble them, the teens' heads were shaved to within a quarter inch of their scalps. Although they were bound together, they were prohibited from speaking to each other or anyone else, except for the armed guard watching them, and were forced to run wherever they went, dragging the chain between them. They slept together, showered together, ate together, used the toilet together, and slept in the same bunk.

The guard led them to a fallen log and told them to chop it into firewood. They did so for sixteen-hour days. One day the guard, a boy not much older than Tommy and Brian, was playing with his gun and dropped it. It hit the ground and fired. The guard jumped, but his charges were too exhausted to react. During their second week in chains, Brian slid his thumb over the wood splitter as Tommy wielded the sledge hammer.

"Hit it," he whispered. Tommy refused. The guard was too far away to see this exchange. "Dude, hit it so we can have a break," Brian insisted. They argued briefly before Tommy relented, and smashed his friend's thumb. The guard took them to the nurses' station, where they learned Brian's thumb was badly bruised but not broken. The nurse bandaged it and they were sent back to the tree. A week later, Stephan Jones noticed that Tommy's ankle was badly infected from chafing against the leg irons. He told his mother, Marceline, who had them cut off.

A year later, one of the boys would make a final, successful attempt to escape Jonestown. The other would die there.

CHAPTER 14

CONCERN

B ack in California, a group of families who had relatives in Jonestown started meeting to strategize and share information. They called themselves the Concerned Relatives, and they were worried sick. Tim and Grace Stoen were members, as were many defectors. Some bought ham radios and eavesdropped on Temple transmissions, but the church learned of their efforts and created an elaborate code to evade them. The group persisted, trying to break the cipher.

One of their prized members was a young woman named Yulanda Williams, who lived in Guyana from April to June of 1977, before finagling a way to leave. She waited until Jones was in a drug-induced stupor before asking him to let her go home. She promised not to criticize the Temple, or the settlement, if she returned to California. Incredibly, Jones agreed, after first warning her that *the angels* (supposed Temple assassins) would find her if she broke her promise, and making her sign a document "confessing" to murdering someone and dumping the body in the ocean.

Back in San Francisco, she attended services at the Geary Boulevard church to keep up appearances, but eventually found her way to the Concerned Relatives. She told them about the various ways Jones controlled residents, by using sleep and food deprivation, hard labor, or even forcing them to eat hot peppers, such as she'd seen Tommy Bogue do. Her anecdotes only ratcheted up the group's fear for their loved ones' welfare.

Steven Katsaris, the relatives' chief organizer, had only recently learned that his daughter was one of Jones's favored mistresses. During her first months in Guyana, Maria sent her father upbeat letters about the project's expansion. But after Katsaris called the church to try to coordinate a visit to Jonestown, he started receiving menacing phone calls. "We know you live on a ranch by yourself," a man snarled into the receiver one night. "If you go, you'll get burned out." The threats only stoked his desire to see his daughter. In a phone patch to the mission, Maria sounded cool and discouraged him from coming, telling him Jonestown had a policy forbidding visits. But Katsaris knew this was untrue; previously she'd written that the settlement received daily guests for medical care or tours. He offered to meet Maria in Georgetown, but she still declined, saying she'd be in Venezuela with her fiancé, Larry Schacht, the camp doctor. Another father in the group told Katsaris that his daughter was also engaged to Dr. Schacht, and later he'd learn of more fake betrothals to Schacht, all designed to throw meddling parents off track: Who wouldn't want their daughter to marry a doctor? Katsaris forged ahead and flew to Georgetown to try to arrange a meeting from there, but at the US Embassy, Consul Richard McCoy told him Maria refused to see him because doing so would "bring back some painful experiences from her childhood." Katsaris looked puzzled, so McCoy elaborated: Paula Adams said Katsaris had sexually abused Maria when she was as girl. It was a bald-faced lie, concocted by Temple leadership several years earlier to discredit Katsaris if he ever spoke out against the church, which he now was.

Undeterred, Katsaris flew to Washington, D.C., to meet with various officials in the State Department and press for an investigation into the Temple. He also met with Guyanese ambassador Laurence Mann, Paula Adams's lover, and paid him a three-thousand-dollar bribe to arrange a meeting with Maria. Katsaris returned to Georgetown, and, after many days of delays, Jones finally sent out his daughter. Her physical appearance astonished him: She was bone thin and had pronounced dark circles under her eyes. More bewildering was her demeanor. The daughter who ended her letters with "I love you and miss you" just a few months earlier, now refused to look him in the eye. She also refused to discuss the supposed molestation, but accused him of being part of a conspiracy to destroy the church. Her speech seemed robotic; her voice lacked conviction. He couldn't help wondering if she'd been coached on how to respond to him. But his hands were tied; Maria was twenty-four years old—he couldn't force her to come home with him. He told his daughter that he'd leave return airfare at the embassy for her in case she changed her mind, and left the country disheartened.

Beverly and Howard Oliver also joined the Concerned Relatives. They'd given their two teenaged sons permission to go to Jonestown for a brief vacation, but then weeks turned into months with no sign that their boys were returning.

As lapsed members, the Olivers knew the media exposes were true, and they feared that Jones's violence and instability would only escalate in the wilds of Guyana. Like other Temple parents, however, they'd forfeited guardianship of their sons as a loyalty test. Their son Bruce was nineteen, but they hired an attorney to demand the return of seventeen-year-old William. A California court ruled in their favor, and they wrote Billy telling him a plane ticket was waiting for him at Timehri airport. Most certainly their letter was withheld by Jonestown's censors, for Billy was quickly flown to Georgetown and married off to a female member who, his parents were told, was carrying his child. In reality, Billy's bride was already in a relationship with another resident, the father of her two-year-old daughter. Jones arbitrarily paired and wed couples, even sending them to Georgetown for marriage licenses, as a way of "proving" to pesky relatives that their kin had found love and happiness in Jonestown.

But the Olivers persisted and flew to Guyana on December 19, 1977, accompanied by their lawyer. The trip, financed by Howard's wages as a security guard, cost them a small fortune, but the clock was ticking: Billy would turn eighteen on Christmas Day, and they were desperate to get him back before he was legally an adult.

McCoy tried to arrange a meeting between Billy and his parents, but the Temple kept postponing it, and a few days after Billy's eighteenth birthday, the Olivers returned to California alone. Jones won the round, but he feared other relatives would be on their way.

Every day, more Temple members were silently disappearing from San Francisco. Edith Roller would eat dinner in the church dining room with a friend one evening, and the next evening, the person would be gone. As the congregation thinned out, the leadership kept her busy typing healing affidavits, letters to the editor, and pieces for the Temple newspaper, the *Peoples Forum*. The extra duties, on top of her full-time secretarial post at Bechtel, caused bursitis to flare up in her elbow and cut into her precious free time.

In her apartment there was a tremendous clash of cultures between Edith, a widely traveled white woman who was conversant in the Hericlitean philosophy, and her roommates, who tended to be uneducated, elderly, black women. Edith insisted on being left alone in the evenings so she could listen to broadcasts of the San Francisco Opera at the kitchen table, but that didn't stop her roommates from bursting in, wanting to chat or rifle through the cupboards for food. She thought they were uncultured, and they thought she was a prickly crank.

Edith found one woman so irritating that she commanded her to stay in her room each morning until she heard Edith leave for work. She suspected, correctly in one case, that some of them were stealing small items from her, such as manicure scissors and tweezers.

The tension came to a head one night when Edith woke in a coughing fit and found that a seventy-five-year-old woman from Virginia had placed a photo of Jim Jones on her chest and was beseeching the demon to come out of her in his name. In her journal, Edith wrote that she was puzzled by this voodoo demonstration, but believed it was prompted by "loving feelings."

It was easier for a loner like Edith to empathize with the plight of her roommates by reading books such as Ralph Ellison's *Invisible Man* and Keith Irvine's 646-page tome *The Rise of the Colored Races*, both of which were on her bookshelf, than by spending time with them.

When a Temple secretary told her to prepare to leave for Jonestown during the first week of January 1978, Edith had mixed feelings. She noted in her journal that Temple handlers prevented one of her roommates from calling her son to let him know she was leaving, and she followed the bad press with curiosity. But she still believed Jones was doing more to promote racial equality than anyone else . . . and that he'd cured her arthritis. Her biggest concern about Jonestown was housing. Some folks thought Jones had promised seniors that they'd each have a private home. Edith hoped this was true. She took comfort recalling video footage of a cottage interior that was shown during a service. The brief segment appeared to be filmed as the cameraman sat, or lay, on a bed; the camera gazed up at a large open window topped by a sheer valance that fluttered in the breeze. After lingering on the valance for a few moments, the camera's focus moved beyond the window to a dazzling white tower of clouds in an azure sky. The footage carried enormous appeal for Edith. There was no voiceover or background noise, just a beautiful silence. She could imagine glancing up from a book to survey this magnificent view herself.

She had no idea, of course, that there were much graver things to worry about in Jonestown than her room assignment. None of the rank-and-file members in San Francisco were privy to the hair-raising conversations between Jonestown and the Geary Boulevard radio room during the September siege, or to the suicide votes. Edith did note in her journal at the time of the crisis, however, that Marcy looked agitated during services. Jones's long-suffering wife had to break the news of her husband's adulterous liaison with Grace Stoen, and the ensuing custody battle, to the California congregation. She was forced to repeat the sordid story at various services for new ears, and looked increasingly distraught and exhausted, Edith wrote: "Marcy asked whether anyone had a problem with this. No one publicly admitted to having a problem." Edith, knowing the leadership read her journals, didn't include her own thoughts on the matter or include any communal gossip.

She spent her final weeks at Bechtel doing what employees tradition-ally do during their last days: taking long lunches and frittering away time with personal business. She was told she'd have her own classroom in Jonestown, and leafed through textbook catalogues at her desk, composing lesson plans.

Her coworkers threw her a good-bye party that was well-attended, and she received a glowing letter of praise from Caspar Weinberger, Bechtel's general counsel and future US secretary of defense. She was cagey, however, when her officemates asked about her retirement plans, telling them she was going to volunteer for an agency that rehabilitated delinquent American youth on the borders of Venezuela. They gave her a blue suitcase as a parting gift.

When Edith called her sister Mabs to tell her she was leaving, she wrote in her journal that her sister's only response was "a sharp intake of breath." Her three younger sisters had kept each other abreast of the

Temple scandals, xeroxing copies of negative articles and mailing them to each other. Dorothy phoned Edith to deride Jones's supposed powers, and they argued. Whenever her sisters told Edith they feared for her well-being, Edith retorted that she was worried for *them*, given the imminent fascist takeover of America that Jones predicted.

Dorothy and Edna flew to San Francisco to visit her before she left. The sisters went to a jazz club to hear a performance by Anita O'Day, but the next day tension erupted again at a lunch Edith hosted at her communal apartment. She'd invited a few Temple friends, hoping her sisters would warm to them and finally understand her dedication to the group. The plan backfired. When Edith tried to draw one of her friends out by asking what brought her to the Temple, Dorothy protested that she did not want to be propagandized. The lunch became awkward as the second guest clammed up and Edith fumed over her sister's caustic behavior. When Dorothy told Edith she was putting sixty-two dollars into an emergency fund in case Edith wanted to return to the States, Edith thanked her but secretly planned to use the money to buy textbooks.

In December, another cord tethering Jim Jones to reason snapped when his mother died in Jonestown. A lifelong smoker, Lynetta was in the last stages of emphysema when she moved to Guyana. She lived in a private cottage with a small mutt named Snooks that she'd brought from California, and rarely strayed from bed. In early December, she suffered a stroke that left her partially paralyzed and died within two days. A few hours after her death, an emotional Jones gathered his followers in the pavilion to notify them. He described his mother's last moments as she gasped for air with her "tongue hanging out, saliva flowing down her face. She couldn't move her eyes." He invited people who knew Lynetta well to take a last look at her. Although she looked horrific while she died, in death she looked "very well, very well indeed," he said.

Lynetta was the one person Jones allowed to call his bluff and get away with it. In Jonestown, when she overheard him bragging about shooting a wild turkey with a pistol at a two-hundred-yard distance, she chortled and called over her daughter-in-law. "That man didn't shoot any turkey," she told Marceline. "Anyone knows you can't shoot anything with a pistol from two hundred yards!"

When she died, her moderating influence also ended. On December 21, in the middle of a rambling screed against the Olivers in the pavilion, Jones abruptly asked his followers:

"How many plan your death?"

Residents murmured among themselves.

"Do you ever plan your death?" he repeated impatiently. "There's a number of you that do not lift your hand and say you plan your death. You're gonna die. Don't you think you should plan such an important event?"

He called on a seventy-five-year-old Texan named Vera Talley.

"Sister Talley, don't you ever plan your death?"

On the tape recording of the conversation, she sounded hesitant.

"No," she finally said.

"And why don't you, dear?" Jones asked.

"I don't know, I just hadn't thought about it," she answered.

"Don't you think it's time to think about it? It's a terrible thing to have it be an accident, like I saw my mother, and in many ways your mother, to be, uh, wasted and just laid in a box. I think that's a kind of a waste, don't you think?"

The old woman was confused; she thought Jones was talking about life insurance: "My husband quit paying it and I didn't have no money to pay it, and I just let it go, and I hadn't thought no more about it."

"I'm not talking about insurance," Jones said impatiently. "I'm talking about planning your death for the victory of the people. For socialism, for communism, for black liberation, for *oppressed* liberation . . . Haven't you ever thought about taking a bomb and running into a Ku Klux Klan meeting and destroying all the Ku Klux Klan people?"

The microphone buzzed loudly, interrupting the dialogue and angering Jones. He admonished people sitting in the back of the pavilion to stop playing with their babies and pay attention.

Maya Ijames, eight, a biracial girl with a cloud of soft black hair, lifted her hand. She, too, was confused.

"What does planning your death mean?" she asked sweetly. On the tape, her voice is shockingly innocent and clear.

In his response to Maya, Jones launched into a diatribe, the essence of which was captured in this sentence: "I think a healthy person has to think through his death, or he may sell out."

The remark revealed Jones's deepest fear, that his followers would "sell out" or betray him if they left the church, as had the former Temple members who'd spoken to the press. He'd rather they die first. "When somebody's so principled, they're ready to die at the snap of a finger," he continued, "and that's what I want to build in you, that same kind of character."

He began discussing various methods of death. "Drowning, they say, is one of the easiest ways in the world to die. It's just a numbing, kind of sleepy sensation."

The crowd was solemn, and their lack of enthusiasm infuriated him. "Some of you people get so fuckin' nervous every time I talk about death!" he shouted into the microphone. He stuck out his tongue and pretended to gag, just as he'd seen his mother do in her last breaths. The crowd laughed uneasily.

An elderly woman refused to smile at his antics, and he turned on her: "You're gonna die someday, honey!" he bellowed. "You old bitch, you're gonna die!"

He started keeping lists of residents who didn't raise their hands when he held votes for revolutionary suicide, and of parents who were "too attached" to their children. He directed the medical team to research ways to kill everyone and encouraged them to be creative; there weren't enough bullets to shoot hundreds of people. Their suggestions would later be found in the materials collected by the FBI.

"It would be terrorizing for some people if we were to have them all in a group and start chopping heads off or whatever—this is why it would have to be done secretly," wrote Ann Moore, twenty-three, Jones's personal nurse and Carolyn Layton's sister. "What a slap in the face to fascists it would be to take our own lives before they could have the pleasure of it." She recommended poisoning Jonestown's food or wells, or perhaps confining everyone to an enclosed space before releasing carbon monoxide fumes into the air. She offered to help kill children.

Gene Chaikin's wife, Phyllis, who was Jonestown's medical director, suggested the community "meet as a group in the pavilion surrounded with highly trusted security with guns. Names will be called off randomly. People will be escorted to a place of dying by a strong personality . . . [where] they are shot in the head. If Larry [Schacht] does not believe they are definitely dead their throat is slit with a scalpel. I would be willing to help here if it's necessary. The bodies would be thrown in a ditch. It might be advisable to blindfold the people before going to the death place in that the blood and body remaining on the ground might increase their agitation."

Marceline Jones, also a nurse, argued that the adults should be allowed to choose their fate, and that anyone under eighteen should be spared. "For many years I've lived for just one reason, and that was to safeguard the lives of children," she wrote her husband. "If some asylum could be arranged for our children, especially the babies and preschool children could be saved for socialism and they are young enough to adjust to a new culture and learn a new language." She volunteered to help kill the adults, if necessary. "I, with Dr. Schacht, would stay back to see that everyone else was cared for humanely."

Michigan native Shirlee Fields, forty, who worked as a dietician and lived in Jonestown with her husband and two young children, thought the community should starve themselves to death. "I feel that if we do commit revolutionary suicide we should do it in such a way that we will be heard in all quarters of the world and get the most publicity we can get for communism. One way I think we can do this is by reference to food. Food and malnutrition is an emotionally packed subject. The idea that we could stop eating or cut down as we are in our heavyweight program occurred to me last night in our meeting. This would be a different way to commit revolutionary suicide and I wonder how many people who believe in suicide would be willing to do this."

In San Francisco, Temple leader Jean Brown pushed to send more aamunition down to shoot everyone rather than have Jones enact any number of the grisly suggestions.

As the nightly suicide debates continued, it became clear to residents that voting against death was not an option. It didn't matter what internal terror they felt; Jones wanted them to die. Every single one of them.

On Christmas Day 1977, which, for the vast majority of residents, would be their last, Jones told them it was Revolution Day, not Christmas. In the pavilion, the group sang odes to socialism and Jim Jones, and performed a skit demonizing capitalism. Temple leaders chastised residents for grumbling that it was the worst holiday they'd ever had.

As New Year's approached, Jones started baiting residents by asking them if they wanted to return to the States. "Who here is homesick for California?" he'd ask the assembly in his gentlest preacher's voice. Woe be the person who dared raise his or her hand. They'd be brought before Jones, who denounced them as "elitists" and "miserable capitalists," and made them sorry for speaking up. One man who always took the bait was Tom Partak, a thirty-two-year-old Vietnam vet from Joliet, Illinois. He wrote Jones several notes asking to return home, and when his requests were ignored, he tried to kill himself with a cutlass. During his confrontation Jones told him he should be shot through the hips before descending from his green chair to slap Partak repeatedly.

Likewise, a free-spirited twenty-four-year-old San Diegan, Rose McKnight, was angry that her two-year-old son was assigned to a dorm with other toddlers. "If I'd known it was going to be like this, I wouldn't have come," she told an acquaintance. For her "counterrevolutionary remark," she was put on the learning crew, a group of people in trouble for offenses ranging from complaining about Jonestown to physically assaulting other residents. The learning crew was housed together in a dorm, prohibited from speaking to anyone, including each other, and required to run from one location to the next. They worked from dawn to dusk doing manual labor, such as splitting wood, digging trenches, or clearing bush, a chain gang without chains. For Rose, a severely obese housewife, the strenuous work in the glaring heat was arduous, but worse yet was the emotional punishment of being sepapated from her son. She learned to choke down her emotions, as Jim Bogue had, to do and say the unnatural.

Shortly after she was released from the learning crew, she wrote a letter home, marveling at the creations of the settlement's kitchen. "Wait 'til you taste our Jonestown—cassava cookies, cassava cornbread, donuts, bread, biscuits, all made in expertly-made wood burning ovens and stoves. They are the best you have ever eaten—and you know how I love donuts!"

Her husband would arrive a few months later, enticed by his wife's breezy missives, completely unaware of the terror brewing in the camp.

CHAPTER 15

CONTROL

Jones continued to send long, fretful letters to Guyanese officials, asking them to take sides in the custody dispute. "It is our understanding from the very beginning that the Guyana government would handle situations like that of my son, John Stoen, with a firm hand, by simply stating that there is no jurisdiction," he wrote to Deputy Prime Minister Ptolemy Reid. "But now we hear that the Cabinet will consider each of the 'allegations' as it arises. This creates for us an atmosphere of insecurity . . . we need to know where we stand."

Although his government allies assured him privately that he would not be arrested, his Georgetown attorney advised him not to leave the project until the arrest order was canceled. Heeding his counsel, Jones thus became a prisoner in his own town, and would not leave Jonestown again until he was carried out in a body bag by soldiers with the US Army's Graves Registration Company.

On November 18, 1977, a year to the day before the massacre, a California Superior Court judge in San Francisco awarded custody of John Victor Stoen to his mother, Grace Stoen, and visitation rights to Tim Stoen, as part of their divorce proceedings. The decree nullified all previous documents granting guardianship to Jim Jones and Joyce Touchette, and directed District Attorney Joseph Freitas, Tim Stoen's current employer, to "take all actions necessary" to secure Jones's compliance in surrendering John John to his mother. Freitas wrote Fred Wills, Guyana's minister of foreign affairs, asking for help enforcing the order. If Jones didn't comply, he wrote, "it will be our duty to apply to the court for a warrant of arrest against Rev. Jones."

Jones didn't comply, so the Stoens flew to Georgetown on January 4. That same day, Jones threatened to play his trump card again. The head of the Temple PR crew in the capital, Sharon Amos, complained in a letter to the Cabinet that "conspiratorial custody harassments" were "bleeding" the project's finances and causing low morale among residents. "Please don't let people push us with any more demands," she pleaded. "Living does not mean that much to us if we have to go through harassment here as we did in the States."

The implied suicide threat brought swift results. The Ministry of Home Affairs issued the Stoens a one-day visa, ordering them to leave the country within twenty-four hours. When the US Embassy intervened on their behalf, a furious Amos tracked down US Consul Richard McCoy. "If John goes, we are all just going to sit down and die," she told him. McCoy would later note that she was very careful not to use the word *suicide*.

"That's a lot of nonsense," he replied.

At a January 7 hearing, Supreme Court Justice Aubrey Bishop ruled in the Stoens' favor on several points, and they left the courtroom confident they would win the case. As they waited for their flight home at Timehri airport, a group of Temple members surrounded Tim and threatened to kill him and Grace if they didn't drop the custody suit.

During the two weeks the Stoens were in Georgetown, Jones held nightly crisis meetings to vent his frustration and paranoia. After a full day of hard physical labor, it was a feat for people to sit still and stay awake deep into the night, despite the hard benches. Some people pinched themselves to keep alert, others jogged in place. Jones decreed that anyone who fell asleep or talked to a bench mate while he was speaking would be assigned to the learning crew. He told residents that the Guyanese government seemed to be cooperating with the Stoens, and warned that the so-called conspirators might fly up again to demand John John, this time backed by a platoon of Guyanese soldiers. He picked people out of the crowd to ask their opinion: Should they fight the invaders or commit revolutionary suicide?

Despite the severe repercussions of being called on the floor, residents still voted overwhelmingly to fight. Jones discounted this option as unrealistic; their ragtag security team was no match for professional soldiers, he said. Besides, he reminded them, they had a "long-standing commitment of one for all and all for one." He pledged that he would die before surrendering John John—and so would they.

Night after night, Jones held his death vote. Security guards nuzzled those who refused to raise their hands with their guns and brought them to the front of the pavilion so Jones could confront them. The meetings wore on until dawn brightened the sky, and people started voting for death just so they could return to their cabins for a few precious hours of sleep. After a while, Jones's obsessive suicide talk lost its shock value and began to bore them.

In the middle of January, US Consul Richard McCoy arrived in Jonestown to do a welfare-and-whereabouts check. During a brief exchange of pleasantries in the pavilion, Jones complained of kidney problems, and McCoy later noted the Temple leader was pale and that his speech rambled. Then the consul got down to business. He came bearing a dozen letters from relatives asking him to check on residents. The Social Security Administration, which had stopped forwarding checks to Guyana during the September siege, also wanted him to talk to twenty recipients to follow up on rumors that residents were forced to sign over their checks to the Temple.

McCoy led his interviewees to the open field next to the pavilion, where he was sure there were no electronic bugs and no one could eavesdrop. He'd heard rumors that troublemakers' heads were shaved as punishment, and while he was talking to a young black man who'd supposedly been disciplined in this fashion, McCoy reached over and yanked his afro to make sure it wasn't a wig. The youngster protested; he'd never had his head shaved, he told McCoy. Everyone he talked to that day told him the same thing: They were perfectly happy in Jonestown.

If residents complained of being depressed or said they wanted to return to California, Jones suggested it was because they weren't busy enough. When there was down time, people tended to grumble.

Jones himself slept in most days, recovering from drug- or booze-induced hangovers. His followers were told not to disturb him because he was doing important work for the cause, and his aides played tapes of him reading the news over the loudspeakers so residents would believe he was awake.

He appointed a surveillance force whose job was eavesdropping on residents and reporting them for negative remarks—especially a desire to go home. His lieutenants made other recommendations for keeping people in line. "Hitler did his indoctrination speeches around six to seven p.m., when workers were home eating and their resistance to change was lower," one of his aides suggested. But Jones one-upped Hitler; his voice droned on for most of the day, and usually late into the night, as residents tried to sleep. Sitting in front of a microphone in his cottage, he read random items over the loudspeakers: his thoughts on guerilla warfare, biographies of revolutionary personalities, textbooks on the structure of the United States government, and whatever else he fancied. Whenever Jones was speaking, everyone else was expected to stop talking and listen, even if it was just a tape recording.

Harriet Tropp complained about the constant noise. "I have entertained the thought that you were deliberately using a known psychological technique of interrupting peoples' thought processes with specific information, so as to keep them in a kind of disjointed state—a state that makes them both more receptive to information fed to them, and less able to do concentrated, (and often treasonous) things . . . whatever your reasons, it is driving me nuts." But her complaint had no impact; instead, Jones upped the ante, announcing residents would be tested on the content of his rambling broadcasts.

The supposed news he read was a blend of fact and fiction designed to convince residents that whatever hardships they endured, it was preferable to live in Jonestown than in America. Most of his broadcasts dealt with the mistreatment of African Americans, who comprised nearly 70 percent of the community. He said black children were being castrated in the streets of Chicago, and that eighty cities had been destroyed by race riots. A sampling of the written exams collected by the FBI reveal the extent of Jones's lies: American newspapers were publishing stories stating that blacks were "better off during slavery," scientists had engineered a way to kill off minorities by poisoning the water and food supplies of inner cities, and the Supreme Court ruled that nonwhites could no longer attend college.

But some people weren't fooled.

"I like to do a critical reading of the news to see if I can spot the bullshit stories and find the real thing," Ron Talley, a thirty-two-year-old Long Beach native, wrote Jones.

Harold Cordell managed to sneak a small transistor radio into Jonestown, and he was also aware of Jones's deceit. In the loft he shared with Edith Bogue, he pressed it to his ear so it wouldn't be overheard. The Voice of America broadcasts he heard were completely twisted by the time Jones recounted the same news. As he ferreted out Jones's lies, he grew increasingly terrified. His family had joined Peoples Temple in Indianapolis, and now he had a dozen relatives living in Jonestown, including his five children, his estranged wife, and his mother. There was only one reason Jones would paint such a bleak picture of the outside world, he figured: to make death more appealing than life.

Residents weren't allowed to use the settlement's ham radio, and relied on letters to communicate with loved ones in the States. Jones gradually cut off this link to the outside world. At first, he complained about paying for airmail stamps on letters sent to people who weren't Temple members. Then he forbade writing nonmembers altogether, saying it showed residents were still attracted to life in the United States. Then he announced that *all* mail would be censored.

"We're not so much worried about *incoming* mail as we are *outgoing* mail," Jones said. "It's the outgoing mail that can be devastating, when people make codes in flowers like some of our people have, and little shit. That's what can really destroy us. So we're not concerned about the *incoming* mail. People say, I don't get my mail. You—you piss me off, 'cause you *do* get your mail. If you don't get your mail, it's because the US government is not letting your mail get through, or your goddamn relatives are just not writing."

This was another lie; he withheld hundreds of letters both to and from residents. These would eventually be deposited in the archives of the FBI in Washington, D.C. Read by a stranger thirty years later, the letters are still sharp with heartbreak and desperation. A father chastises his ex-wife for taking their children to Guyana without his knowledge. A brother dying of cancer asks his sister to come home for a final visit. A mother is notified that her daughter has overdosed on reds and is in serious condition. A husband wants to know when his wife will be returning from her mission trip. Parents offer to pay the return airfare for their adult children. The censors summarized each letter for Jones, before writing: "Shall he/she get the letter?" More often than not, his reply, scrawled next to the summary, was "Do not give letter." Often residents weren't told when one of their relatives died; Jones didn't want people clamoring to go home for funerals.

Those relatives who didn't receive mail contacted the State Department, and US Embassy personnel singled out their loved ones in Jonestown for interviews. To curtail suspicion, Jones ordered everyone to write their families upbeat letters. Mentioning that it rained every day could get a letter nixed, as could talking about the heat. As a result, letters home were full of bland non sequiturs: "I am really happy here." "We eat meat every day: chicken, pork, beef and fish." One recipient complained that the letters appeared "as if they had been written by machines." "It is very obvious that the letters I have received have been written according to rules and saying only approved-of things," another wrote his ex-wife, who was in Jonestown with their five kids, including the thirteen-year-old son of whom he had primary custody. Another woman objected that her mother, who always called her children by pet names, used their given names in letters written from Jonestown, and that her misspellings were crossed out and corrected in someone else's handwriting. Others noticed that Jonestown letters arrived unsealed, or that the page bottoms were cut off. Toward the end, Jones insisted that all letters home be written in front of censors, because, he said, "They know how little words can be taken wrong and be used by the CIA."

Edith Roller arrived into this maelstrom on Friday, January 27, 1978. The boat trip thrilled her. As old friends greeted her in the pavilion, she heard Jones announce her arrival over the PA system. He was in the radio room, only a few yards away, surveying the incoming group. He stated that she had fled the CIA and taken refuge in Jonestown. She found his words puzzling, but was flattered by the personal welcome.

Soon afterward, a hubbub erupted in front of the radio room. Jones was berating an old man who'd told a newcomer that "You can't get out of Jonestown," before asking the person if he'd brought any liquor with him. Edith made a note of the odd exchange in her diary.

She ate dinner in the dining tent, but got permission to skip the mandatory Friday night socialism class; she felt too tired and dirty. She hadn't washed or brushed her teeth during the two day river journey, and her luggage was missing, compounding her discomfort. A friend lent her a clean shirt and escorted her to her residence. As she walked past rows of cottages, she must have recalled, again, the videotape footage of the fluttering valance, the towering white clouds. The peace and quiet.

But when she reached cottage number 48, in the last row and facing the jungle, she was dismayed to find it had no front door. Inside were four sets of bunk beds and a loft. The construction crew was run ragged trying to house the flood of immigrants, her friend explained, adding that Edith should be grateful: her cottage wasn't as crowded as most.

The movies hadn't shown the full interior of a cottage. She now saw that the cozy room her imagination had constructed around that window was a chimera. The cottage's three windows were covered with wooden slats, and the interior walls were unpainted, rough-hewn lumber. The bunk-bed mattresses were thin slabs of foam. She resolved to decorate her space, at least, and make it look more welcoming.

She felt self-conscious undressing with the wide-open door, and climbed into the top bunk, just in case a jungle creature padded inside during the night. She slept poorly. Her ankles were riddled with bug bites, the mattress was too thin, the blanket too thick. She listened to the cries of animals outside the gaping door, and ruminated on the confrontation she'd witnessed that afternoon. "You can't get out of Jonestown." What did he mean? By the time she fell asleep, the security guards were already roving between the cottages, banging on walls to wake people up.

More disappointments were in store. When her luggage finally arrived, she watched a supervisor confiscate her extra clothing, and the prescription drugs she took for menopausal hot flashes, telling her that everything was communal in socialist Jonestown.

She was eager to start teaching, but learned there was no classroom prepared for her, as she'd been told in San Francisco. She was shocked by how poorly equipped the school was—there was a dire shortage of books, papers, and pencils—and wrote Temple staff in California suggesting immigrating members pack teaching materials in their luggage. "NO GO," someone wrote next to her suggestion. The letter was also a no go, and never sent, probably because of this criticism.

On her second day, Edith visited Christine Bates, her former roommate. Bates had sent Edith a letter stating she was "very happy" in Jonestown and Edith tracked her down to a massive dorm filled with dozens of seniors, many in triple-level bunk beds. The crowded quarters made Edith glad for her doorless, yet quiet cottage. When the two women were alone, Bates confided to Edith that she'd suffered from various illnesses since she arrived in Jonestown, despite boasting on the promotional movies shown in San Francisco that "she'd never been so healthy."

The visit only increased Edith's anxiety. In her resignation letter from San Francisco State University, she'd written, "I have learned in my life experience . . . in particular in the intelligence service, that concealing the truth, consenting to secrecy and pretense is practically always a mistake. To put it another way, truth really is intelligence, and intelligence truth."

In Jonestown, she'd be forced to endure a life of pretense and secrecy with everyone else.

The community held an extra layer of distress for an introvert like Edith Roller. From the time she lined up outside the clinic every morning to get the pill that controlled her hot flashes, to the time she bunked down in her cottage, which soon housed twelve women, she was surrounded by the crush of humanity. She waited in long queues at breakfast, lunch, and dinner. Jonestown overwhelmed her; she had few moments of privacy.

She squabbled with her roommates in cottage 48, just as she'd done with her roommates in apartment 47 at 1029 Geary Street. She scolded them for talking after lights out, and for tracking mud on the wood plank floor. If someone dared move her shoes from the place where she put them, she'd be furious. Nonetheless, her roommates helped themselves to her sewing supplies and hand mirror, and by turns ignored her or exasperated her to the point of tears. A few got so fed up with her complaints that they curtained off their side of the cottage to create a barrier against her.

And she grew close to Bates, about whom she'd once written in her journal: "I am having as little communication with Bates as possible. I don't want to hear any more about her ills. I save considerable time by not having to listen to her." Bates made Edith a pillow using a swath of the Indian silk Edith brought from California. The silk pillow and a small Mexican painting from her friend Lorraine cheered her private space, which consisted of her bunk bed and the wall next to it. The tiny space where she stored her personal effects was her queendom, her small island of control amid the mayhem.

A few weeks later, when she was finally given a class of teens, and another of barely literate seniors, she busied herself making lesson plans. She taught socialism and English. When she arrived, the school staff was debating teaching methodology. Most of the pupils were African Americans who spoke an inner-city vernacular, and the teachers wondered how to best serve them: Should they teach them standard English, Black English, or a combination of the two? After much discussion, they agreed to permit Black English in classroom conversations, but insisted students learn to read and write in standard English. (The Jonestown school was ahead of its time: In 1996, the Oakland school board would pass a resolution that also allowed the use of "Ebonics" in the classroom.)

The school was comprised of two open-sided long tents set side by side near the pavilion. The tarps leaked from numerous holes when it rained, and although each tent was subdivided into makeshift classrooms by bookshelves and chalkboards, the noise from one class spilled into the next. Edith frequently had to shout to make herself heard over the din of the band practicing, the rain, or Jones babbling over the loudspeakers. (Classes were usually allowed to proceed when he was speaking.)

She wrote in her journal that she "planned to sneak up [on] her high-school students with poetry." But when she read them selections from

Robert Frost, Ogden Nash, and A. E. Housman, they looked bored, and when she announced she planned to continue with Shakespeare, they protested outright. They wanted poets they could relate to: black poets like Langston Hughes and Maya Angelou, not pedantic old white men. She agreed, and a happy compromise was made.

More often, however, she lost patience with her teenage charges. She didn't know how to relate to them, nor they to her. She was stiff, rules oriented, and tragically unhip in her Peter Pan collars and thick glasses. Her young pupils were rowdy when they entered the classroom, and talked to each other or fell asleep while she lectured. Some liked to provoke her by asking her a stream of irrelevant questions and watching as she became increasingly exasperated. She suspected Tommy Bogue was stealing her pencils. It was a game, pissing off Professor Roller. Her classroom was a far cry from the respectful, quiet place of learning she fantasized about as she perused textbook catalogues during her last days at Bechtel. Once, her class overheard another teacher lecturing on the same topic as she was, and they stood in unison and deserted her for the other classroom.

Her greatest satisfaction came from her older students, who were truly grateful for the opportunity to learn. In her basic English class, most of the black seniors could only read at a third or fourth grade level. Some couldn't write. She used children's books to teach them. When Jones started testing the community on the news, her senior students panicked. They struggled to understand complex geopolitical notions, let alone write about them. Their fear only grew when Jones said that anyone who failed the news test twice would be assigned to the Learning Crew. Edith started to write Jones a memo suggesting he rely more on teaching rather than testing to improve residents' political awareness, but then wondered if it would be construed as a criticism, and decided not to give it to him. Instead, she started producing a special senior edition of the daily news, simplifying the concepts Jones spoke of and typing them up on a large-font typewriter.

She encouraged her older black students to take pride in their cultural heritage, and spent her free time fashioning a large map of Africa from a blue bed sheet and paper flour sacks to teach them geography. As her students pinned the continent's fifty-three countries to the sheet, they were "deeply impressed" with its size, she wrote in her journal. For many of them, it was the first time they'd learned about their roots.

She became particularly close to one of her students, a seventy-seven-year-old black woman from Texas named Eddie Washington. Washington arrived a week after Edith, and like Edith, she was unmarried, childless, and alone in Jonestown. At the pavilion rallies, Eddie started saving Edith a seat at one of the front benches, which had seat backs. It took Jonestown for Edith to surmount her classism and reach out to an unschooled black senior like Eddie. Jonestown was the great equalizer. For the next nine months, Edith and Eddie sat side by side in their front pew, witnessing the man they once so admired plunge into madness.

CHAPTER 16

RELEASE

On February 2, two representatives from the US Embassy, Desk Officer Frank Tumminia and Deputy Chief of Mission John Blacken, flew up to the settlement for a routine visit. Tumminia would later testify that Jones appeared "rational, though he exhibited a distinct persecution complex." He was more concerned about the residents. Many appeared "drugged and robot like" when they responded to his questions, he later testified. But he was a pencil pusher, not a psychiatrist; he couldn't detect any signs of violence, or indications that people were being held against their will. He didn't see any weapons or anything else that would hint at coercion. He was forced to take everything at face value.

Tumminia had no way of knowing how carefully Jones had rehearsed for the diplomats' visit. Only the day before, officials from the Soviet embassy visited Jonestown, and in preparation, Jones micromanaged every detail of their tour, from the red shirts donned by residents to the band playing "The Internationale" in the pavilion as they arrived.

For the US Embassy guests, Jones told residents to avoid red, and instructed entertainers to sing "God Bless America." Several classes were staged to impress the guests, and Edith Roller was asked to fill a seat in a contrived history class. If residents were asked where John John was, they were to reply "I don't know."

One of the people Tumminia interviewed was Hyacinth Thrash. Her family was concerned because she hadn't written them, while Zippy had penned several glowing reviews of Jonestown. Hy couldn't bring herself to lie, and she was nervous during the interview. "I'm fine," she told Tumminia. "Tell my family not to worry."

Everyone was hewing closely to the script until the guests entered the senior dorms, where an eighty-three-year-old Texan named Katherine Domineck complained that she'd fallen from the top of a triple-decker bunk.

As soon as the visitors left, Jones summoned the entire camp to the radio room. There, for a solid hour, he cursed the old woman for ruining his careful preparations as his henchmen shook their fists in her face. Edith noted in her journal that he proposed isolating potential troublemakers during future visits.

Domineck's confrontation left Hyacinth deeply shaken. She'd never seen Jones turn his fury on a black senior, a woman, no less. In California, he was always so caring toward seniors, pausing to compliment them or lay a soft hand on their shoulder. His apparent concern, and his out-spoken endorsement of equal rights, prompted many African Americans to join the Temple and donate all their earthly goods to his cause. He'd promised them that, in Jonestown, they could walk around without fear of getting mugged. They now feared Jim Jones. Hy was glad she'd kept her mouth shut. She was crippled, thin, only five-foot-two; if Jones sicced his heavies on her, there'd be nothing left.

Not long after Edith Roller arrived, the region's first dry season began. The intense equatorial sun desiccated seedlings and shriveled vines, and the entire community—seniors, school kids, even four-year-old children—pitched in to form a bucket brigade to save their crops.

Despite these painstaking measures, the settlers still couldn't eke enough sustenance from the soil. Food—the *lack* of it—became a sore subject. Meat scarcely graced their plates. The piglets were felled by a mysterious illness that Jim Bogue knew only as *baby pig disease*. They were born perfectly healthy and suckled eagerly at the sow's teats, but after a few days, they wandered around the pen crying weakly, before collapsing from dehydration. Bogue figured the sow's milk supply was inadequate, so he tried changing the sow's food, injecting the piglets with sugar water, and warming them under heat lamps. Nothing worked; few survived to maturity.

The chickens were also dying, from disease and human error. The coops lacked proper ventilation and hygiene; as a result, the chickens became ridden with parasites, and viral and bacterial infections. To keep the chicks from pecking each other to death, inexperienced workers trimmed their beaks but sliced off the tips of their tongues in the process, causing them to starve to death. When Edith Roller arrived, the chickery was only producing an average of 270 eggs per day while the settlement's population topped nine hundred.

At the weekly agricultural meeting, the most pressing concern of the audience was filling their stomachs. "How long's it gonna take for the bull to be eatable?" someone asked. "How soon will the cows be ready for milking?" asked another. A man gave an overview of the garden: how many feet planted of mustard greens, shallots, and cabbage, how many pounds harvested of okra, squash, and bora beans.

"Any questions?" he asked in conclusion.

"Plant more next week," someone wisecracked, prompting a laugh from the crowd.

Jones urged the agricultural committee to find a crop that could feed one thousand people on a regular basis. The committee recommended cassava. The starchy tuber is high in calories, thrives in poor soil, tolerates drought, and grows year-round, which makes it a staple in many poor tropical nations. Every part of the plant is useable. The roots can be prepared like potatoes or ground into flour, the leaves boiled as a potherb. But cassava, while hardy and plentiful, is also very low in vitamins and minerals, which is why malnutrition is rampant in countries that rely on it. In March, the garden supervisor announced that there would be no vegetable harvest for thirty to sixty days, except for cassava leaves.

Edith noted the food problem soon after her arrival. To start with, residents were only served two meals a day on Sunday: breakfast and an early dinner. Jones explained that, since residents only worked a half day on Sundays, they didn't burn as many calories and could forgo lunch. Breakfast was usually a starch—sweet rolls, a scoop of rice—containing hardly enough calories to tide anyone over for an entire day.

On her first Sunday, the community was abuzz: Word got around that they'd have barbecued pork for dinner. Jones sold most of the pigs that survived to maturity downriver; now that he wasn't pulling in thousands of dollars from offering plates each week, he said the community needed to sell its surplus meat and produce to help defray the cost of running the project. But when residents made their way through the meal line that evening, they were handed a bowl of rice topped by a watery gravy of greens with a few shreds of meat, and they were angry. Only two hogs had been slaughtered to feed nine hundred people. The groans and complaints that ricocheted through the dining tent were reported to Jones, who got on the PA system and scolded residents for their ingratitude. It was too expensive to put a pork cutlet on every plate, he said, so they had to get their protein from other sources, such as legumes. When the grumbles continued, he dispatched the "Jonestown police" to the dining area to discourage further insubordination.

But with hunger clawing at their bellies, they couldn't think of much else.

The next week, when residents rejoiced at being served a fried chicken dinner, Jones made them feel guilty for it, lamenting that it cost him $2,000 to provide it. He told them to savor it because they wouldn't get another chicken dinner for two months.

Because the farm couldn't produce enough food to feed everyone, Temple members in Georgetown were dispatched to the capital's produce markets and wharfs to beg for scraps. Farmers gave them bruised and overripe produce, and boat captains let them pick over their nets. This refuse was shipped upriver on the *Cudjoe*.

As the months passed, some desperately hungry people resorted to stealing food, wolfing down seed peanuts and raw sweet potatoes, or unripe fruit from the orchard. Others swiped food from the plates of the seniors or toddlers they cared for. A guard arrested a group of children, including a seven-year-old boy, for picking fruit off trees.

But while Jones kept his followers hungry, he kept the small refrigerator in his cabin well-stocked. It is telling that Jones drank Diet Pepsi; a survivor would bitterly remark that Jim Jones was the only person who got fat in Jonestown. During the pavilion meetings, he sipped cold drinks and chewed ice to ward off heat as his congregation sweltered, and he ate heaping plates of food as their stomachs churned.

In San Francisco, Jones once told an aide that the way to control people was to "keep them tired and poor." In Jonestown, he kept them tired, poor, and hungry.

One night, when Stanley was guarding the front gate, he decided to visit a nearby kiosk. He was friendly with the proprietor, a man who lived in the house adjoining the shop, and reckoned he'd hit him up for a cold beer. Stanley woke the man, who indeed kindly offered him beer and cigarettes. The contraband was like manna from heaven, a break from the relentlessness of Jonestown. But as Stanley walked back to his post, he heard the tractor-trailer lumbering up the road from the community's center toward the gate and realized the other guard had radioed back to report him AWOL. He started sprinting, but the tractor got to the gate first. Lee Ingram, one of Jones's top enforcers, rode in the trailer. "Get in," he ordered Stanley.

As they drove back toward camp, he could hear Jones shrieking into the loudspeakers: "Alert! Alert! Everyone to the pavilion!" People streamed down the paths, groggy, pulling on robes. Stanley was shoved to the front of the pavilion, where Jones called him a motherfucker, a spy, and accused him of fraternizing with the enemy. Next, the horde descended on him. The violence of the catharsis meetings skyrocketed in Jonestown. People felt trapped and hopeless, and hitting someone during a confrontation was a way to release their frustration. Jones encouraged it. At one point, as the group pummeled Stanley with their fists and feet, he dropped to his hands and knees and crawled through the forest of legs, and his assailants turned on each other. Stanley stood on the sidelines watching the chaos in disbelief.

"Y'all are some damn fools!" a guard finally yelled. "Stanley's over here watching y'all."

Jones assigned Stanley to the learning crew, where he chopped firewood for weeks, prodded along by a rifle.

It was hard to control the many unhappy people in Jonestown. Jones warned residents that dangerous animals lurked in the jungle, waiting to attack them the moment they stepped off the property, and that fear alone kept many residents from attempting to flee. But some people who'd been there longer, such as Jim and Tommy Bogue, knew this was just bluff. Although there were jaguars and pumas in the surrounding bush, they were rarely seen because they fled human encounters.

Jones constantly invented new ways to humiliate or scare residents into submission. His son Stephan used a boa constrictor to terrify people, including a five-year-old boy named Norya Blair. The child "screamed and cried as Stephan said he would tell the snake to bite him," Edith Roller wrote in her journal. Another time, Jones ordered the snake to be hung around the neck of an emotionally disturbed woman named Kay Rosas, who refused to work. Rosas begged for forgiveness, but Jones terrorized her further by ordering Stephan to take her to see "the tiger," stating that the "Fucking tiger hadn't been fed tonight." Jones didn't actually have a tiger at his disposal, but that didn't stop him from using the *idea* of a tiger to manipulate people. He also came up with a punishment called Big Foot. Children were led to a dark well where, they were told, Big Foot lived. As guards hung them upside down by their ankles, adults hiding inside the well tugged at their arms. Afterward, the kids would be led back to the compound, sobbing and distraught, thus "verifying" the monster's existence for others.

Jonestown principal Tom Grubbs suggested a new method of behavior modification. He wrote Jones a memo suggesting troublemakers be confined to a small, enclosed space, that was "light tight, well ventilated, and soundproof." Eventually, he settled on a shipping crate, which was lowered into an earthen tunnel that the community used for dry storage.

"The theme idea is to deprive *all sensation* as much as possible," Grubbs wrote. He explained that a supervisor would sit beside the crate to monitor the occupant, but would not communicate with the person for the first three days. Then, the second phase, as Grubbs envisioned it, began: "Short communications disparage all selfish, capitalistic behavior characteristics *specifically*. Communications should be 10–30 seconds long and not more often than once an hour. Statements need to be carefully thought out for clarity, brevity, emotional and intellectual impact. At this time the monitor does not engage in 2-way conversation at all.

"Beginning about 30 hours after the onset of hallucinations, the substitution phase is initiated and with it the first 2-way communication. . . . My studies never mentioned any of the subjects as going insane, but that they did pass through disorientation and re-orientation and that it took nearly a week to appear *'normal'* after the experience."

The first person sentenced to "the box," as it came to be known, was Dana Truss, seven, who was in trouble for slapping another child. At the time, Dana's mother was in California, desperately trying to get her back. She'd been told that Dana, accompanied by her grandma, would only be at the project for six to eight weeks, as a kind of educational field trip. But two months had turned into nearly a year, and she'd hired a lawyer who was provoking Jones's ire.

Groups of schoolchildren were brought over to witness Dana's confinement. Edith Roller joined one of the groups, and wrote in her journal that Dana cried out for water as principal Grubbs sat taking notes. He dismissed Dana's pleas, saying she was just trying to get attention, and the children listened with wide eyes as their playmate screamed. If they misbehaved they'd be next, they were told.

The path to the box passed the cottage of Hyacinth Thrash, who rarely made it to rallies anymore and thus wasn't aware of its existence. She saw kids released from the box walk by her, shaking and disheveled, and called out to them, "What happened?" but they only quickened their pace, refusing to talk to her.

CHAPTER 17

DRILL

O n the evening of February 13, 1978, a ham-radio aficionado in Bethesda, Maryland, was twirling the dial on his transceiver when he picked up a distress call from South America. The frantic man on the other end of the line identified himself as Larry Schacht, a doctor stationed at a mission village in Guyana. He needed to consult an obstetrician about a breech birth; the woman's life was in peril. The ham patched Schacht through to his neighbor, Albert Greenfield, an ob-gyn.

Schacht told Greenfield that his patient was pregnant with twins and two weeks overdue; she'd been in labor for fourteen hours and wasn't progressing. Schacht explained that he was a general practitioner and had no experience with what he feared was a breech delivery. Furthermore, it was impossible to airlift the woman to Georgetown: The nearest jungle airstrip was unlit and covered in fog.

Greenfield urged Schacht to perform an emergency C-section. He talked him through the entire procedure, starting with how to place the woman on the operating table. Schacht mentioned that the only anesthesia he had on hand was ether, and as Greenfield hung up, he had little hope that the mother or her twins would survive the ordeal.

The next day, the ob-gyn asked his neighbor to radio the project to check on the patient's status. To his relief, he was told that the mother had lost two pints of blood, but was doing fine, as were her twin girls. The *Washington Star* published a story on the birth, and Ambassador Laurence Mann honored Greenfield in a ceremony at the Guyanese embassy in

Washington, D.C. The obstetrician humbly told the press that the real hero of the story was Larry Schacht.

But there was one problem: the birth story was a complete fabrication. An Amerindian woman did deliver twin girls in Jonestown, but she did so vaginally, according to a survivor who assisted with the birth.

Jones concocted the entire tale as propaganda.

Laurence Eugene Schacht came from a family of progressive Jews living in Houston. His parents were communist sympathizers. His older brother Daniel was arrested for wearing an army uniform during an anti-Vietnam protest in a case that eventually went to the Supreme Court. He won on free speech grounds, and the court revoked an obscure law prohibiting citizens from wearing uniforms while ridiculing the military.

In Texas, the Schacht family was harassed both for its ideologies and heritage. Vigilantes fired shotguns at their house, burned a cross on their lawn, and threatened to kill them in letters and late-night phone calls. Schacht's high-school classmates remember him as a Bob Dylan wannabe, a dark and brooding kid who liked to sing folk songs about injustice. But in his late teens, he started using crystal meth, supplied by a friend who was a chemist. The drug made him paranoid; he told his friends that the FBI was following him.

In 1969, he had a vision telling him to go to California, an acquaintance would later tell the FBI, and once there, he had another vision telling him to join Peoples Temple. He arrived in Redwood Valley with a stepladder of injection marks scarring his forearms. The Temple dried him out and sent him to medical school, and he graduated from the University of California at Irvine with high honors.

But a mere five weeks into his required internship at San Francisco General Hospital he disappeared. He wrote his family that he was going to complete his residency in Guyana, but the truth was later revealed: Jones had ordered him to Jonestown. Schacht procured and administered various narcotics to the Temple leader while he was in California, and Jones wanted him to continue this personal care in Guyana.

The lack of hands-on experience that doctors gain during their residencies hindered Schacht in Jonestown, where he paused frequently during patient consultations to thumb through reference books.

When the Guyanese Minister of Health, Hamilton Green, heard the twenty-nine-year-old was practicing medicine in his country without a license, he tried to stop him. In the United States, doctors are legally required to complete at least three years of a residency before they can practice medicine, and in Guyana, the requirement is a year. Green wanted Schacht to complete his residency at a Georgetown hospital, but Jones refused to let him leave Jonestown. Privately, Jones feared Schacht wouldn't return to the settlement if he let him go. Publicly, he tried to prove Schacht was indispensable by fabricating the C-section story.

Jonestown residents regarded Schacht as a strange bird. Survivors would describe him as a loner who was "extremely intelligent but emotionally unstable." One man complained to the FBI that Schacht "enjoyed giving prostate exams to men who didn't need them."

As the sole doctor for nearly one thousand people, a third of whom were senior citizens, Schacht was overwhelmed by his caseload. He frequently used the settlement's ham radio to consult with the Medical Amateur Radio Council (MARCO), a group of ham-radio users working in health care who tuned their sets to a certain frequency every evening to provide free consultations to far-flung listeners. Schacht's questions were so simplistic—about basic procedures to set broken bones or treat skin rashes—that the MARCO members were surprised to learn he was a practicing physician.

Schacht worked fifteen to sixteen hours a day, after which, he told Jones, he resorted to knocking himself out with Valium. He was always behind on his appointments, and worried that his coworkers would write him up for a poor attitude or job performance.

Like Jones, he had depressive tendencies, and he self-medicated to control his moods.

"I am a pisser when I wake up, hate to face an onslaught of human needs. Spoke today about wishing I could blow my brains out," he wrote to Jones on January 1, 1978.

His one free day each week was Wednesday, when he stopped healing Jonestown residents and instead researched ways to kill them. When Jones directed the medical team to find a way to carry out the mass suicide, Schacht responded with enthusiasm. He ordered a microscope, slides, and test tubes for his makeshift lab and asked the nursery to save empty baby-food jars for him, as they worked well for growing microbial cultures. A few weeks later, he wrote Jones that he felt encouraged because he'd succeeded in producing a culture that looked like the botulinum bacteria under the microscope, but that may have been tetanus. In another update, he noted that he was working on twenty-one different cultures, including a fungus that could be injected into people to make it look like they had died from meningitis. "I need a good book on forensic medicine—[something that] tells many different ways people are actually killed," he wrote. "There is a good chance I can develop germicidal means—botulism and staphylococci in process now. But with time pressing in (and) my confidence level low, my expertise is lacking in this area. I am quite capable of organizing the suicide aspect and will follow through and try to convey concern and warmth throughout the ordeal, have told the rest of the team this and Joyce Parks and myself will commit suicide last after graduating our adult comrades on the team."

Through his research, he decided botulism was the best bet for mass death: The botulinum toxin is the most poisonous substance known to exist; a single gram is capable of killing more than a million people. It causes death by paralyzing muscles—including the chest muscles—resulting in respiratory failure. The toxin is also fairly easy to produce. Its spores thrive in homemade preserves, and its cheap and easy production have made it the biological weapon of choice for murderers ranging from Pancho Villa to Saddam Hussein. And surely Schacht must have heard of the fifty-nine people in Michigan who were hospitalized in 1977 after eating contaminated jalapeño peppers at a Mexican restaurant; it was the largest reported outbreak of food poisoning in US history.

But botulism is not a perfect killer. It is slow acting. Symptoms, including slurred speech, weak muscles, and difficulty swallowing, take up to seventy-two hours to develop, and death can take days.

Another culture he succeeded in growing, staphylococcus aureus, wasn't an ideal killer either. Commonly known as *staph*, the bacterium thrives in unrefrigerated meat and dairy products. Although faster acting than botulinum toxins, staphylococcal toxin's worst effects—vomiting, diarrhea, and fever—are rarely fatal.

Undeterred, Schacht returned to his lab.

* * *

On the same day that the *Washington Star* published an article on the alleged C-section, Guyana's principal newspaper, the *Guyana Chronicle,* ran a letter to the editor blasting the Temple. The *Chronicle* had printed a puff piece a few days earlier describing the agricultural project in glowing terms, and the angry reader accused the Temple of aggressive self-promotion and chastised the paper for publishing "hand-outs . . . from persons who may have their own purposes to serve." The author was no one less than the powerful Minister of Development, Desmond Hoyte.

When Temple staff in Georgetown read the letter to Jones over the radio, his paranoia skyrocketed. He called the letter a slap in the face, and feared that the entire Guyanese cabinet was distancing itself from him. To make matters worse, one of his closest allies, Foreign Minister Fred Wills, had recently been fired for allegedly mishandling funds.

By the early months of 1978, the negative press and rumors swirling about the Temple had reached the Guyanese populace. A large community of Guyanese expatriates lived in the United States, where they clipped news articles about the controversial church and mailed them home. When Jordan Vilchez and other members panhandled in Georgetown, they were asked blunt questions: Were residents free to leave Jonestown? Was there an armed guard posted at the entrance? How was the project financed?

A former government official railed against the church on a popular Georgetown radio station: "Who are these people from Peoples Temple and who knows anything about them? Who are they to drive around town with a foreign license plate—what would happen if we were to go to America and drive around with our plates?"

Jones feared the Stoens would use the divisiveness to their advantage. His aides shot off a new round of thinly veiled suicide threats to Guyanese officials, pressing them to take a stand on the custody case. "Why in hell's half acre can't a community of 1,000 people who have no indulgences or excesses but their own voluntary commitment to Guyana be guaranteed the safety that none of their residents will be moved?" Sharon Amos wrote cabinet members. "Are we wanted here or what?"

Hoyte's letter to the editor seemed to confirm Jones's fear that Hoyte, Prime Minister Burnham's heir apparent, had it in for him. Previously,

Hoyte had complained about the settlement's use of the Guyanese Defense Force planes to airlift patients to the capital, and five days later, the army started billing the Temple for flights.

On February 16, at six in the morning, shortly after his Georgetown staff read him Hoyte's letter, Jones got on the loudspeaker and ordered everyone to the pavilion. Edith wrote in her diary that by the time she reached the meeting space, the entire membership was crowded beneath the corrugated metal roof.

Jones was livid. He ranted about shakeups in the Guyanese government, and suggested the CIA was behind them. The *Cudjoe* crew spotted Guyanese soldiers in Port Kaituma, and Jones feared they were amassing to attack Jonestown.

In her diary, Edith noted that Jones slurred his words. He complained of a tooth infection, and periodically an assistant made a show of putting a "temporary filling" in his mouth. Most likely, he was high.

Jones asked his followers for their take on the situation, and radioed his Georgetown reps to clarify the views of different government officials. He suggested the crisis could force the group to leave Guyana, and asked for opinions. Long lines of residents formed. Some suggested returning to the United States. Others wanted to move to a communist nation: Cuba, the Soviet Union, or various African countries. Edith wrote Jones a note suggesting they send able-bodied members to Africa to join a revolution. A guard carried her note to Jones, but he chose not to read it aloud. She then stood to make the same suggestion to the crowd, but her voice was drowned out in the hubbub. Jones shot down each alternative: They had too many nonworkers, he said, too many seniors and young children, for any country to take all of them, and he refused to leave anyone behind.

Hours passed. A meager breakfast was served. Armed guards escorted groups of people to urinate behind a nearby building.

As the day wore on, Jones effectively dismissed any option but revolutionary suicide. In the late afternoon, he told the astonished group that mercenaries were on their way to attack them.

"It's all over, they're coming in right now to kill us," he announced. He argued that it was better for them to die by their own hand because the CIA-backed soldiers would surely torture them as they had done to socialists in Chile. He leapt from one paranoid scenario to the next, each ending with mass suicide.

After residents realized it was futile to argue with him—as he would just outtalk them or berate them into submission—his aides carried a large vat to a table at the front of the pavilion, along with towers of paper cups.

He commanded them to line up and drink the "potion"—a dark liquid that he said would take about forty-five minutes to do its job. He assured them it was painless; they'd just feel as if they were falling asleep. After ensuring everyone had "crossed over," he'd drink it himself.

Some protested. They didn't understand the jumps in his logic, or why he wanted to die over a letter to the editor. Guards forced these to drink first, marching them to the table and standing over them as they drained their cup, then leading them into the field next to the pavilion to lie down and wait for death. This intimidation stifled further rebellion. Seniors were allowed to remain seated and nurses carried trays to them. Everyone else joined the line. Someone asked Jones about the nursery workers and the babies, as well as the people working in the kitchen and at the piggery. "They've already been taken care of," he said.

The planning commission members who'd partaken in the suicide drill in San Francisco wondered if it was another loyalty test. Small children failed to grasp the gravity of the situation. "Oh boy, I'll get off the learning crew!" yelled a seven-year-old boy named Irvin Perkins. The line wound through the pavilion and stretched behind it to the radio room. It moved slowly. Some people had to be coaxed to drink. To others, suicide was more appealing than another day in Jonestown. Those who wanted to live sized up their options as they drew closer to the death vat. If it were just another loyalty test, and they refused to drink, they'd be branded as anarchists, or worse, traitors, and face days, weeks, or even months of harassment. Armed guards surrounded the pavilion, and Jones, sitting impassively in his green chair, warned that anyone who tried to flee would be shot.

While some people went mute with disbelief and others sobbed with abandon, Tommy Bogue and Brian Davis joked around. "That's not poison," Tommy whispered to his friend. They laughed at the people who drained their paper cups then immediately dropped to the ground convulsing.

They looked ridiculous, whether they were dying or not. Guards dragged them to the field by the arms. Tommy didn't give a damn about socialism; he couldn't wrap his brain around most of what Jones said. He was tired of the constant gloom and doom, the exhaustion, lousy food, and the tension. When Principal Grubbs showed his class the box, Tommy fantasized about climbing into it. Grubbs said it was soundproof; he wouldn't have to hear Jones's drivel anymore. He'd be left alone.

When Jones saw the two boys joshing around, he bellowed into the microphone. "What are you laughing about?" Guards hustled them to the front of the pavilion, where Tommy didn't miss a beat: "We're just so happy to be dying for the cause, Father," he responded in a sincere voice. He knew what he was supposed to say. Jones ordered them to get back in line. It was a turning point for both boys: They now knew Jones could not read their minds. He couldn't even tell they were lying. He had no paranormal powers.

Stanley Clayton was incredulous. From where he stood, he had a good view of the people lying in the field. Some fidgeted, smoothing down the sharp stalks of field grass. Others whispered to each other. They sure didn't look like they were dying.

Edith Roller was alarmed. She thought mass suicide was unwarranted. Her roommates had told her about the September siege, when Jones started advocating death, and now, as the sun sank below the jungle canopy, she was deeply afraid. The line inched forward, trancelike. Even small children were silent, their eyes luminous with the magnitude of the event, sensing their parents' consternation.

She wondered if Jones would really go through with it, and studied him as he sat in his throne chair observing his followers drink what he'd told them was poison. While their faces were rife with anguish, his seemed unmoved, even detached. She recalled how he often said life was just pain for him and that he regretted being born, and decided that, yes, he was fully capable of making them all die.

She'd only been in Jonestown three weeks, and she was very clear about one thing: She did not come to Guyana to end her life. She came to help, to do something useful with it. She wanted to teach, to write the history of Peoples Temple.

She tried to distance herself from what was happening by intellectualizing the event. She thought of rebels who'd died bravely for their beliefs, including the Revolutionary War hero Nathan Hale, and Jose Rizal, martyr of the Philippine Revolution. She regretted that she'd no longer be able to read poetry. Shakespeare came to mind. *Hamlet,* as well as Henry IV, in which Feeble states, "We owe God a death." She thought about her sisters, and her friend Lorraine. She was sure they'd dismiss Jones as a lunatic when they got the news, and possibly her as well.

As she drew closer to the table, she formulated her last words to Jones. She'd recommend he tell the world, over the ham radio, that they had died to protest fascism. In a peculiar way, she enjoyed the experience. Everything was so vivid and profound. Time slowed, even as her thoughts raced. She felt a new fondness for the members around her, for her new friend Eddie Washington. They would die together.

She was annoyed that she left her watch in her cottage—her room-mates had been rushing her to get to the pavilion—and wondered if the first people who drank the potion were already dead. The thought amused her: What difference does time make when you're waiting to die? She was used to timing all her activities for her journal entries, but she'd never be able to write: "I died at 5:30 p.m. on the 16th of February 1978." She tried to psych herself up for her last act, resolving to be a credit to herself, to drain the cup without hesitation. Afterward, she'd calmly sit on the grass and watch the last wisps of sunset fade, and then, after a few minutes, pass out.

Her reverie was interrupted by Jones's voice. He was crying.

"You didn't take anything," he said quietly. Tears ran down his face. "You had only punch with something a little stronger in it."

He'd conducted the drill to learn which of his followers would obey him during an emergency, and which would defy him. The people who collapsed or felt dizzy during the ritual were merely experiencing the power of suggestion; he added: "The mind is very powerful."

The next day, Jones asked residents to write up their impressions of the exercise.

"As far as my thoughts after I drank the solution—I was trying not to think at all," wrote Queens, New York, native Maria McCann, twenty-five.

"It is so amazing to me how we live here from one day to another. One day we are drinking a death potion and the next day we're producing in the fields as though we have a long life before us."

Parents who'd brought their children to Jonestown believing they were giving them a better life were deeply troubled. "My children took the day good except for Leanndra," wrote Carol McCoy, who'd followed Jones from Indiana. Her daughter, who turned nine on the day of the crisis, was "scared, cried and couldn't understand. She felt this way before when we talked about death. I don't know quite what to say to her except to make her feel death would be so much better. She spent the night with me on her birthday and was afraid to go to sleep because she was afraid she wouldn't wake up."

In her journal, Edith was circumspect. "Was this movement to come to naught, to a pile of dead bodies and an abandoned agricultural experiment in the small country of Guyana?" she wrote. "Is this what (Jones) will be remembered for?"

She recalled a service in which he'd promised his congregation: "If you stay with us, your fondest hopes, all that you ever imagined you could be, will be fulfilled."

"I didn't feel that I had achieved all I could do and I knew others had not," she wrote.

Her diary and hundreds of other personal notes were part of the fifty thousand pieces of paper the FBI collected in Jonestown after the killings. They tell a tale of individuals who came to Guyana expecting Eden but found hell instead. Gathered from the settlement's mud by agents looking for clues to explain the largest mass murder-suicide in modern times, the slips of paper tell the real story of Jonestown: not of a brainwashed people who killed themselves and their children "at the snap of a finger," but of idealists who realized, too late, that they were trapped in a nightmare.

CHAPTER 18

HYACINTH

Hyacinth Thrash certainly never heard Jones mention suicide before she moved to South America. She didn't venture to the pavilion for the punch drill, but Zippy told her about it later. Some people went into hysterics, believing they were actually dying, Zip said, "but it was more of a pretend thing." The sisters laughed about it.

Hy rarely attended community meetings since the September siege; she used her lame leg as an excuse. When she did, she was offended by what she'd see: the violence, Jones braying about his sexual prowess or squalling about spies hidden in the jungle. One night, she watched him eating peanuts and popping pills at the same time. Another night, he shot a pistol into the air and growled, "I ought to kill everyone last one of you." On yet another occasion, he forced a sixty-year-old woman who'd complained about Jonestown to take off her clothes and parade naked up the aisles. Hyacinth couldn't stand being party to the woman's humiliation and covered her eyes with her hand as she passed. The next day, Hyacinth met the woman on a path, and she turned away in shame. "Don't you turn your face!" Hyacinth told her, before embracing her, right there in broad daylight. Was she the only one who noticed that Jones was going crazy?

Since her arrival six months earlier, the quality of life in Jonestown had steadily declined. At first her breakfast tray contained juice, coffee, and pastries, but now it was usually rice and gravy, which tended to be lunch and dinner as well. She didn't understand why Jones kept selling their produce and meat in Port Kaituma when they didn't have enough food to feed themselves. She kept hoping Jones would at least save the chicken gizzards for them; in the South, folks ate them battered and deep fried; the very thought made her mouth water. Once, a staff member walking back from Jones's cabin brought leftovers to Hy and her roommates, a regular meal of meat, salad, Jell-O, and coffee. Hy was astonished; she had no idea such delicacies existed in Jonestown anymore.

There were other signs of trouble. She'd learned that Jim and Marcie had separated. She'd found their separate cottages strange, but assumed it was because Jones worked late and Marcie wanted to sleep. When her roommate Esther Mueller told Hy that the couple hadn't lived as man and wife for years, she was shocked. In the States, they'd always presented themselves as a unified front, father and mother, although Hy refused to call them anything other than what she'd always called them: Jim and Marcie.

From her porch, where she liked to catch the afternoon breeze, she could see Jones's cottage in one direction, and Marcie's in the other. Once she heard a racket and looked down to his cottage to see him cursing at several young women who were waiting on him, dressed only in their underwear.

At meetings, Jones sometimes called on residents to testify to his skills as a lover. "You ain't been fucked until you been fucked by Jim Jones," one woman said. Then he called on a male resident, who said the same thing. The audience laughed uncomfortably, while Marcie hung her head. Hy wondered why Marcie didn't call the police to put him in a nuthouse.

One night, around midnight, Hy heard a noise outside her window and looked out to see Marcie struggling with two of her sons. "I've taken this for fourteen years and I'm not going to take it any longer," she heard Marcie yell. Her sons urged her to quiet down before she woke the entire camp, and ushered her back to her cottage.

Hyacinth secretly hoped that the trouble between Reverend and Mrs. Jones would lead to the failure of the project, so that everyone could go back home. She was confident she and Zippy could rebuild their lives from scratch again, as they'd done in Indianapolis and in Redwood Valley.

She started keeping tabs on Jones's lies. Once he chastised a woman who requested a fan, saying, "I don't know why you can't take the heat.

I'm Father here, and I'm taking it." But Hyacinth knew he slept to the hum of an air conditioner. He also claimed that he ate the same food as everyone else, but of course she knew this was also a lie. When she heard him rambling over the PA system, she picked up a book and tried to tune him out. Once he got on the loudspeaker to admonish residents, "You ought to be like Hyacinth and Zip. They never complain," which made her snort with bitter laughter. Although the sweat was running down her back and her stomach rumbled, she knew to keep quiet.

But as the months wore on, she felt more helpless and alone. When Jones didn't send his mother's body back to the United States for burial, she began to suspect that he wasn't going back either. In her moments of despair, she recalled the Bible stories she learned as a girl: the travails of Job, David and Goliath. Jones made the sisters sell their big family Bible before they left California, saying it cost too much to ship. But she knew of other seniors who'd sneaked their Bibles in and kept them hidden lest Jones take them away. In the communal bathrooms, when they ran out of newspaper to use as toilet paper, Jones passed out a shipment of Gideon Bibles. Hy refused, and collected rags and pieces of paper instead. Zippy got angry whenever Hy mentioned God. White people wrote the Bible to justify slavery and to keep blacks poor and ignorant, Zip told her, repeating Jones's teachings. He often read them Bible verses that sanctioned slavery, such as Ephesians 6:5: "Slaves, obey your earthly masters with respect and fear, and with sincerity of heart, just as you would obey Christ."

"What did God ever do for us?" Zip snapped, "Jim has done everything." Hy didn't dispute the fact of slavery; her own ancestors were slaves. But Paul wrote in Galatians that when a person believes in Jesus Christ, they were "neither Jew nor Gentile, neither slave nor free, nor is there male and female, for you are all one in Christ Jesus." That was Hy's belief, that Christ would free her. She knew that many black folks of her generation couldn't read or write—but they could pray, and she was certain God heard their prayers.

During one meeting, Jones gave her a long, hard look, and she wondered if he could read her treasonous thoughts. Residents who held onto Christianity infuriated Jones; when eighteen-year-old Jair Baker got caught writing "Jesus Saves" in class, he was sentenced to the learning crew. Once, Dr. Schacht told the audience that an elderly male resident who'd just died made the mistake of calling out to Jesus from his deathbed instead of Jim Jones.

Nonetheless, Hyacinth kept praying to the God of her youth for deliverance. She didn't dare get down on her knees for fear of being reported, but prayed ceaselessly in her head.

CHAPTER 19

STANLEY

Sex had long been one of Jones's primary hang-ups. Although he had sex with both women and men, he argued that he was the only "true" heterosexual on earth. In San Francisco, he put male members of the planning commission on the spot by making them "admit" their attraction to other men. In Jonestown, he took this manipulation community-wide. He ordered residents to write up their sexual fantasies and to list the names of other members—both male and female—that they were attracted to. Most gave Jones the lurid details they thought he wanted to hear. Others gracefully evaded his prying. Zippy Edwards, who'd never married, wrote Jones that she was attracted to "flowers, trees, nature's beauty."

His profanity and sexually explicit commentaries at meetings rankled some seniors and parents with small children present, and Jones singled them out for mockery. He told them not to be so "uptight," and pressured them toward groupthink. A single individual could overthrow the system, and on Jonestown's final night, he'd need residents to obey his order as one.

Despite bragging at length about his own "fucks," Jones didn't allow his members the same freedom. The "relationship committee" approved romantic pairings, and casual liaisons led to the learning crew. But furtive sex still happened. The people needed release. The toolshed—off the beaten path, next to the garage—was a popular place for liaisons, but couples snuck into the thatched hut worrying that their partner would rat them out afterward, and sometimes, they did.

One night, Jones decided to make an example of a couple that was caught having forbidden sex. As the band struck up a seductive version of "Red Roses for a Blue Lady" he ordered them to disrobe and copulate. Edith described it in her journal: "the crowd, including children, watched attentively with laughter and cheers as Ellen was helped to undress and Chuck took off all except his red shorts. Jim chided some of the seniors for their disapproval, saying this demonstration would be good for children, show them 'there's nothing in it' and might even cure some cancers. 'In fact, I'm sure it will.' . . . Chuck tried to perform while Ellen played the role of the frigid female, but he was unable to 'get it up.'" Jones finally let them sit back down, saying, "You couldn't have seen a show like this on Broadway."

As the couple was humiliated at the front of the pavilion, Stanley Clayton took a long look at Ellen Klingman's naked body and became aroused. Ellen had a reputation as a flirt; she worked in the bakery, where she gave free samples to attractive men. Now that he knew the thirty-one-year-old married mother of four was "hot"—and that her husband wasn't in Jonestown—he decided to pursue her. He considered himself a "player" in the States. Seducing—or attempting to seduce—women was a pastime for him, payback for an unaffectionate mother.

His feelings for Janice were complicated. He loved her, but he also loved spreading himself around. Being faithful would give her a power over him that he wasn't ready to concede. And yet Janice stayed, hoping he'd outgrow his wanderlust. During their mandatory three-month separation, they'd met frequently in the tool shed, and now they shared a loft together.

Stanley's chance at Ellen came in early April. Janice was in Georgetown for an eye doctor appointment, and he was feeling randy. He hunted Ellen down during Sunday afternoon free time and, with a wide carnal smile, invited her back to his loft. She didn't hesitate. But once they were naked and fully charged, a pang of guilt crept into him—a new sensation for Stanley. When he had kissed Janice goodbye, he felt the same pang. "I can't do it," he told Ellen. She left disappointed.

But Sebastian McMurry, a security worker who'd gone to Berkeley High with Stanley, had seen the couple enter the cottage. They'd also seen Sebastian, and when Ellen balked, Stanley reassured her. "He's cool," he said. But Sebastian—who was close to Jones's sons—was not cool with rule-breaking, and reported them. That night they were on the floor. Stanley tried to defend himself—they did not have sex, he insisted—but the reputations of both parties made guilt a foregone conclusion. They were assigned to the learning crew.

When Janice returned, Jones convened a special meeting to inform her publicly of Stanley's betrayal. There were no private lovers' quarrels in Jonestown: every conflict was paraded before the crowd. According to protocol, Janice was supposed to slap Stanley, but she didn't want to hurt him; she knew how damaged he was already. "Just do it!" Stanley whispered to her, but she refused. As a result, Janice also was sentenced to the learning crew. And so the three of them—Stanley, Janice, and Ellen, worked side-by-side, carrying prefabricated cottage frames from the wood factory to the residential area.

The whole business infuriated Stanley. He'd done the *right* thing for once, and he still got in trouble. Now he and Janice were doing hard labor in ninety-degree heat and, like everyone else on the crew, prohibited from speaking to anyone but their crew supervisor. Janice gave him dirty looks; he shot her back pleading ones. His anger surged with each new indignity. He got tired of the supervisor barking orders and, in protest of his treatment, refused to drink water.

That night, he was confronted again. When he didn't show remorse for his behavior, Jones's primary enforcer, Johnny Brown Jones, marched him into the darkness as Jones and Charlie Touchette followed. After the pavilion slipped from view, they stopped, and Touchette pressed a handgun to Stanley's head.

"So you wanna die, huh?" Touchette asked.

"Go ahead and kill me because I'd rather be dead than be here," Stanley answered.

When Jones saw that Stanley wasn't intimidated, he told Touchette to lower the weapon. Stanley repeated his defense that he was unjustly accused—he didn't have sex with Ellen—and Jones switched gears. "You should never oppose the office," he told Stanley in a confiding tone, "or others will follow suit." He made a deal with Stanley: he'd take Janice and him off learning crew if Stanley acted scared when they returned to the pavilion, as if they'd roughed him up. Stanley agreed.

"I learned my lesson," he told the crowd, pretending to cower. When he returned to his seat, his buddy Ed Crenshaw pressed him for details, but Stanley kept up the ruse.

Jones, however, wasn't finished meddling in his relationship.

During a rally a few nights later, a counselor walked up to Janice as she and Stanley sat together and, taking her by the hand, led her to Dr. Schacht. Schacht had written Jones several notes describing his fantasies about black women, and now, as Stanley watched in disbelief, Jones announced Dr. Schacht and Janice were now a couple. Janice deserved better than a two-timing troublemaker, Jones told the crowd.

That night, Stanley talked to Janice for hours in their loft, apologizing for his bad behavior and promising radical changes, begging her not to dump him for the doctor. Although Janice resented being handed from one man to the other like a prized dairy cow, she was still angry with Stanley and wasn't quick to soothe him. She was moved into Schacht's cottage the next day.

Jones continued the drama. He announced to the community that Dr. Schacht "was introduced" into Janice, and told Stanley, "You have learned what life is like."

But then Janice refused further advances by Schacht. She preferred her Stanley—her big, flawed, sexy bear hug of a man over the depressive, pale weakling that was the camp doctor. Schacht was crestfallen. "Life is shit, except for socialism," he told the pavilion crowd. "I want to die a revolutionary death, and I've been hesitant and afraid, but boy, it look(s) good."

Jones was also upset and blamed Stanley for everything. The debate went on for hours, as residents rehashed Stanley's past trespasses, and Jones recounted everything he'd done for Stanley, including springing him from jail and allowing him to live in the church. On a tape recording of the confrontation, you can hear Stanley being slapped, and Jones's admonitions for people not to rip his shirt, which he had paid for. Stanley himself barely speaks. He shut down, just as he did when his mother beat him.

His silence only fueled Jones's fury.

"How in the hell do I know, when you won't be loyal to a woman, how in the hell do I know what the fuck you're going to do on the front line, when we're here facing a goddamn war? You don't ever talk. Nobody opens your mouth."

The couple's sex life was exposed, as Jones grilled Janice on her method of birth control, and Stanley on how long he could maintain an erection. Jones, who'd been swilling booze all evening, became increasingly vulgar, bragging that he could stay hard for "eight hours straight."

"Woo, that's strong brandy!" he called out. "I'm drunk!" Jones chastised those who refused to laugh at his antics. "You smile, bitch, or I'll pour it up your vagina," he threatened one woman, and he asked another woman who stood to speak: "Do you want to fuck?"

"Drink it up!" someone yelled.

He proceeded to fart, burp, piss behind a blanket, and finally vomit, but the meeting continued deep into the night.

"The only fuck I want right now is the orgasm of the great fucking grave," he bellowed.

As Stanley stood in front of Jones with blood dripping from his lip, he brooded. *My, how the Reverend Jimmy Jones had fallen,* he thought bitterly. *How he was reduced.*

He and Eddie Crenshaw sometimes talked about high-tailing it out of Jonestown. But it was more jive talk than anything. It was just blowing off steam. Eddie would never leave his wife, Francine, and their one-year-old baby girl. And Stanley, for his part, couldn't abandon Janice, who remained loyal to Jones, despite everything. He'd promised her that they'd be together forever.

CHAPTER 20

RELATIVES

C onfined to his jungle dystopia, Jones's only line of communication to the outside world was his ham radio. He conversed deep into the night with his lieutenants in San Francisco and Georgetown, issuing directives, keeping tabs on the opposition, ranting about conspiracies, and managing the farm. Carried over public airwaves, these conversations were anything but private.

Dozens of amateur radio operators in the United States eavesdropped on Temple transmissions for various reasons, not the least of which was the fact that most of Jones's top aides were women and most hammies—as they were called—were men. The Temple's female operators had "real sexy voices," one man later told the FBI.

The stateside hobbyists patched calls from Jonestown through to phone numbers around the United States in exchange for a postcard confirming the exchange, called a QSL Card. (Radio shorthand for "I confirm receipt of your transmission.") Operators collected these cards as avidly as boy scouts did badges, and displayed them on their radio room walls. The more exotic the locale, the more prized the card. Jonestown's was in high demand. The settlement's calling card included the station's identification number, WB6 MID/8R3, and one of two illustrations. The first was of the Jonestown logo, an outline of Guyana containing an image of the sun rising over rows of plants, the second was a triptych of photographs—a black woman peering into a microscope, a pair of hands holding a cassava stem, and a white man and a biracial boy using an acetylene torch. Temple operators took to the airwaves offering a QSL card to anyone willing to patch a call through for them, and almost always found a taker.

But ham-radio operators soon started complaining about Temple operators to the Federal Communications Commission, which governs wireless communications. The FCC's rules forbid business communications, broadcasting outside authorized frequencies, obscene language, messages in code, and require operators to identify their station at ten-minute intervals. The Temple routinely violated all these rules, and the government agency started monitoring the Temple's transmissions. Although Jonestown was outside its jurisdiction, the FCC repeatedly cited the Temple's San Francisco station, WA6DTJ, for violations. The church just paid the fifty-dollar penalty and continued breaking band rules. This contemptuous disregard irked many ham users, who in turn refused to patch through the group's calls. Jones, always one to overreact, interpreted this rejection by a loose group of hobbyists as part of the widening campaign to destroy him.

In mid-March, the Jonestown leadership sent an open letter to Congress charging several government agencies, including the FCC, with harassment. One sentence of the letter stood out: "I can say without hesitation that we are devoted to a decision that it is better even to die than to be constantly harassed from one continent to the next." It was signed by Pam Bradshaw, a Jonestown health worker whose sister, Sandy, was the probation officer who smuggled guns to Guyana. Although the weird message from a fringe group living in South America didn't do more than raise a few eyebrows in the US Capitol, it set off a firestorm among the Concerned Relatives.

Yulanda Williams, who'd promised never to criticize the church as part of her bargain with Jones, finally decided to go public. On April 10, 1978, she signed an affidavit about the "teaching and practices of Rev. James Warren Jones in Guyana, South America." In it, she charged Jones with taking residents' money and passports, censoring their communications with the outside world, and preventing them from leaving. Jones would "rather have his people dead than live in the United States," she stated. She revealed everything in damning detail: the atmosphere of terror, the lies passed off as "news," the bizarre punishments.

Her affidavit confirmed the worst fears of friends and families with loved ones in Jonestown. The next day, a group of about fifty people, including relatives, former members, and a cadre of reporters, descended on 1869 Geary Boulevard. Tim and Grace Stoen were there, as were the Olivers and Steven Katsaris. When they knocked on the front door, there was no answer. As they walked around the building, they could see Temple aides scowling down from the upper-story windows. At the street level, every door was locked. When the group reached the back parking lot, which was enclosed by a chain-link fence, they saw a man near the fleet of buses and called him over. It was an associate minister named Hue Fortson. As the news cameras rolled, Katsaris slipped Fortson a sheaf of papers through the closed gate. On the first sheet were the words "An Accusation of Human Rights Violations by Rev. James Warren Jones."

The document charged Jones with holding their family members captive and called him to task for the suicide threat in the letter to Congress.

"We frankly do not know if you have become so corrupted by power that you would actually allow a collective 'decision' to die, or whether your letter is simply a bluff designed to deter investigations into your practices," it read. "Has this 'decision' already been made or is it to be made in the future? If made, when and where? Were our relatives consulted? Did anybody dissent? By what moral or legal justification could you possibly make such a decision on the behalf of minor children?"

It was signed by twenty-five relatives of thirty-seven Jonestown residents. Stoen, who would file lawsuits against the Temple on behalf of several members and relatives, told reporters that many families had been too afraid of reprisals to speak out against Jones prior to that day. One grandmother who told a radio station that she was worried about her granddaughter in Jonestown, for example, later received a letter from the girl stating she was "sorry to hear she called the radio station, but since you did, I will not be writing you anymore."

The group asked Jones to allow their family members to return to California for a seven-day visit, at their expense. Afterward, they promised not to interfere if their kin wanted to go back to Jonestown. If Jones didn't comply with their request, the group told reporters, they'd consider hiring mercenaries to rescue their relatives from the jungle camp.

The confrontation made the next day's papers, including the front page of the Santa Rosa *Press Democrat*, which ran a photo of Steven Katsaris handing the accusation to Fortson.

That night, an agitated Jones summoned the community to the pavilion.

"Several of your relatives, nearly all of your goddamned relatives, have signed a petition," he announced. "They got a powerful backing. I wouldn't be surprised there's not a fascist coup in the making in USA, certainly there's a reactionary hold in elements of government, (or) these fuckers wouldn't stand (at) our door." He accused the group, falsely, of throwing rocks into the parking lot and threatening to "shoot our people," but he did not reveal the content of the petition.

The Concerned Relatives were the latest addition to the powerful conspiracy threatening to destroy their movement, he said. He riled up the crowd, then asked residents who were related to the petition signers to describe how they'd torture their family members, given the chance. He recorded their statements, most of which were given in flat, hesitant tones, on cassette tapes and punctuated their sentences with his high, hyenalike laugh.

He ranted for hours, skipping from the treachery of the relatives to that of the CIA and of the Guyanese government, which was still pressuring Dr. Schacht and Don Fields, the pharmacist, to complete their residencies in Georgetown.

He then turned the conversation, again, toward suicide. "We can make an incident in history," he said. He was already scripting their last statement to the world: "We'll say we have died in protest to thus thus thus . . ."

A woman stood to speak. "I feel that, if we took a stand . . . where we all decided to die, that it might never be interpreted correctly in history, and that we owe our commitment to socialism to stay alive as long as possible."

Angry at her objection, Jones cut her off. "You pricks don't want to face a white night, because you're not capable of facing a white night," he yelled.

As the night wore on, residents became increasingly dismayed.

He paused from his rants to ask a question in a soft, confiding voice.

"How many are still glad you came?"

It was a set-up, a question he asked often. A few poor souls always fell for it, and Jones's face darkened when he saw them.

"Catch 'em," he ordered his guards. "That's what you're supposed to do is catch 'em. Anybody don't have their hand up. Catch 'em."

On April 17, Jones responded to the Concerned Relatives in a press conference held via shortwave radio at Charles Garry's office. The event had been meticulously planned, the press release much debated by Temple leaders. As the reporters sat in Garry's office, Harriet Tropp, in the Jonestown radio room, read a statement denying the Temple had sent the letter to Congress in one breath, and defended it in the next.

"Any person with any integrity or courage would have no trouble understanding such a position," she said. "Before we will submit quietly to the interminable plotting and persecution of this politically motivated conspiracy, we will resist actively, putting our lives on the line, if it comes to that. This has been the unanimous vote of the collective community here in Guyana. We choose as our model not those who marched submissively into gas ovens, but the valiant heroes who resisted in the Warsaw ghettos. Patrick Henry captured it when he said, simply: 'Give me liberty, or give me death.'

"The group of Concerned Relatives is a cruel, monstrous hoax," she added scornfully.

Several residents whose relatives signed the petition got on the radio to denounce their family members as child molesters, drunks, drug addicts, racists, and terrorists. "Leave us alone," was the overwhelming message. But listen carefully to the tape and you can hear Jones and Tropp whispering lines to people as they sit at the microphone. The residents' voices are stilted, their intonation wrong, the delivery mechanical. It's evident they're reading from prepared scripts, many unwillingly.

A few nights later, Jones asked his followers to raise their hands if they thought they were going to live a long time. Of the sixteen people who raised their hands, only two would. He continued to warn them to be prepared for a mercenary attack, and on Saturday, April 22, as residents sat in the pavilion a little after midnight, shots from automatic weapons rang out in the darkness. People fell to the dirt floor and scrambled for cover under the benches. The guards switched off the banks of overhead lights, but there was a delay turning off the light over the stage, where Jones was sprawled on his stomach, barking orders into the microphone. He urged everyone to keep still, and then narrated the drama as it unfolded. The security guards were scouring the bush for the invaders, he told them. Then, "We got one of them!" He got up and left the pavilion to investigate, wanting to see if the captive had valuable intelligence information. He was gone for almost an hour as his followers lay on the hard ground in terror.

Edith Roller, crouched under a front row, reached up to grab the pillow she'd started bringing to sit on as the rallies got longer and longer, and slid it under her head. She thought it strange that guards lit flares around the pavilion—the bright light would make the residents sitting ducks—but an aide said the flares meant the danger was over. Jones finally returned, saying the wounded intruder had been carried away by his companions. There was no intruder, of course; Jones staged the event with the help of his guards.

He reconvened the meeting to analyze the group's reaction to the crisis. Complaints were heard about adults who tried to save themselves before children, thereby putting their individual survival before the community's, and about residents who didn't follow instructions. The biggest complaint, however, was about the number of people who fell asleep. These Jones assigned to the learning crew, furious that they didn't take his "emergency" seriously, or perhaps didn't believe there was an emergency, or any mercenaries, at all.

CHAPTER 21

THE EMBASSY

On May 10, US Consul Richard McCoy returned to Jonestown. Again, he asked the residents he interviewed if they wanted to drive away with him. Again, no one accepted his offer. In a perfunctory report, he wrote that it was improbable that residents were being held against their will. "In general, people appear healthy, adequately fed and housed, and satisfied with their lives on what is a large farm." The Temple spun his report in a press release announcing that the State Department had "refuted" the charges of the Concerned Relatives. Three days later, on May 13, Jones's forty-seventh birthday, one of Jones's top aides defected.

Debbie Blakey, twenty-five, had been a Temple member for seven years. She rose quickly through the ranks to become one of Jones's sexual intimates and a church financial secretary who helped establish the church's overseas bank accounts. In Guyana, she also worked on the PR crew, a position that gave her access to various diplomats, including Consul McCoy. One day, she finagled a way to be alone with him and asked him to help her get out of the country. He issued her an emergency passport and flew back to the States with her. On the plane ride home, Blakey told McCoy about the dire situation in Jonestown. The conversation left him frustrated. Like the Concerned Relatives' charges, Blakey's accusations were too broad, he'd later testify: They lacked damning details, and she wouldn't name individuals who could be charged with specific crimes. She told him the residents he interviewed were too afraid of reprisals to accept his offer to get out, but that seemed beyond comprehension to him. As a representative of the

United States government, he could guarantee them safe passage home. Furthermore, he couldn't understand how a single man could wield that kind of power over so many people.

The same day Blakey defected, Jones called an alert at two in the afternoon. Field workers sprinted, sweating and dirt-smeared, to the pavilion. Seniors stopped cleaning vegetables and sewing toys and hobbled over. Attendance was checked. Residents would remain in the pavilion until six the next morning—a full sixteen hours.

Jones announced that a member had defected who could do more harm than Tim Stoen, and that the defector's lies would prompt the government to attack them. During the ensuing discussion, various people suggested seeking refuge in Cuba or Russia. Jones brushed their comments aside, saying the Temple's brand of communism was "too advanced" for either country, and that he would no longer be allowed to lead them if they moved.

"Revolutionary suicide is the only acceptable answer," he repeated. He picked a cross section of residents—children, parents, black, white— to record statements explaining why they were willing to die for the cause, saying the tape would be released to the world press after they died.

One of the people he recruited was Edith Roller:

"I am Edith Roller, and I have had a very varied life," she said into the microphone in a measured voice. "And I've always been distressed by the poverty and the discrimination especially against people in the underdeveloped areas of the world, and among the black people of our own nation and other minorities. It seemed to me when I joined Peoples Temple, it was an ideal society of egalitarian justice and love." She emphasized the word "when," and a perceptive listener could interpret this to mean that her view of the church—and Jim Jones—had changed. "I pray and hope that this tape will at least survive in portions so that [the world] can know what we stood for. I'm glad that my death will mean something. I hope it will be an inspiration to all people that fight for freedom all over the world."

She'd later write in her diary that she "did not approve" of revolutionary suicide, but "intended to assent to whatever decision was made."

After dinner, which was served in the pavilion, Jones took a suicide vote.

"At all times those in favor of revolutionary suicide were in the majority," Edith later wrote. "However I felt that these were strongly influenced by his advocacy. The number of those opposed grew as thoughtful statements were made. I mentioned the world situation which seemed to be turning in favor of liberation movements [and] against the US and might result in war, which could be helpful to us."

In the middle of the night, it began to storm. Raindrops pelted the corrugated metal roof like hurled stones, drowning out the baleful discussion. Residents huddled on the benches in grim silence, knowing Jones would not let them go to bed until they gave him what he wanted.

"When we resumed, opposition to the proposed suicide declined, (and) those in favor of carrying it out tonight seemed more determined," Edith wrote. "I became convinced by the tired eyes of [Temple leader] Sharon Amos that I would be wrong to persist."

On the next show of hands, Edith raised hers. The vocal opposition had fallen to about twenty people. Somebody asked about the Temple members who weren't in Jonestown. Would they also die? Jones said that San Francisco members were all adults who "would know what to do." But he decided to delay the suicide until a group of newcomers who'd just landed in Guyana reached the camp.

Edith crawled into her bunk bed as dawn broke over the compound, eager to deliver herself to blissful unconsciousness.

A survivor would later say of the suicide votes, "I figured if we just quit arguing with him, we could get some sleep." One wonders how many other Jonestown residents felt coerced into voting for their own deaths. Certainly Edith did, and it's safe to venture that many others did, too: On the next day, most of the students in Edith's adult reading class said they didn't understand what the crisis was about; they'd simply raised their hands because they knew they were expected to do so.

Jones, however, was encouraged; with every white night, the number of residents publicly opposing suicide fell. At some point during the crisis, perhaps when the downpour silenced the debate, he wrote instructions for what was to be done with the Temple's money after he died:

"In view of the death of myself, and the destruction of my life's work brought about by provocateurs . . . it is the community's and my desire to have all of our funds that we have always intended to go towards the fostering of the spread of Marxist-Leninism to either Cuba or the USSR, whichever nation can readily receive the funds." The note would be found in a safe deposit box at a Panamanian bank months after the massacre.

Back home in San Francisco, Debbie Blakey recorded an affidavit stating that Jones had grown so paranoid that he was no longer able to distinguish between fantasy and reality. By keeping Jonestown residents exhausted, underfed, and afraid, he'd weakened their resolve to the point where it would be possible for him to "effect a mass suicide," she warned. "On behalf of the population of Jonestown, I urge that the United States Government take adequate steps to safeguard their rights. I believe that their lives are in danger."

In Washington, McCoy briefed his superiors in the State Department on Blakey's allegations. In the past, he'd called Jones's threats "nonsense." He found it impossible to believe that nine hundred people would line up and kill themselves; it just wasn't civilized behavior. But Blakey seemed like a rational person, and her stories worried him. He lobbied the State Department to formally ask the Guyanese government to investigate Jonestown, but was told the First Amendment prohibited interference in the privacy and religious freedom of American citizens. Blakey's plea for help was circulated among embassy workers in Georgetown before being filed away in their "general fund of information," he would later testify.

The Guyanese government was also stumped about what to do. The national chief of police, Skip Roberts, told McCoy he'd found no evidence of gunrunning and that whenever he or other officials asked the group, "Are you all going to kill yourselves?" the answer was always "No."

Jones dismantled the isolation boxes—he'd constructed a second—after Blakey disclosed their existence to the media, fearing regional authorities would come looking for them. Harriet Tropp pressed him to go further. "The more 'secretive' we need to be, the more vulnerable we are to 'defectors,'" she wrote him. "If our structure is more able to be publicly examined, then we are less vulnerable. Outsiders would be able to walk around the project, observe meetings, etc."

But Jones did the exact opposite. He sealed off Jonestown from the outside world completely.

A reporter for a small California paper who flew to Guyana at the end of May discovered this firsthand. Kathy Hunter had written several flattering stories about Jones when he first moved to Ukiah from Indiana, but more recently, she'd penned sympathetic portrayals of Timothy Stoen and Steven Katsaris, prompting Jones to place her on his list of enemies.

Hunter assumed she'd be welcomed in Jonestown, based on her past friendship with Jones. But after she checked into her Georgetown hotel, mysterious fires were set in the hallways and bomb threats were called in to the front desk. When she went out, hostile Temple members surrounded her on the street, demanding to know what she was doing there. Georgetown officials did little to reassure her, and in fact suggested she leave the country for her own safety. She did. Upon returning to California, she related her ordeal to the media, which only heightened curiosity about Jim Jones, and what he was hiding.

A month later, the Guyanese government booted another snooping journalist from the country. Gordon Lindsay, on assignment for the *National Enquirer*, had received no answer to his repeated requests to visit Jonestown, so he flew to Georgetown to try his luck from there. But Jones had forewarned the government about Lindsay's arrival, arguing that bad press for Jonestown was bad press for Guyana. Lindsay never cleared customs and boarded the next plane out. Undeterred, he flew to Trinidad and chartered a small aircraft with a photographer. The plane circled the settlement several times at low altitude, enraging Jones, who told officials the plane had "violated Jonestown's airspace," as if the camp were now a sovereign country. Jones suspected, correctly, that the tabloid was working on a smear piece, and ordered Charles Garry to get it stopped.

As pressure on the isolated community grew, Jones kicked his death plan into high gear. It was obvious that the farm wasn't sustainable, and Jones was increasingly becoming an embarrassment to the Burnham administration. He pressed Schacht to hurry up with the suicide plan.

"Cyanide is one of the most rapidly-acting poisons," Schacht wrote him a short while later. "I had some misgivings about its effectiveness, but from further research I have gained more confidence in it, at least theoretically. I would like to give about two grams to a large pig to see how effective our batch is to be sure we don't get stuck with a disaster like would occur if we used thousands of pills to sedate the people and the cyanide was not good enough to do the job. I also want to order antidotes just in case we may need to reverse the poisoning process on people . . . cyanide may take up to three hours to kill but usually it is within minutes."

He requested an Australian medical journal called *Anaesthesia and Intensive Care*, whose November 1974 issue carried an article on acute cyanide poisoning. He even provided Jones with a cover, lest it raise suspicion among the San Francisco aides assigned to track it down for him: "We could say that a child was brought into our free medical clinic who had ingested rat poison containing cyanide and we want this article on the subject."

Written by an anesthesiologist at St. Vincent's Hospital in Sydney, the scholarly study described the cases of two patients who'd swallowed cyanide in suicide attempts, but who were saved by the diligent actions of emergency workers. In clinical detail, the author described the generalized hypoxic cell death caused by cyanide. Simply put, the poison prevents the body from absorbing oxygen, causing suffocation at a cellular level. It is an agonizing death. One sentence in the article—which was intended to help emergency workers save poisoning victims—gave Dr. Schacht the information he was looking for: "In adults, the lethal dose of ingested cyanide salt is 250 mg."

He placed an order for one pound of sodium cyanide from J. T. Baker, a chemical company in Hayward, California. The order, which cost $8.85, was for enough poison to kill 1,800 people.

CHAPTER 22

THE WIDENING GYRE

The extreme duress of life in Jonestown made people crack. They didn't care about socialism if it meant chronic hunger, exhaustion, and fear. Their days were ruled by anxiety. They ate their miserable food in silence and filed into the pavilion each night with trepidation: Would this be the night they'd be called on the floor? Would this be the night Jones made good on his death threat? They worried about being reported for some blurted aside, and stopped confiding in their spouses and children. They withdrew into depression and apathy and cynicism.

Some tried to gain favor by informing on people who didn't smile or praise Dad enough. Larry Schacht reported patients who took pain poorly, such as Helen Snell, seventy-six, who cried out when he stuck a needle in her foot. Jones himself sometimes administered pain tests during rallies to determine how residents would respond to torture, telling them, "I don't trust you if you can't take pain."

As Jones receded into a chemical haze, he spent more time in his cabin and less time with his people. He appointed a triumvirate to manage the community's daily operations, which included his longtime mistress Carolyn Layton, Harriet Tropp, and Johnny Moss Brown—one of the few African Americans in leadership. The internal surveillance team kept an eye out for strange behavior, and even reported Jonestown principal Tom Grubbs: "Yesterday he went to the very back of the cottages and looked around the jungle for a while. This is not the first or second time he has done this." Some residents informed on themselves before others could do so, hoping their voluntary confession would soften their punishment. It was hard to know whom to trust. Loyalists divulged their partners' pillow talk. Grubbs's girlfriend, Bea Orsot, told Jones about Grubbs's private fears, dreams, and sexual proclivities. He suspected she was informing on him, but she denied it. At the end of October, Grubbs would find himself in trouble after telling Orsot that he thought Jones was deliberately brainwashing the community.

One night, Vince Lopez, the fifteen-year-old teen who'd flown to Guyana with Tommy Bogue, found himself the focus of Jones's rage. His guardian, a defector named Walter Jones who now lived with Grace Stoen, was filing lawsuits in California trying to bring him home, and this did not endear Vince to the Temple leader.

Vince's mother died in childbirth when he was in first grade, and his father was a heroin addict who was in and out of prison; he was eleven years old and homeless when a juvenile court in Oakland sent him to a foster family that belonged to Peoples Temple. (He was one of twenty-two foster kids sent to Jonestown.)

In Guyana, Vince was often on the learning crew for sleeping during meetings or cracking cynical jokes.

"Did you get any of the bacon they sent you?" he asked one befuddled senior. "How tall are you?" he asked another. When the woman asked why he wanted to know, Lopez replied: "The woodshop wants to know how long your casket should be."

One night, Jones gave Vince the chance to dance his way off the learning crew. He ordered the boy to imitate a Pentecostal Holy Roller by running up and down the aisles pretending to speak in tongues. Vince refused to make a fool of himself. The crowd shouted encouragement, but he refused to budge. One of Jones's guards threatened him: "He told you to do it, punk, now you run up the fucking aisle." Vince still wouldn't move.

"You're a goddamn masochist!" Jones finally yelled, before telling his guards to "Get him out of my sight."

The next time Tommy saw Vince, a week or so later, his friend was doing the "Thorazine shuffle" down a pathway. When Tommy called to him, Vince barely lifted his head. Frightened and confused, Tommy veered away. Something was obviously very wrong with Vince, something that was allowed to happen.

Soon afterward, Tommy was sentenced to scrub pots all night in the kitchen, alone, when he made a strange discovery. Opening the fridge, he was surprised to find a tray of vanilla milkshakes. He couldn't resist. He took a few sips from each, making sure the liquid in all the glasses was even when he was done. The next day he felt loopy; everything was slow and surreal. He complained to his mother, and, after much prodding, she elicited his transgression. "Don't drink those shakes," she warned. "Those are Jones's shakes. Now you know they have something in them."

But Jones didn't drink the milkshakes himself; he gave them to people he wanted to squelch. To prepare for visitors, Joyce Parks would regularly sedate troublemakers, such as a woman who grew distraught upon learning her dogs had been sold in California without her consent. Other unruly residents were assigned to the special care unit, where they were given a choice: they could either swallow tranquilizers voluntarily or be forcibly injected with them. What happened in the SCU eventually became an open secret, and Jones would read the names of residents who were in danger of being confined to the SCU over the PA system.

Drugging people allowed Jones to control them without leaving evidence of physical harm. Eavesdropping ham-radio operators would later tell the FBI that in the colony's last months, Jonestown operators ordered a tremendous amount of drugs and syringes. Sedatives were always requested in one thousand doses, enough to subdue Jonestown's entire population.

But Jones's narcotics-buying spree was hampered in October 1978 by the passage of the Psychotropic Substances Act, which cracked down on recreational abuse of drugs.

In San Francisco, Temple leader Jean Brown couldn't find injectable tranquilizers such as Valium. "The only way it can be gotten is if you get a personal prescription, which someone with blood pressure problems is attempting to do," she wrote Jones.

A week later, Jones told Joyce Parks, a camp nurse who traveled frequently between Jonestown and Georgetown, to buy all the tranquilizers and disposable syringes she could get her hands on, and within two days, she'd located 100 vials of Thorazine. In this piecemeal fashion, Jones built up an impressive opiate stockpile; indeed, the first doctor who entered the Jonestown pharmacy after the massacre said it contained enough psychotropics to keep every resident continually sedated for two years.

One of Jones's more egregious abuses of power was his drugging and rape of a young woman named Shanda James. Jones's preferred female body type was rail thin and white. Shanda, nineteen, was the first African American woman he pursued. When she rejected his advances, Jones committed her to the SCU. Stanley Clayton happened to be there at the same time, sick with the flu. The beds in the SCU cottage were only separated by curtains, and one day Stanley watched as Jones walked past him and pushed aside the curtain where a doped-up Shanda lay. A few minutes later, he heard heavy breathing and the bed moving. He was outraged. When he told Ed Crenshaw what he'd seen, his buddy warned him to be quiet, lest he himself be drugged into silence. When Shanda was released, her friends were shocked at her appearance. She clung to a railing of a walkway, barely able to stand, as her blue bathrobe hung open exposing a breast. Jordan Vilchez walked by her with a group of field-crew workers, but didn't stop. "We got so used to not questioning things, to minding our own business," she'd later say. "Life became a series of odd things."

Shanda herself, in a lucid moment, wrote Jones a confused note: "I cannot sit down for ½ hour before I fall asleep. . . . I don't know what I'm taking but it really affects me. I feel awful." When she finally realized what was going on, she swallowed a handful of oral contraceptives to avoid getting pregnant, and became violently ill.

As residents grew more desperate, there was a rash of violence, runaway attempts, and mental breakdowns. Jones accused people of faking emotional disorders to get out of work, and threatened to shoot runaways in the legs. Some launched quieter protests; Tennessean Alleane Tucker, forty-nine, was reprimanded for singing slave songs in the field.

Residents wondered why they should exert themselves weeding vegetables or hauling lumber when they were repeatedly told that they'd have to die or abandon Jonestown for another, uncertain, location. Farm coordinator Jack Beam told Jones that residents' apathy was just as serious as the garden infestation. The Jonestown leadership considered different ways to motivate people, such as honoring a worker of the week, handing out wooden beads as merit badges, or dubbing subliminal messages into the music cassettes played over the loudspeakers—"produce for socialism," or "remember the news."

Harriet Tropp suggested implementing Soviet-style production goals: six-month, one-year, two-year, and five-year plans. "The Soviets found such planning to be the key to motivation and building community initiative," she wrote Jones. "It will provide a kind of psychological balance for the effect of the White Nights on the kids—they will develop the determination to sacrifice for the collective, but also have the accompanying sense that we are building something, and not just going from one day to the next." Division supervisors duly submitted their long-range goals: a five-year swine breeding plan, a new school with proper walls where students would be sheltered from rain and noise, a 100-acre citrus orchard, and dozens of other improvements and structures designed to reduce crowding and "make the place more liveable."

Jones, of course, had no interest in making Jonestown more livable. He was plotting his "orgasm of death."

He reinforced his bleak outlook with carefully selected books and movies. In the evenings, mandatory films included *No Blade of Grass*, a horror movie about a virus that decimates the world's grain crops and plunges the world into chaos, *The Pawnbroker*, a grim portrayal of a Nazi death camp survivor, and *Night and Fog*, a documentary on the horrific medical experiments performed on children at Auschwitz and Majdanek. Jones screened the films repeatedly, pausing the reel to interject his own nihilistic commentary. His gloom was contagious. "I saw the movie 'No Blade of Grass,' last night, which was a perfect reminder of what you have taught us to expect for the future to come," Liz Ruggiero, twenty-four, wrote Jones. He read aloud from the memoirs of Chilean socialists who were tortured by the Pinochet regime, commending their bravery, and adding: "There should be no fear of death here, and I am very impatient with you that still fear death, which is the last enemy that we've overcome in many a White Night." The Jonestown library stocked five hundred copies of *The Question*, the account of a French-Algerian communist named Henri Alleg, who was brutalized by the French military for supporting Algeria's independence. As children sat in their parents' laps, Jones read gruesome descriptions of Alleg's torture before making his point: It was better for the community to take their own lives than to let the enemy torture them to death. The lesson took. A survivor would later testify that "You got to the point where you thought, what would you rather do? You would rather kill yourself first before they got ahold of you."

Edith Roller's journal is remarkable in that it is the only known document to chronicle daily life in Jonestown. She spent mornings typing up her handwritten notes from the previous day, sitting on her lower bunk with a typewriter perched on a shipping crate in front of her. In the resulting pages, she recorded Jones's mental decline by quoting his bizarre pronouncements and describing his cruel behavior. "I think I'm a mutation that dropped off some asteroid," he announced one night. She listed the conspiracies he saw everywhere. The chickens were dying because the CIA had injected them with a disease. The spy agency had also injected cancer cells into Marceline. The US Senate Armed Services Committee was funding the Concerned Relatives. A shadowy entity called the Eureka Research Association had been contracted to kill him.

Edith was cautious in her reflections, knowing the Jonestown leadership scrutinized her writings. Nonetheless, a subtext of quiet desperation emerges. "I spent a most frustrating and tiring day," she frequently wrote, or "I had a very bad day at the end of which I felt completely demoralized."

She was dragged into Jonestown's darkness against her will. Twice, Jones called her to the front of the pavilion to slap someone during a confrontation. Even in discipline, he wanted the appearance of integration and selected her when he needed a white person to join an attack. The first woman she hit was Michaeleen Brady, a thirty-five-year-old Long Beach, California, native. Brady, who was there with her two daughters and four of her siblings, suffered from mental-health problems that frequently got her in trouble, and had just been released from a two-week stint in the isolation box for assaulting her boyfriend. She emerged looking "very haggard" and "fearful," Edith noted in her journal. Three days later, Brady was on the floor again, this time for threatening a security guard with a cutlass.

During Brady's confrontation, two black women slapped her in the face before Jones ordered Edith to do the same. But Edith felt sorry for Michaeleen. The two women had once shared a security shift at the San Francisco Temple, patting down visitors as they entered the building. When Jones called on her, Edith stood with great reluctance and walked to where Brady cowered before the Temple leader. She paused before raising her hand and cuffing Brady lightly on the cheek. Several onlookers chided Edith for not hitting her hard enough.

A few weeks later, Brady showed up at Edith's adult literacy class, accompanied by a guard. She asked Edith if she could sign up for the class, and Edith noted in her journal that Brady seemed drawn to her. Most likely, she sensed in Edith a welcome bit of humanity.

Four months after her arrival, however, Edith reported another resident for saying she wanted to go home. A Nashville native named Lovie Jean Lucas, seventy-four, confided in Edith that she was lonely, preferred cities, and didn't realize that she couldn't return to the States when she came to Jonestown. "She is a senior, seems well educated, is not likely to try to leave the area, but we have orders to report all negative comments," Edith noted in her journal. Before leaving California, members signed a release promising to "work diligently" at the settlement and "to keep a cheerful and constructive attitude," or else they'd be "responsible for any and all costs and other obligations incurred in" returning home. This wording led many Temple members, including Lucas, to believe they'd be free to leave Jonestown any time they wanted to. In March, when Jones announced "No one leaves until all are here," alarm rippled through the settlement.

Nonetheless, Lucas, who owned a barber shop located a half block away from the Geary Boulevard church, wrote Jones that she'd "got a strong instinctive urge to get ready, and pack and so I did—I'm all packed." If he let her go home, she promised to send him a "box of jewelry" each month. Instead, Jones publicly berated her for wanting to return to racist America.

It was now an offense to even utter the words, "I want to go home." Danielle Gardfrey, thirteen, was assigned to the learning crew for doing so, and Jones warned Mary Baldwin, fifty-two, that she'd be condemned to a hospital bed for saying she didn't like Jonestown.

Jones purchased this building at 1502 N. New Jersey Street in Indianapolis in 1956 and described it as a church whose "door is open so wide that all races, creeds, and colors find a hearty welcome to come in, relax, meditate, and worship God." (Roger Stacy)

Jim Jones in 1971, about forty-years-old, at the height of his faith-healing crusade. That same year he purportedly fathered a child with a married congregant named Grace Stoen. (©*Indiana Star*)

Jones working the pulpit at his church in Los Angeles, wearing his trademark sunglasses. By the mid-seventies, he denied the existence of a Christian god altogether. (California Historical Society [CHS])

Jones with Temple children. A dimple in the negative created what he claimed was the white "aura of love" radiating from his heart to the girl on his right side. The image was a bestseller among Temple members. Seven of these children died in Jonestown. (Al Mills)

Jones bought this former Masonic temple at 1859 Geary Boulevard in San Francisco in 1972. Many Temple members lived in warrenlike cubicles on the upper floors or slept in the sanctuary, while Jones's family lived in an apartment on the third floor. Today a U.S. Post Office occupies the lot. (CHS)

Jones poses next to fruit supposedly grown
in Jonestown—as well as the bag the fruit
was purchased in. Although billed as a model
agricultural cooperative, the settlement would
never be self-sufficient. (CHS)

A staged photo of a cottage interior in
Jonestown. To lure as many of his followers
to Guyana as possible, Jones used videos and
photographs to depict the settlement as the land
of plenty. (CHS)

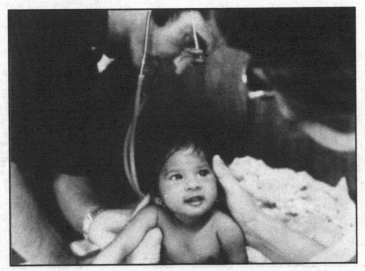

Dr. Larry Schacht examines an infant in Jonestown. When Schacht wasn't delivering
babies or tending to sick residents, he was busy trying to find a way to kill off the
entire population of Jonestown. (CHS)

Gene Chaikin, a lawyer originally from Los Angeles, left Guyana when he realized Jones was mentally unstable, but the Temple leader refused to let Chaikin's children leave Jonestown, so he was forced to return to the settlement. (CHS)

Jim Bogue immigrated to Guyana in 1974 along with a small group of pioneers and was quickly named farm manager. He hoped living in the community would help his faltering marriage. (CHS)

The Simon family in Jonestown: (left to right) Jose Simon, Al Jr., Crystal, Al, Bonnie, and Summer. Al and his father were Pomo Indians, and this photo was used in a Temple brochure to demonstrate the racial inclusiveness of the settlement. (CHS)

Edith Roller was one of many college-educated progressives who were drawn to the Temple's stated mission of furthering racial, social, and sexual equality. (CHS)

Brian Davis, Tommy Bogue's best friend. The two boys tried to escape Jonestown together a year before the massacre, but were captured by Jones's security guards. (CHS)

The Temple became family to Stanley Clayton, a rage-filled seventeen-year-old from a broken family in Oakland. A Temple member who worked as a probation officer negotiated an early release from jail for him, and he lived in the church sanctuary. (CHS)

Hyacinth Thrash and her sister Zipporah Edwards first heard of Jim Jones in Indianapolis when they saw his integrated choir perform on television in 1955. They followed him to California and then to Guyana. (CHS)

Tommy Bogue (back row, left) was sent down to Jonestown in July 1976 to "straighten him out." He enjoyed the experience until Jones moved down a year later, bringing with him an air of gloom and doom that would affect the entire community. (CHS)

Infants in the Jonestown nursery. The day before the massacre, Marceline Jones would tell reporters that thirty-three babies were born in the settlement. None of the babies in this picture survived. (CHS)

Sharon Amos worked with Jones's public relations crew in the capital of Guyana, where she kept a finger on the pulse of official opinion toward the church. (CHS)

Jonestown as seen from the air. The two long school tents are next to the pavilion at the community's center. The thick jungle surrounding the settlement deterred many residents from trying to flee. (FBI)

Troublemakers—residents who tried to escape or didn't toe the line—were injected with tranquilizers and confined to the "Special Care Unit." (FBI)

The northwestern region of Guyana where Jonestown was located was alternately scorched by droughts and drenched by rainstorms, making crop production a challenge. Here, Jones joins a bucket brigade. (CHS)

Women prepare eggplant in the communal kitchen. The amount and quality of food in Jonestown steadily declined during the last year, and toward the end most meals consisted of rice and watery gravy. Most residents lost tremendous amounts of weight. (CHS)

Congressman Leo Ryan poses with members of the Houston family the day before the massacre. The girls' grandfather asked Ryan to investigate whether Temple members were being held against their will in Guyana. (FBI)

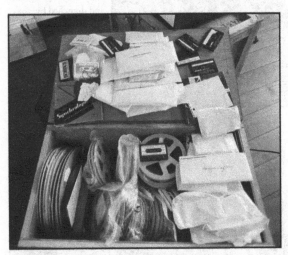

Agents with the Federal Bureau of Investigation collected some 50,000 pieces of paper and 1,000 audiotapes from the colony after the massacre to try and determine whether there was a conspiracy to assassinate Congressman Leo Ryan. (FBI)

Christine Miller was the only dissenting voice heard on a tape Jones recorded during the mass murder-suicide. "I think we all have a right to our own destiny as individuals," she told Jones. Her objections were shouted down by other Temple members. (CHS)

Residents sized up the jungle and their chances of getting through it alive. "Sometimes I feel like getting away from it all," Brenda Warren, sixteen, wrote Jones. "I walk by the bush and say, 'I could just leave,' but I don't really have the courage as I say I do."

Edith Roller knew better than to ask to leave. She was particularly annoyed by the tedious rallies, and after one meeting that lasted from dusk until dawn, she wrote Jones a memo suggesting ways to expedite them. When she showed the note to one of Jones's secretaries, however, the woman warned her not to criticize "the office," so she threw it away. That did not stop her from keeping a thorough accounting of the problems riddling the settlement in her journal.

She noted each meal she ate in her diary, and as the months passed, there was less and less protein. Dinner was "a chowder of fish heads and greens," or "curried chicken necks." Sometimes, her plate only contained a few slices of watermelon or pineapple. Often she was hungry.

When the farm analysts met in July to predict the settlement's harvest for the next six months, they were discouraged. In ideal conditions, without excessive rain, drought, or equipment breakdown, they calculated that the farm would only produce enough beans to feed residents every third day and enough rice to feed them once a week. By the middle of August, Jim Bogue reported that the garden was worse than he'd ever seen it. The soil was so ridden with pests and disease that seedlings emerged from it deformed and dying. Field workers handpicked beetles and worms off the plants, but there was no way to stop the onslaught of the acoushi leaf-cutter ants, which could strip entire plots of cassava to leafless stalks overnight. Bogue suggested visitors bypass the fields altogether, a major defeat for the farm that the Guyanese government touted as a "model of cooperative agriculture."

Jones complained constantly about how much it cost to feed residents. Some of his aides collected donations from neighboring farms in the North West District, but these were paltry; on one sweep, they were given 380 overripe mangos, 100 oranges, and forty-eight pineapples— far from enough to sustain one thousand people. The entire country was undergoing a food crisis, and the government was forced to import staples such as rice.

Most, if not all, residents lost tremendous amounts of weight due to a combination of insufficient calories and a plague of intestinal parasites. Their ribs stuck out, they felt wan and passive.

In the final months, dinner was reduced to lumpy flour gravy served over rice. Jim Bogue preferred to eat his in the shade, where he wouldn't see the telltale shapes of the weevils infesting the rice. In San Francisco, Jones had railed against the injustice of a world where two out of three babies went to bed hungry; now, he was imposing that same injustice on his own people.

The lack of roughage gave Edith, and many others, chronic constipation. Because Jones was too cheap to buy real medicine, health workers passed out green papaya or plantain as a laxative, but this did little to help. Edith was also one of many residents who suffered from athlete's foot: The heat, humidity, crowded quarters, and poor hygiene in the communal showers caused outbreaks of the fungus, as well as of ringworm. A "sore table" was set up in the pavilion to treat residents' various skin afflictions with ground cassava powder and Irish vine. But these homeopathic remedies didn't work either, and Edith's itchy feet added to the torment of the endless nighttime meetings.

Naturally, Jones's followers wondered why he didn't use his paranormal powers to cure them or multiply their food as he'd supposedly done with the KFC dinner in Redwood Valley. He had a ready answer: Doing so would take energy away from him that he needed to keep their enemies at bay.

Edith's physical discomfort only added to her crankiness. She thought of her friend Lorraine and her three sisters constantly, but rarely wrote them. After a censor vetoed her second letter home several times over perceived criticisms of the project, she delayed making the required "corrections," and then lost her desire to send it altogether. Like many residents, she volunteered to return to the States to "take care of traitors," and when Jones complained about money, she wrote him saying she'd be willing to return to her Bechtel job and send her wages down to the project. It was the closest she'd get to directly asking to go home.

Whenever possible, she sought out the solitude of her cottage. She sneaked back between classes, or on a rare night when there wasn't a required function in the pavilion. Alone on her bunk bed, she'd console herself with poetry. She'd brought along the collected works of her favorite poet, W. B. Yeats, and although she'd donated the book to the school library, she checked it out frequently herself.

Surely she must have found a new and terrifying insight into his most famous poem, "The Second Coming":

Turning and turning in the widening gyre
The falcon cannot hear the falconer;
Things fall apart; the centre cannot hold;
Mere anarchy is loosed upon the world,
The blood-dimmed tide is loosed, and everywhere
The ceremony of innocence is drowned.
The best lack all conviction,
While the worst are full of passionate intensity.

CHAPTER 23

ESCAPE

D espite the odds, many residents still clung to the hope that somehow, someday, they'd get out of Jonestown alive. Human instinct is to survive; surrendering to death is unnatural. The younger, stronger residents fantasized about sprinting through the jungle, and the older, weaker ones prayed for divine or governmental intervention.

Hyacinth Thrash alternately implored God to save them, and fell into depression. Some days, she didn't even bother getting out of bed. She could hear Jones's scaremongering lies over the PA system as she lay on her mattress: racists had taken over the United States; residents should be happy to be safe in Jonestown. Then he'd start up with the suicide talk again. One day, Hy started to say, "Maybe we'd be better off dead . . ." but stopped herself. She thought about taking up her cane and hobbling into the jungle, but she feared she'd fall and wouldn't be able to pick herself back up.

One night, Hy saw Zippy slip from bed and sit down at the small table in their cottage to fill a page and a half of paper with her neat schoolgirl cursive. She'd seen her sister do this before, and knew she was writing Jones another love letter. When Zip left for breakfast the next morning, Hy read it. "I know that it was not by chance that I turned on my TV that Sunday morning and you were there," Zip had written. "I never will forget the feeling that came over me when I heard you speak. I knew at once that I had found what I had been looking for . . . I am blessed to be here." Hyacinth remembered that same morning with bitterness. She threw the note in the trash, but later worried that her action would be discovered, and took it out again.

As far back as Redwood Valley, Jim Bogue recalled Jones asking his followers if they were willing to die for the cause, if they would lay down their life for the brothers and sisters sitting beside them: their black, socialist family. Bogue always thought it was just idle talk and theatrics.

He was certain that Jones never mentioned revolutionary suicide before Guyana, and he was very worried. Whenever Jones kept hinting that something might happen, it eventually did. There were several occasions when Jones mentioned that he was so afraid for so-and-so who'd betrayed the cause, or associated with outsiders, or held back money and warned that some harm would befall the person, and sure enough, it did. They'd suffer a stroke, crash their car, get mugged. Bogue had no idea, of course, that Jones had engineered such mishaps, including chemically induced "strokes."

Bogue's sole concern, as Jones stepped up his suicide drive, was finding a way to get his children out of Jonestown alive. He got them into the church, and now he had to get them out.

Since Jones was constantly badgering residents to come up with ideas to make money, Bogue proposed gold prospecting. The ruse would allow him to roam the bush around the colony and start forging a path toward freedom. He didn't know a thing about gold, other than that it was worth nine hundred dollars an ounce and that Guyana seemed lousy with it. He'd seen wildcat miners in rubber boots trudging up the road to Port Kaituma clutching small bags of the precious metal. They didn't have any sophisticated equipment, yet they collected it by the handful from streams. Why couldn't he do the same? Gold seemed to be all that the cursed jungle was good for. The leadership agreed to give him a go at it, even ordering prospecting guides and pans for him.

He set off into the jungle with his handpicked collaborator, another disgruntled Jonestown resident named Al Simon. Bogue found a kindred spirit in Al, a Pomo Indian who was born on a reservation in Middletown, California. Like Bogue, Al was soft-spoken and introspective. Neither man was in Jones's inner circle, nor aspired to be. The two men had worked together in various farming capacities at the settlement, and something in Bogue's gut told him Al was trustworthy. It was possible to get a sense of another resident's true feelings by reading their body language during Jones's harangues: a wince, a sigh, a moment's hesitation during a death vote. It was risky to approach another resident, however, and it took months for Bogue to broach the topic of escape with Al. At first, they talked about the failure of the farm. This conversation eventually led to a discussion of other failures, including those of Jim Jones. The men cautiously agreed that Jones couldn't be a seer, and compared notes on the lies they'd caught him telling.

Al was also deeply unhappy in Jonestown. His wife, Bonnie, was a true believer and a security guard who flirted openly with other men, but Al was intent on saving his three small children and his father. In the rallies, he sat with his two-year-old daughter, Summer, sprawled out in his lap sleeping, while Crystal, four, and Alvin, Jr., six, dozed on the bench beside him. He was thankful that they were too small to understand most of the discussions. Like Bogue, he suspected Jones would make good on his threat, and subtly let him know he opposed it. Al had never feared death until his children were born, he wrote the Temple leader: "I felt that the lives of my kids meant more than mine. I had a fear of dying because I felt since I helped bring them into the world, I felt I couldn't die because they were so little. . . . I feel all the children here should have a right to live to carry on."

As the months passed, however, it became increasingly clear to him that Jones didn't give a damn about anything, even children.

After Jones approved Bogue's gold prospecting endeavor, the two men used machetes to carve out a path behind the sawmill. They planned to hack a trail to the narrow-gauge railway that ran between Port Kaituma and Matthew's Ridge several miles away. One advantage of Jones's drug addiction was that he stopped micromanaging the settlement; the men could be gone an entire day without raising suspicion. Bogue sent Jones periodic updates saying he'd found a promising streambed that had a "good rock formation, good water source," always adding that he'd need more time to suss it out.

Jim's two older daughters were onboard with the plan. He'd whispered it to Teena, twenty-two, when she was on his planting crew, and to Juanita, twenty-one, when they worked together at the piggery. They agreed to keep the secret from their mother, who was so trusted by Jones that he sent her to Georgetown to do public-relations work. Bogue was vague with his son Tommy, who talked in his sleep, but warned him to stay off the learning crew. It would be impossible to retrieve his son if he were under armed guard.

Marilee, nineteen, was another matter. Bogue felt as though he'd lost his youngest daughter to Jones as well as his wife. Since the beginning, both had been what he called "100 percenters." The chasm between him and his youngest daughter only widened during his long absence as a pioneer. When the time came, he planned on grabbing her, kicking and screaming if need be, and dragging her to freedom; she'd thank him someday.

As the two men discussed who else to let in on their plan, they felt as though they were playing God, deciding who would live and who would die. Bogue decided not to confide in his Jonestown wife, Luna Murral. Even though the couple slept side by side every night, he couldn't decipher what her true sentiments were—if her fervor for Jones was real or pretend. She held trusted jobs as a counselor and a nurse. If he did invite her along, what about her five school-age kids? If she told them, they might tell others and blow their cover.

Al worried about evading his wife and finding a way to gather his children when the moment came. The Bogues assured him they'd help carry his three little ones. But what about Al's sister, brother-in-law, and niece, who'd once dated Tommy, and who were also in Jonestown? All of the Bogue girls had boyfriends there, too. Such was the tapestry of Jonestown. Families were entwined and extended. Ultimately, the two men narrowed the list to their offspring. Despite his best efforts, Jones hadn't broken their instinct to protect their children, and it would only take one loudmouth to land them all in the special care unit. They wouldn't have two chances to get it right.

Jim Bogue's daughters fretted that their dad wouldn't be strong enough to hike out. He'd lost nearly fifty pounds in Jonestown, and weighed less than one hundred as he forged the path. His daughter Juanita stole eggs for him from the chicken coops, which were near her job in the piggery, and boiled them in a can in the jungle. Al gave him some cured pork he'd swiped from the smoke house. The protein fueled their resolve.

As they worked, they fine-tuned the details of their plan. The army base commander in Matthew's Ridge had requested Bogue's help locating ground water, and Bogue planned to take the opportunity, when they were alone, to ask him for shelter. He'd made a point of chatting the man up whenever he brought a load of sweet potatoes or cassava to sell to the base, and felt he'd be receptive to his request. After the base commander gave him his word, they'd wait for the right moment to lead their children to the railroad, where they'd flag down a train and ride to the base, and from there, contact the American embassy. He was still struggling with how to word his request. He worried that the base commander would repeat his disclosures to another resident, or even to Jim Jones. He recalled Jones warning them that the army was under orders to return runaways to the settlement. He hoped this was another of his lies.

The men's progress was agonizingly slow. The rain forest was dense with vines and saplings, and in some stretches, they'd hack for hours, until their muscles shook, only to clear few yards. Blisters caused by his water-logged boots covered Bogue's feet, but his resolve to save his family was a powerful anesthetic.

Somehow their plan would succeed; they had to believe it. The opposite was unfathomable.

CHAPTER 24

CHAOS

In late summer, the Temple contacted author Donald Freed to see if he was interested in writing a history of the church. Freed came highly recommended by Temple counsel Charles Garry. The men knew each other through their work with the Black Panthers: Garry represented the group and Freed wrote a book about them. Like Garry, Freed was progressive and politically engaged. Even more appealing to Jones, Freed believed in conspiracies. He'd coauthored the screenplay for a movie called *Executive Action*, which blamed President Kennedy's assassination on a shadowy military industrial complex opposed to his liberal policies, and he wrote a book suggesting the same cabal killed Robert Kennedy.

When Freed heard there was a large group of American socialists living in Guyana that claimed to be harassed for its ideology, his interest was piqued, and he readily accepted Jones's invitation to visit the colony.

Jonestown spent weeks preparing for the author's visit. In the pavilion, Jones rehearsed the answers to questions Freed might ask, as indicated in this tape recording:

> Jones: How's the food here, madam?
> Female resident: The food is wonderful.
> Jones: [angry] I don't know what wonderful means. What kind of
>   food do you have?

Female: We have chicken, we have pork, beef. . . . We also have
   plenty of fruits, vegetables.
Jones: Okay. Uh, tell me, do you put people in boxes here and bury
   them in boxes?
Male resident: No, uh, I . . .
Jones: I'd look more shocked—I'd look more shocked than that.
Male resident: No, we haven't, you know . . .
Jones: I'd say "What?! Hell no! What prompted that question?"

Cottage supervisors coached residents for hours on responses to twenty-
five negative questions Freed might ask. Afterward, Jones's lieutenants went
from cottage to cottage making sure everyone had memorized their lines.
They were told to refer to Jones as "Jim," not "Dad" or "Father," to avoid
being considered cultish. They were to lie and tell Freed that families lived
together. They were to say they didn't believe in suicide—it was a selfish act.

"It's important that we all appear happy and exhibit satisfaction and
know how to avoid the warning kind of question or not give information
which can be used against us," Jones instructed residents. "Everyone is to
smile constantly and make the victory sign to each other in passing."

Jones selected an entourage to serve as Freed's escorts/chaperones, and
even scripted the escorts' seemingly spontaneous jokes.

Freed arrived in August. During his visit, the front rows in the pavilion
were carefully integrated, and instead of forming the usual long lines in
the dining tent, residents were served meals sitting down. The food was
better, so naturally, residents looked happier. Several cottages were fixed
up as model residences with fewer beds, to diminish rumors of over-
crowding.

Jones encouraged the author to get a physical exam during his tour
to try out the settlement's superlative medical services. He assented. During the eye exam, Freed was given drops that blurred his vision for ten
hours, and while he found this odd, a later interaction with Jones caused
him more concern. Jones, who didn't take off his dark sunglasses for the
entire visit, was strolling along a pathway with Freed when he casually
mentioned the results of Freed's rectal exam: He told the writer that he suffered from a type of gonorrhea that was only transmitted by homosexual
encounter. Freed, a recent widower, wasn't gay, and told Jones as much,

politely suggesting the results were erroneous. But Jones blithely brushed aside his protests, assuring Freed that he was open-minded; he himself had been forced to have gay sex with his followers to keep them dedicated to the cause. As Reverend Jones continued to regale Freed with tales of his sexual exploits, Freed became increasingly uncomfortable. Yet he looked around at the smiling faces of people flashing the V sign at him and was inspired. Jonestown appeared to be a triumph, despite its eccentric leader.

During Freed's visit, Temple leaders collected residents' biographies for him to use in his book. Edith Roller was asked to interview her students and transcribe their histories, and the exercise gave her a deeper empathy for them. Her younger students told her of struggling with drugs, both dealing and using, while her older ones described the violence and loneliness that plagued their existence in the ghetto. These testimonials were meant to prove that Jonestown was a haven for the downtrodden.

For several nights, Freed spoke to the pavilion crowd about the supposed conspiracies behind the deaths of Martin Luther King Jr. and President Kennedy. As Edith took notes, she struggled to keep up with Freed's jumbled stream of thought. His talk of sinister forces intent on destroying progressive movements was tailored to the crowd, especially its leader. Freed told the crowd that Tim Stoen was a CIA agent before he joined the Temple, without citing any evidence, which prompted Jones to suggest that Stoen was a spy even while he was a Temple member.

One night during Freed's visit, Jones summoned Edith to the head table to brag about her success teaching elderly African Americans how to read and write. Freed seemed touched by her efforts, Edith wrote in her journal, and she was flattered by the attention. But she also noted, as she stood at Jones's side, what he and the other Temple leaders were eating—chicken breasts compared to the giblet gravy served the rank and file.

When Freed returned to California, his doctor told him there was no such thing as gay gonorrhea. He would eventually view Jones's strange lie as a clumsy attempt to blackmail him. Still, despite his misgivings, Freed agreed to help Jones uncover the supposed conspiracy against the church. He enlisted his old friend Mark Lane, attorney and conspiracy theorist extraordinaire, to help him. Lane was Freed's coauthor on the *Executive Action* screenplay. The duo's first mission for Jones was to interrogate Joseph A.

Mazor, a private detective who'd worked with the Concerned Relatives. Although Mazor no longer worked for the group, Jones wanted to know if he had an inside scoop on the relatives' plans.

Under the guise of paying Mazor $25,000 as a consultant on a movie about Jonestown, Lane and Freed rented a suite at a hotel overlooking San Francisco's Union Square, and proceeded to interrogate him over a September afternoon.

Mazor had a reputation as a con man, and indeed, Mazor's web of lies rivaled those of Jones himself. He told Freed and Lane that he'd led an armed expedition of Venezuelan poachers to Jonestown to rescue children for the Concerned Relatives in September 1977, but changed his mind after noting there were no fences circling the camp and residents moved about freely. When Freed and Lane asked him whether he noticed anyone else outside of Jonestown at the time, Mazor volunteered that, as his group retreated, they'd encountered a band of ultra-right-wing terrorists who were laying siege to Jonestown.

At Jones's invitation, Mazor flew to Jonestown, where he repeated the fallacious expedition story to Jones's lieutenants, thereby "confirming" that Jonestown was under mercenary attack during the September siege. Jones was delighted.

Mark Lane arrived in Jonestown just after Mazor left. He later said Jones never left his cabin during the day while he was there, but emerged at night to interrupt discussions of proposed strategy with long, rambling asides. But Jones's strange behavior didn't stop Lane from promising the Temple leader that he'd get to the bottom of the conspiracy. A man who'd cry conspiracy over sour milk, Lane did not hesitate to present Jones's most paranoid fears as truth. "Even a cursory examination reveals that there has been a coordinated campaign to destroy Peoples Temple and to impugn the reputation of its leader," he wrote Jones. He proposed conducting a full-scale investigation, and at the beginning of October, he flew to California, where he posed as a journalist to interview Temple critics Kathy Hunter and Steve Katsaris. A few days later, he and Don Freed held a press conference at the San Francisco church, where they announced plans to file a "massive, multi-million dollar lawsuit against all the agencies of government" for attempting to destroy the Temple. He even got the "facts" of Mazor's story wrong, telling reporters that an Interpol employee led a killing force of twenty men armed with guns and rocket launchers through the jungle to fire at the compound for six days.

A skeptical reporter asked why the mercenaries continued firing their weapons after noting the absence of fences.

"That's a good question, we don't have a satisfactory answer," Lane hastily replied, before making his main point: The United States was trying to undermine Jonestown because it was embarrassed by the success of the socialist experiment.

Media coverage of the conference was paltry and derisive. The *San Francisco Examiner* buried its story and described Lane's lawsuit as targeting "virtually everybody but the Coast and Geodetic Survey." KSAN radio reporters mocked Lane's findings, then feigned concern that the lawyer would accuse them of being CIA agents for disagreeing with him. The *Chronicle* sent two reporters to the conference, but didn't publish a word on Lane's allegations, furthering Jones's contention that San Francisco's largest paper was part of the vast plan to destroy him.

Charles Garry thought Mazor's jungle tale was "bullshit," he told Temple leader Jean Brown. He was also repulsed by Lane, whom he considered an amoral opportunist who was tapping into Jones's paranoia for profit. When Jones told Garry that Lane believed Stoen was a government plant all along because he belonged to the Rotary Club, Garry laughed aloud in disbelief; he'd once been a member of the service group himself.

Garry had already peppered Washington, D.C., with Freedom of Information Act (FOIA) requests and failed to uncover any government interest in the Temple. Only the FBI sent him its information on Jim Jones, which consisted of four letters Jones himself wrote requesting his "file." Garry stopped believing Jones's conspiracy hype, and focused on defending the church from mounting lawsuits brought by former members. But Garry's inability to crack the supposed conspiracy angered Jones, who suggested Garry might also be "in the pay of the CIA." For his part, Garry suspected Jones hired Lane as a red herring, hoping the conspiracy fable would divert attention away from Temple scandals. After the massacre, Garry would accuse Lane of being "morally responsible" for the mass deaths because he'd ratcheted up Jones's paranoia.

A turning point in Lane's relationship with Jones came when he single-handedly squelched the damaging exposé commissioned by the *National*

Enquirer, something Garry had been unable to do. Lane managed to get a draft of Gordon Lindsay's story, which ran nearly one hundred pages and was based on interviews with twelve former members. It described Jim Jones as a "mixture of Moon and Manson," and quoted Stoen saying Jones was "bored with life" and got "his kick out of power." It revealed the affair between Paula Adams and Ambassador Mann, and described horrific conditions in Jonestown, including children who "all have ringworm, parasites, hair missing, gashing wounds on their legs."

The unpublished article also dropped a bombshell: The Los Angeles District Attorney's Office wanted to extradite Jones to testify in several extortion cases brought by former members who said the Temple leader threatened them when they balked at giving him their homes.

When Gordon Lindsay called Garry for a comment, the lawyer refused to confirm or deny the charges. But Lane did more than that—he made several stern phone calls to the *Enquirer* threatening libel, prompting the tabloid to kill the story. An elated Jones told the community that night: "We got a new set of attorneys now. I ain't dealing with 'old toupee Garry' now. By God, you open your mouth, [Lane] threatens to sue your ass."

After the massacre, Lane would say Lindsay's article was "absolutely, 100 percent true."

Over the summer and into the fall, Jones told residents that their survival depended on Russia. If the Soviets let them set up a cooperative there, he led them to believe, they could avoid revolutionary suicide. Although many of the African American residents were worried about rascism in the USSR, the move was obviously preferable to the alternative. Gene Chaikin, Tom Grubbs, and Dick Tropp ordered books on Russian geography and researched locations that had warm enough climates to support long growing seasons. They submitted a list of preferred areas to Jones on October 25, marking the east coast of the Black Sea as their top choice.

Residents signed a petition asking the Soviet Union for permission to immigrate and attended mandatory Russian language classes. Edith Roller and a few others who knew a little Russian taught these, aided by books and records. To make sure residents did their homework, Jones instituted a new policy: As residents stood in line for a tray of food, aides asked them a question in Russian. If they answered incorrectly, they were sent to the back of the line. The collective effort to learn the foreign language and possibly avoid revolutionary suicide prompted a renewed camaraderie among residents as they helped each other learn vocabulary words and saluted each other on the muddy pathways with *"Privyet!"* (Hi!) and *"Kak dela?"* (How are you?).

In Georgetown, the Temple PR crew courted the Russian embassy. Sharon Amos continually badgered a junior diplomat named Feodor Timofeyev for an answer on whether the group could move to its "spiritual motherland." Their meetings had a distinctly Cold War flair, with Timofeyev switching on a radio as soon as Amos walked into his office because he assumed that the CIA had bugged it.

Timofeyev hemmed and hawed for months, as Amos gave him different reasons for the move's urgency: Jones believed the Guyanese cabinet was becoming more conservative and would turn against him; he feared Venezuela would reclaim the Northwest territory, including Jonestown. Finally Jones taped a personal message for the Russian diplomat: "Are we or are we not welcome in the Soviet Union?" he asked. "If the Soviet Union is out, I don't think that I can make it." Even Timofeyev grew tired of Jones's paranoid obsessions. "The Temple thinks every movement of the moon deals with it," he told Amos.

In all likelihood, Jones was just stringing residents along with the notion of moving to Russia. After all, the poison was already ordered, the death plan already in place. But that was a secret he didn't yet want to divulge to his followers, so he made it look like Russia was a viable alternative, cruelly toying with their hopes once again.

Jones suffered another blow three weeks before the end, when his lover and financial secretary, Teri Buford, defected. She'd flown back to San Francisco to be deposed by Garry in a lawsuit and disappeared. Buford was one of the few Jonestown residents privileged enough to travel freely and plot her escape.

Although Buford sent numerous memos to Jones supporting the "last-stand" plan, she got scared when she realized he was actually going to go through with it. In Guyana, Jones had grown increasingly tyrannical, and the plan appeared less like Custer's valiant final stand and more like the Nazis' final solution. She'd witnessed Jones's mental deterioration on an intimate level. He'd become abusive during sex, pointing guns at her or choking her and telling her what a big rush it would be for him if she died. When she joined the church Buford believed Jones was God, but by the time she escaped, she knew he was a madman. It became apparent that Jones didn't care if the farm succeeded, or whether his people were fed, or healthy, or happy. The only person who mattered to Jim Jones was Jim Jones. "This is the age of the antihero," he told Buford, "I will go down in history, mark my words." Shortly before she left Jonestown, she crossed paths with Marceline, who told her, "A person on these kinds of drugs doing these kinds of things might be psychotic." Teri didn't respond to the leading remark, fearing Marcie was testing her loyalty. A few days earlier, Jones had drawn her aside to tell her he had $3 million in the safe in his cottage, and that it only cost $500 to hire a hit man.

On the day she left Jonestown, she was so stricken with fear that Jones could read her traitorous thoughts that she silently counted from one to ten, repeatedly, until the dump truck dropped her off at the Port Kaituma airstrip.

In the States, she contacted Mark Lane for legal advice, worried she could be prosecuted for her Temple activities. They'd worked on legal strategies together in San Francisco, where she complained that Lane was constantly coming on to her. When she returned to the States as a defector, he readily agreed to represent her, although he was still on Jones's payroll.

In October, Sharon Amos raised the stakes with Timofeyev. She told him Jones was dying, hoping the information would spur Russia's decision. Of what? the diplomat wanted to know. Amos gave him different answers on different days. He had a mysterious ailment that gave him 106-degree fevers, she said. He had a bad heart. He had lung cancer. Timofeyev, who smoked three packs of cigarettes a day, asked if Jones was a smoker. When Amos said he wasn't, the consul was incredulous, so Amos told him Jones contracted cancer from talking on the radio too much. This made Timofeyev more dubious, and when pressed, Amos admitted Jones's illness was a hoax. The medical department had even sent diseased cells to a laboratory, she confessed, because they "were just trying to see how far [the government of Guyana] will go thinking Jim is dying."

Soon afterward, Timofeyev told Amos that the Soviet Union would not allow the group to immigrate. He explained that it was nearly impossible for a single person to get permission to move to Russia; it would be that much harder for a thousand.

That night, Jones relayed the news to the startled community: The Russians had rejeceted them. The Soviets would only take his immediate family he said, and he wasn't about to abandon his followers. The residents were heartsick at the news; death now seemed inevitable. Some fell into a numbed apathy. Others retreated inward, and stopped speaking altogether. Marceline tried to rein in her husband's murderous impulses. After Debbie Blakey's defection, she publicly protested Jones's cryptic statement that "When Mrs. White drops by, she makes us all equal. [We] should see Mrs. White now and again." Marcie knew *Mrs. White* was a code term for death. She later publicly apologized for disagreeing with her husband. Marcie wasn't told of his first mass suicide threat, on September 11, 1977, until after the crisis was over, and whenever she was included in the secret discussions of the last stand, she made it abundantly clear that she was opposed to killing children.

Jones's Georgetown allies also grew weary of his pushiness and bizarre threats. In October, Jones recorded a private message of "utmost gravity" for the Minister of Home Affairs, Vibert Mingo. In it, he repeated his litany of gripes regarding the custody suit before launching into a lecture on socialism. Sharon Amos reported back to Jones that while the tape played, Mingo rummaged through papers on his desk and then covered his face with his hands in apparent exasperation. Afterward, Mingo canceled his weekly meetings with Amos altogether.

Jones developed a persistent cough and strange fevers, and played these up for sympathy. He told his followers that he had lung cancer and with the strains upon him, could only expect to live three or four more years. For this reason, he said, all complaints must stop.

Dr. Schacht, with his limited expertise and equipment, couldn't get a clear diagnosis of Jones's maladies, aside from a urinary tract infection. Government officials assured Jones that he wouldn't be arrested if he came to Georgetown for medical care, but they refused to commit their promises to writing, so Temple aides asked his personal physician from San Francisco, Carlton Goodlett, to examine him. Goodlett was wary of making the trip; after moving to Guyana, Jones called him several times via shortwave radio, always in the middle of the night, to complain about the mounting conspiracies against him. Goodlett suspected Jones was suffering from manic depression. But when Marceline Jones personally showed up at his office in August and begged him to go, he relented. In Jonestown, he found the Temple leader had a temperature that ran to 102.8 degrees, and a deep, nonproductive cough. The X-rays were normal, however. There was no sign of cancer, tuberculosis, or pneumonia. He reassured Jones that he wasn't dying, but urged him to get a bronchoscopy to rule out a possible fungal infection in his lungs.

On his return to San Francisco, Goodlett met with Marceline and other Temple leaders at 1859 Geary Boulevard. He cautiously alluded to Jones's drug addiction and mental instability, and recommended he be taken immediately to a Venezuelan clinic for treatment.

"You know he's not going to do that," Marcie responded.

"If you can't convince him, then take him," Goodlett said.

Jones's followers sensed their leader was losing control of himself. When he read the news over the PA system, his tongue lolled in his mouth as he slurred or mispronounced words. Sometimes he even sounded some words out, as though he were speaking a foreign language. He blamed his vocal impairment on exhaustion, illness, or the sound equipment. His temper grew worse, and he raged over the loudspeakers about perceived slights. At one point, he ordered nearly twenty people to be medically sedated. A survivor who passed by Jones's cottage in the final weeks recalled overhearing Jones yelling "White night! White night!" over a trivial matter before Marceline prevailed in shushing him: "No, Jim! That's *not* necessary!"

As Jones deteriorated mentally and physically, he spent entire days holed up in his cabin, attended by his dark-haired concubines. Toward the end, he feared his followers as much as they feared him. He stationed armed guards outside his door and warned residents to stay away from his cottage lest they find themselves "in a lot of trouble that's meant only for mercenaries." He carried a .357 magnum revolver in his waistband and gave Carolyn and Maria lighter-weight .25 caliber pistols. He assigned two guards to watch his food being prepared so that no one poisoned it, and ordered an antidote in case someone still managed to do so.

Deep in the Guyanese jungle, Jones created a vacuum of reason where his madness played out unfettered. He staged more "mercenary attacks" with the collusion of his sons, which kept residents afraid and obedient.

Jones even managed to keep his subterfuge hidden from Carolyn Layton, according to a memo she sent him in Jonestown's last weeks. "Someone must viciously hate you and think you a threat or the shootings and assassination attempts would not have taken place," she wrote. "I think logically it must be CIA there."

In the same letter, she reflected on the cursed atmosphere of the camp. "Eventually we will have some defection, perhaps a young person leaving or a senior . . . if we make a stand or decide to die, how are we going to do it . . . do you give everyone pills?"

From these sentences, it's apparent that she didn't even know of Dr. Schacht's cyanide experiments. Although many Temple members had a piece of the puzzle, no one knew the complete layout of Jones's macabre plan. Thirty years later, survivors would still be struggling to find and fit all the pieces together.

CHAPTER 25

NOVEMBER

Congressman Leo Ryan, a Democrat from San Mateo, California, was known for his brash style. He wasn't afraid to go undercover to expose injustice; he posed as a substitute schoolteacher to document living conditions in the slums of Watts, and as an inmate at Folsom Prison to investigate the penal system.

Although Ryan had casually followed the Temple scandal in the Bay Area press, his interest piqued when an old friend and constituent told him he had family in Jonestown. Sam Houston's son, Bob, was a Temple member who had died under mysterious circumstances a few years earlier. The day after Bob defected, he was crushed to death by a freight car in the railyard where he worked. Now, Bob's widow was in Guyana with his two teenage granddaughters, and Sam Houston was worried about them.

The Concerned Relatives felt that Leo Ryan was their last hope. Despite the dire warnings of Debbie Blakey and Yulanda Williams, the State Department was too fearful of violating First Amendment freedoms to press Guyana to investigate Jonestown, and it was increasingly apparent that Jones had the cabinet in his pocket anyway. This seemed especially obvious in the John Victor Stoen custody case; the presiding Guyanese judge, Justice Aubrey Bishop, quit the case after receiving phone calls from people with American accents who threatened to hurt his family if he ruled against Jim Jones. When the case returned to the docket, Chief Justice Harold Bollers didn't reassign it, but simply let it stagnate, as the court had done with the arrest warrant, which was signed but never activated.

The failure of Guyana's judicial process infuriated Tim Stoen, who told the State Department that he was prepared to retrieve his son by force if necessary.

Congressman Ryan's offer to help seemed a more realistic way of recovering John.

On November 1, the congressman sent Jones a telegram:

Dear Reverend Jones,

In recent months my office has been visited by constituents who are relatives of members of your church and who expressed anxiety about mothers and fathers, sons and daughters, brothers and sisters who have elected to assist you in the development of your church in Guyana.

I have listened to others who have told me that such concerns are exaggerated. They have been supportive of your church and your work. Your effort, involving so many Americans from a single U.S. geographic location, is unique. In an effort to be responsive to these constituents with differing perspectives and to learn more about your church and its work, I intend to visit Guyana and talk with appropriate government officials. I do so as part of my assigned responsibilities as a Member of the House Committee on International Relations . . . .It goes without saying that I am most interested in a visit to Jonestown, and would appreciate whatever courtesies you can extend to our Congressional delegation.

Although Ryan described his mind-set as "open and honest," Mark Lane insinuated to Jones that the congressman's sole purpose in coming— with an NBC camera crew in tow—was to smear the Temple. Based on Lane's assessment, Temple aides wrote NBC a letter accusing the television network of being part of a "McCarthy-like web" spun to destroy the church, and flatly refused to allow the crew entry to Jonestown. Lane, for his part, wrote Ryan a letter accusing him of conducting a witch hunt, to which the congressman coolly replied, "The Committee does intend to leave as scheduled."

Jones worried that if Ryan were allowed to visit, at least one disgruntled resident would leave with him. That would create a snowball effect, he feared; the defector would talk to reporters upon returning to California, generating more pressure on the colony. Despairing, Jones told the Guyanese government, "We prefer death to this kind of harassment." If Ryan and his entourage were allowed into the settlement, he continued, it would be a "grave mistake."

On November 7, US Consul Richard McCoy's successor, Doug Ellice, flew up to Port Kaituma. The new consul was leery of Jones even before meeting him. When he took the Guyanese post, Temple members in San Francisco had flooded him with letters praising Jones. The mass mailing was shoddy work: Every letter carried the same date and format, even the same misspelling of his name. He was irritated by the stunt, and told Sharon Amos that his job as an American diplomat in Guyana had nothing to do with people living in California.

Ellice and Vice Consul Dennis Reece conducted their welfare and whereabouts interviews in the field next to the pavilion; no one complained or accepted their offer to leave. During lunch, the Jonestown Express sang "America the Beautiful," and residents stood and pressed their hands to their hearts. It seemed obvious to the guests that the song was chosen for their benefit. When Jones appeared after a long time, he was wearing a gauze mask and walked with the help of two assistants. He complained that he had a fever of 105 degrees, but both Ellice and Reece noted that his palm was dry when they shook his hand, as was his forehead. While Jones's mask hid his chronic lip-licking—a dry mouth is a common side effect of drug abuse—it couldn't hide his mental impairment. At one point, the visitors noted, Jones tried several times to spell a simple word that he didn't want a nearby child to hear before giving up in frustration.

The visit was cut short by an approaching thunderstorm; the pilot wanted to fly back to Georgetown before it hit. As the officials skimmed the settlement in the plane, they noted in their report that they didn't see "barbed wire, any guards, armed or otherwise, or any other physical sign that people were being held at Jonestown against their will."

The State Department passed along the information to Ryan. As a result, the congressman's staff was more concerned about travel logistics and wardrobe choices than they were about potential violence. The Temple and Ryan's office were still negotiating the possibility of a visit, despite

Jones's bluster, when the *Chronicle* published an article about the planned trip. The paper quoted Ryan as saying that he was going to investigate the living conditions of more than a dozen minor children and other relatives of constituents, and that he intended to stay down there "as long as it takes to find out what is going on."

His comments made it clear to Jones that the congressman was on a mission. When he announced Ryan's intended visit to Jonestown residents, he described him as a hostile racist, and swore that the politician would never set foot in the project. He was worried, however, that Ryan's party might try to sneak in from the Kaituma River, and warned that they would suffer the consequences if they did so.

On November 9, he ordered the adults to line up and sign a resolution stating their refusal to see Ryan or his entourage.

In Jonestown's cramped cottages, gossip was rampant about Ryan's visit, as well as Jones's physical deterioration. The Temple leader could barely walk; his face and body were swollen with edema, his hands puffed to almost twice their usual size. Naturally, some residents pondered taking advantage of his weak condition to make a break for it, and Jones seemed to sense this temptation. "See if you can make it to any railway," he told the pavilion crowd eight days before the end. "See if you can get to any passport. Try. I dare you to try. You don't know who you're talking to. Just because I don't use the language of the church, I am that which they call God. . . . I will see you in the grave. Many of you."

Dr. Schacht was ready for Ryan. Although the paper trail doesn't reveal whether his experiment on a large pig was successful, it does show that he began to stockpile cyanide. He placed multiple orders for the poison, including a pound of sodium cyanide, and three 500-gram bottles of potassium cyanide.

Toward the end, survivors would say, Dr. Schacht walked around muttering to himself and was constantly shaking, as if he were sick. The military prosecutor who performed his autopsy detected large levels of Thorazine in his system, perhaps taken to steel his nerves as he plotted the deaths of more than nine hundred people, almost a third of whom were children.

* * *

The week before Ryan flew to South America, Harold Cordell witnessed a large drum of chemicals arrive aboard the *Cudjoe*. It was Cordell's job to take an inventory of items shipped to Jonestown, and the drum wasn't on the manifest. Furthermore, no one knew who ordered it. Agronomist Russ Moton read the label and told him it was a poison that was highly lethal if it were mixed with water and swallowed. Cordell sent the drum to the warehouse, but its presence lingered in his mind. He wondered if Jones were planning to poison the congressman and his party—or if he were planning to poison the entire community by dumping the chemical in the wells. He whispered the news to Edith Bogue late one night as they lay in their loft, and the wall of suspicion between them collapsed. They both confessed to being terrorized at what Jonestown had become. There was an urgency now; Jones had the means to make good on his suicide threats. After they cleared the air, they began to plan. How could they save their kids? How could they even raise the subject of escape with them? What if their children reported them? Lately, Tommy had been asking Edith strange questions: "If he and his sisters left the church, would she stay?" She wondered if he was going to run away again. Between them, Harold and Edith had nine children in Jonestown. They schemed and schemed but each time returned to the same fear that their own kids would turn them in if they broached the topic of escape; they had been trained to do so.

Word of the mysterious drum of chemicals raced through the community. The young woman who washed Hyacinth Thrash's hair told her about it, adding darkly that Hy might not need a cane much longer. Hy didn't understand. "You mean I'm gonna get healed?" she asked in a hopeful voice. The young woman didn't answer.

The tension of those last weeks could have sparked in the air. On Sunday, November 12, Joyce Touchette told the three George children—the Amerindian children she'd adopted in Jonestown's early days—to pack their things and go back to their mother. They did so. Something ominous was brewing in Jonestown, they told their mom, and they were scared. But she was too poor to feed them, and sent them back against their will.

Five days before the end, when Jones told the group that he was prepared to make a great sacrifice, Jim Bogue knew exactly what he was referring to. He and Al Simon were ready. Their pathway to freedom was finished; they were just waiting for the right moment to lead their children out. Bogue was due in Matthew's Ridge on Monday, November 20, to consult with the army about finding groundwater; they'd have to bide their time until then.

CHAPTER 26

RYAN

The congressman kept adding members to his entourage. One of Jones's top lieutenants, a Vietnam vet named Tim Carter, returned to San Francisco posing as a defector to infiltrate the Concerned Relatives and kept Jones apprised of Ryan's latest plans.

By the time the congressman arrived in Guyana shortly past midnight on Wednesday, November 15, his party included the NBC crew; reporters for the *Washington Post*, the *National Enquirer*, and the two San Francisco papers; as well as over a dozen relatives, including the Stoens, the Olivers, and Steven Katsaris. Jones was beside himself.

His Guyanese allies did their best to help him obstruct the visit. Minister of Home Affairs and Immigration Vibert Mingo told the Temple that Congressman Ryan and the NBC crew were cleared to enter the country, but that he would revoke the visas of the other reporters. He made good on his word. When *San Francisco Chronicle* reporter Ron Javers landed at Timehri airport, he was detained on a trumped-up currency violation: He'd exchanged $100 for Guyanese dollars in California, and customs officials told him it was illegal to bring the local currency into the country. They held Javers at the airport for twelve hours until the American Embassy intervened. Meanwhile, the Concerned Relatives and the other journalists arrived at their hotel to find their reservations canceled. They spent the night in the lobby, and, the next morning, an immigration official showed up and restamped their passports to reduce their permitted stay from five days to one. Again, the American embassy intervened.

On Wednesday afternoon Ryan and *Washington Post* reporter Charles Krause drove to the Temple's headquarters at 41 Lamaha Gardens, where they were met by the stony faces of Sharon Amos and Jim McElvane, the church's six-foot-seven security chief, whom Jones had summoned to Guyana the previous day. The congressman asked to speak to Jones over the radio, but Amos said Jones was too ill to do so. Some of the Concerned Relatives had followed Ryan to the Temple house, and they also were refused entry. The group then met privately with Ambassador John Burke, who told them his hands were tied: Jonestown was private property; if they tried to force their way in, they could be arrested for trespassing.

On Thursday, Ryan held a press conference at his hotel and stated he was worried about the mental health of the Jonestown residents. Despite Jones's repeated declarations that Ryan would never enter the community, the congressman announced he'd chartered a twenty-passenger plane and was flying up to Port Kaituma the next day.

That night, Jones held a rally:

Jones: "I can assure you, that if he stays long enough for tea, he's gonna regret it . . . son of a bitch. You got something to say to him, you want to talk to him?"

Crowd: "No!"

Jones: "Anybody here care to see him?"

Crowd: "No!"

Jones: "I don't know about you, I just wanted to be sure you understood where I'm coming from. I don't care whether I see Christmas or Thanksgiving, neither one. You don't either. We've been debating about dying 'til, hell, it's easier to die than talk about it . . . I worry about what you people think, because you're wanting—trying to hold onto life, but I've been trying to give mine away for a long time, and if that fucker wants to take it— he can have it, but we'll have a hell of a time going together."

On Friday, November 17, Charles Garry and Mark Lane flew to Georgetown. When Garry discovered Lane was on the flight, he refused to sit next to him, still furious at him for inciting Jones's paranoia. But when the duo arrived at Lamaha Gardens, however, they agreed on one thing: Jones should welcome Ryan into Jonestown. Refusing him admittance would only validate the congressman's contention that Jones was hiding something, and when he returned to Washington, he'd probably hold hearings on the matter.

The lawyers met with Ryan at his hotel, and he told them his chartered flight was leaving that afternoon. When they radioed the news to Jones, the Temple leader started ranting about conspiracies. Garry interrupted him.

"Cut the horseshit," he said. He gave Jones two alternatives: He could either tell the congressman to go to hell or he could let the delegation in. Garry told Jones that if he refused Ryan, he would resign as Temple attorney. Jones fell silent for several moments before saying in a weak voice, "Very well."

The twin prop DeHavilland Otter carrying the congressional party soared toward the northwest rain forest as scheduled. On it rode Congressman Leo Ryan; his aide Jackie Speier; Deputy Chief of Mission Dick Dwyer; an official with the Guyanese Ministry of Information named Neville Annibourne; Garry and Lane; four members of the Concerned Relatives, Beverly Oliver, Anthony Katsaris (Maria's brother), Jim Cobb, and Carolyn Houston Boyd (the Houston girls' aunt); and a group of eight journalists that included NBC reporter Don Harris; NBC sound technician Steve Sung; NBC producer Bob Flick; *San Francisco Examiner* reporter Tim Reiterman; *San Francisco Examiner* photographer Greg Robinson; *San Francisco Chronicle* reporter Ron Javers; *Washington Post* reporter Charles Krause; and *National Enquirer* freelancer Gordon Lindsay.

The relatives who knew their chances of getting into Jonestown were slim, including the Stoens and Steven Katsaris, volunteered to stay behind.

While the plane was aloft, Jones had his aides radio the Georgetown air traffic control tower to report that the Port Kaituma landing strip was too muddy to use. But the Otter's pilot flew over it anyway, and found it in perfectly good condition. He got permission to land, and touched down at three forty-two.

The Temple's yellow dump truck was parked on one side of the airstrip, and several Temple members stood beside it, including security guards Jim

McElvane and Joe Wilson, and Jones's advisor Harriet Tropp. Tim Carter, the defection ruse over, was also there, and when Dwyer attempted to introduce him to the congressman, Carter walked away. A lone policeman approached the party and stated that he had orders to keep them out of Jonestown; in fact, they weren't even permitted to leave the airstrip.

The Temple aides invited Jones's lawyers to the settlement, and as they drove away on the dump truck, Congressman Ryan gathered the press to make a statement. He'd always assumed that the Temple leader wouldn't let him into Jonestown, and was about to condemn this rejection when the truck came racing back: now Ryan, Speier, Dwyer, and Annibourne were invited in. Garry told the reporters and relatives that he'd try to get them in later that afternoon or the next day. Alone on the airstrip, the group took shelter from the scalding sun under the airplane wings, and the newsmen paid a couple of teens to fetch them cold beer.

As the congressman's group drove down the three-mile dirt road leading to Jonestown, it hit a barricade: Logs had been deliberately strewn across the road, making it impassable. They waited for the bulldozer to arrive and clear the way. When they finally pulled into the settlement, around five that afternoon, Marceline Jones greeted them cheerily, with nary a mention of the barricade. She brought them to the pavilion, where she offered them iced tea and showed them a display of handicrafts. When she started leading them on a tour, however, Ryan politely insisted on speaking to Jones. He wanted to settle the matter of the group stranded at the airstrip as soon as possible.

Thirty minutes later, Jones arrived wearing a red shirt and sunglasses, flanked by his lawyers. Ryan cordially explained that his purpose in coming was to determine whether residents were being held against their will, and told Jones that the best way to silence his critics would be to admit his entire party. Pressured by his lawyers, Jones made only one exception: Gordon Lindsay, who'd penned the scathing article for the *National Enquirer*.

As the dump truck turned around to retrieve the rest of the entourage from Port Kaituma, Jones watched it go with apprehension.

"I hope to God I have done the right thing," he said, to no one in particular.

* * *

The truck returned just after sunset. The pavilion was packed, and residents stared openly at the guests as they walked through the crowd to a table near the stage where Jones sat with his advisors. As the reporters immediately began peppering Jones with accusatory questions, the visiting relatives sought out their family members.

The night before Jones had warned residents: "As far as your relatives coming up to talk to you, be civil, but don't get engaged into long conversation with them . . . tell them how happy you are, tell them what your food is, how much food, that you wouldn't go back to the United States if someone were to give you a ticket tomorrow." If they disobeyed these orders, they'd be on the floor, he warned.

Beverly Oliver took a walk with her two sons, and asked them if they'd received any of her letters. They hadn't. She then asked why they hadn't written her, and they replied that Jones had said she was a CIA agent, and that she and the rest of the Concerned Relatives wanted to kill everyone in Jonestown.

Maria Katsaris refused to return her brother Anthony's embrace, and during dinner, she made weird comments about the guests' food being poisoned. Temple security chief Jim McElvane came over and sat next to them, precluding any private conversation.

Meanwhile, Ryan and Speier camped out at a table set to one side of the pavilion, interviewing residents. To counteract rumors that Jonestown was bugged, they showed people a card instructing them to nod their heads if they wanted to leave. No one did. But Speier noted a patterned response to questions and wondered whether residents were too intimidated to be honest with her. Furthermore, several residents she wanted to speak with were supposedly sick or otherwise unavailable. Ryan brought letters from worried family members, and these, as ordered, were duly handed to Temple censors, unopened, as soon as the residents left his table. FBI agents would later find them in a file marked "Letters brought in by Ryan."

Earlier, residents were served a hearty dinner of barbecued pork, biscuits, callaloo greens, and punch, as well as the first coffee they'd tasted in months. They knew the food was for show, but it was delectable just the same, and such small joys were hard-won in Jonestown.

At the lead table, Jones raged about conspiracies. As he careened from one topic to the next, his tongue lolled sloppily in his mouth, making the reporters wonder whether he was high or, perhaps, mentally ill. Their uneasiness was only heightened when Jones abruptly stated, "Sometimes I feel like a dying man." He repeatedly mentioned death, but when the reporters asked about the mass-suicide threats, he acted offended. "I only said it is better that we commit suicide than kill," he said, adding that he'd rather kill himself than give John Stoen back to his mother. As if on cue, the six-year-old was trotted out so Jones could point out physical similarities between them, even making the boy bare his teeth to "prove" they had the same dental structure.

As the newsmen grilled Jones, the adult residents cast worried glances in his direction while their children, oblivious, horsed around. The band played the Guyanese national anthem, and then "God Bless America." A robust black youth named Poncho Johnson sang "The Greatest Love of All," a tune elevating hope and self-reliance, and a well-dressed young couple got up to dance, as scripted.

Anthony Katsaris invited Maria to take a stroll so they could be alone. She accepted, but when he asked her pointed questions, she was surly and evasive. Their exchange became heated, and when he grabbed her arm to stop her from walking away, she yelled for the guards. Frightened, he returned to the pavilion before they showed up.

After the talent show, Marceline interrupted Ryan's interviews to introduce him to the crowd. In the NBC footage of the event, he was casually dressed in slacks and a red-and-blue-striped polo shirt, but spoke with a statesman's aplomb. He noted that he'd run into a former student from his days teaching high school, as well as an old classmate of his daughter. Then he got down to business, telling the audience: "This is a congressional inquiry. I think that all of you know that I'm here to find out more about questions that have been raised about your operation here, but I can tell you right now that, from the few conversations I've had with some of the folks here already this evening, that whatever the comments are, there are some people here who believe this is the best thing that ever happened to them in their whole life."

The residents' applause, which lasted a full minute, reverberated off the metal roof. The NBC cameraman turned his lens from Ryan to pan over the ecstatic crowd for a few moments, then returned to the congressman, who waited for the noise to subside with an awkward smile. He attempted to speak several times, but was drowned out each time by applause, whistling, shouting, and drums. The ruse was working.

Around eleven that night, residents started to fade into the darkness toward their cottages, and the press and relatives boarded the dump truck for a guest house in Port Kaituma. Despite the newsmen's protests, Jones only allowed Ryan, Speier, Dwyer, and Annibourne to spend the night in Jonestown. As Dwyer stood off to one side of the pavilion, a young man named Vern Gosney walked up to him and whispered that he wanted to get out of Jonestown "immediately." Dwyer told Gosney that it was too late to arrange anything that night, but that he'd be happy to help him the next day. Later, when Dwyer told Ryan about the encounter, the congressman showed him a note Gosney slipped NBC reporter Don Harris earlier in the evening. It stated simply: "Vernon Gosney and Monica Bagby. Help us get out of Jonestown." Gosney, a former heroin addict, had moved to the community with his five-year-old son, hoping to stay clean, only to realize Jones himself was a junkie.

Nevertheless, Dwyer went to bed that night feeling satisfied with the visit; the congressman had been warmly received, and only two people wanted to leave.

On Saturday, Jones gave the residents a free day, but he scripted the seemingly relaxed atmosphere of the camp: the girls' drill team practicing their dance moves under an awning, a group of teens playing basketball, children watching cartoons in the pavilion.

Congressman Ryan was up shortly after dawn to resume his interviews, and since he was running out of time to complete them, he asked Dwyer to talk to Gene Chaikin for him.

Gene was in the infirmary; as usual, Jones had him drugged and hidden from view. Medical records show that he was admitted a few hours before Ryan arrived, and prescribed Valium by Dr. Schacht. Although Ryan had visited Gene the evening before, there had been too many people around for a private conversation, and something about Gene's demeanor unsettled him. Ryan handed Dwyer a letter from Gene's brother. Ray Chaikin had asked the congressman to show his brother the letter, but not to let him keep it—he was worried that Gene would be harassed if it was found on his person.

When Dwyer got to the infirmary, he found Gene lying on a cot and asked him to accompany him to the building's small deck, before handing him the letter. In it, Ray Chaikin pleaded with his brother to take advantage of Ryan's visit to come home; he'd included an airplane ticket. Dwyer asked Gene if he wanted to leave, but Gene shook his head. "They just don't seem to understand that my home and family are here now," he said. He told the diplomat that he hoped Ray would someday visit him in Jonestown. Dwyer jotted down a release on the back of the envelope that allowed him to disclose their conversation to Ray, and Gene signed it. Dwyer returned to the pavilion; Gene Chaikin was never seen alive again. His medical chart shows that on November 17, he refused to eat, and on November 18, he refused water. After Dwyer left, he was given 10 mg of Valium, a strong dose usually reserved for patients suffering from high anxiety.

The Temple dump truck was two hours late picking up the reporters from their Port Kaituma boardinghouse. By the time they reached Jonestown, at ten-thirty in the morning, the newsmen were anxious for a scoop. Marcie started her canned tour, but they grew restless and broke off on their own. *Washington Post* reporter Charles Krause walked up to a large dorm called the Jane Pitman Gardens, and when no one answered his knock, he tried pulling back a shutter to look inside. Someone on the inside held the shutter in place, so he jumped to the conclusion that the inhabitants were being held against their will. He demanded to be let in. An aide told him that the residents merely wanted to protect their privacy, but he insisted, and was finally allowed to enter with the other reporters. They found a group of elderly black women inside, none happy at having their quarters invaded by pushy young white men. The reporters noted that the living space was crammed with bunk beds, but also that each woman had personalized her space with embroidered pillows and quilts.

In the pavilion, a group of children watched *Willy Wonka and the Chocolate Factory* as the NBC crew set their camera equipment for a final interview with Jones. The Temple leader sat in a chair dressed in the same red shirt and sunglasses as the night before, and NBC correspondent Don Harris sat down facing him, wearing a light-blue leisure suit. Harris again asked Jones about the rumors of mistreatment and imprisonment. Jones again denied everything. Harris then pulled out Gosney's note and handed it to him. Jones read it in silence, before looking at Harris with disgust.

"People play games, friend," Jones said. "They'll lie, they'll lie. What can I do about liars? Are you people gonna . . . leave us, I just beg you. Please leave us." The print reporters, crouched out of range of the television camera, scribbled his words in their notebooks. "If it's so damn bad, why is he leaving his son here? Can you give me a good reason for that? I'd take my son with me."

As Dwyer stood nearby, waiting for the interview to conclude, a grandmotherly woman with white hair and cat's-eye glasses walked up to him. "We want to leave," Edith Parks said. The Parks family had planned to escape through the jungle, but discovered that morning that the plastic bags containing clothing and food that they'd hidden in the bush were missing, and feared Jones was onto them. There were seven people in her party, Edith told Dwyer. The diplomat pulled Ryan aside and asked him to tell Jones that more people wanted to leave, and then he walked to the radio room to call for a second plane.

As the cameras rolled, a pallid Jones walked up to the Parks family. "Please don't go with him," he begged them. The Parks family had been with him since Indiana; it would look very bad if his longtime followers abandoned him now. "Wait a week or two," he said, "and I'll give you your passports and five thousand dollars."

It was a provocative offer. Like all Temple members, they'd signed over all their material wealth to the church and would be going home dirt poor. The family debated his proposal for a few minutes before rejecting it. Once the delegation left, they reasoned, Jonestown would again become a sealed village and they would be regarded as traitors. Emboldened by their decision, Jerry Parks didn't mince words with Jones. "You held us here as slaves and now we are getting out," he said.

Jones turned and walked away. Gone was the gloating, the crowing, the preening vulgarity. He sat on a bench, alone, his shoulders slumped.

Tommy Bogue saw Edith Parks talking to Jackie Speier and panicked. Everyone had been ordered to stay away from the guests—or else—and here was Mrs. Parks speaking with the congressman's aide in plain sight. It was obvious to him that she was asking for help, and he sprinted away to find his dad. Jim Bogue told Tommy to gather his sisters and head to the sawmill for an emergency meeting.

Tommy rushed to the sawmill with Teena; Juanita and Marilee followed. Already there were his dad, Al Simon, Al's two little girls, and Al's dad, José Simon. There was no time to delay, Jim Bogue told the group. Jonestown was unraveling, and he was sure that Jones would call the final white night as soon as the congressman left. They wouldn't live to see tomorrow if they stayed. He glanced at Tommy, who was wearing a red nylon basketball jersey and shorts, and shook his head. The boy was practically naked, and they had to trek through miles of brambles, biting ants, and mosquitoes to reach the railroad.

Al hadn't been able to locate his boy, six-year-old Alvin Jr. "I'm gonna get him and I'll be right back," he told the group. Bogue promised they'd wait for him; the two men had forged the path together and together they'd hike it out. A few minutes after Al left, Jim's estranged wife, Edith, sauntered up the path with Harold Cordell. Bogue cursed under his breath, fearing they'd been sent as spies.

Edith asked to speak with Teena. They walked to a log a short distance from the sawmill and sat down. Edith told her daughter about Tommy's strange questions, and asked her whether she thought he was planning to run away again.

Teena started to cry. "Are you going to turn Tommy in?" she asked her mother. Edith assured her she'd never inform on anyone again. She mentioned the container of poison Harold unloaded from the boat, and Teena cried harder. "Mom, so help me, if this is a trick . . ." she started to say, but Edith stopped her. "It's not a trick," she said. "I'm afraid for our lives."

As they were talking, Juanita showed up. She looked from Edith to Teena with suspicion. "Mom is with us," Teena told her.

Next, Marilee arrived, belatedly responding to Tommy's summons. Everyone knew she couldn't be trusted. They loved her, but she was a true believer. They forced the conversation onto another subject. When the time was right, they'd jump her.

As the group waited for Al, two security guards ran up and asked if they'd seen a young woman named Leslie Wilson and her two-year-old boy; Wilson's husband, a security guard, suspected she'd fled. They hadn't, and the guards left. But the fear fluttering in their hearts made it clear that it was time to move.

Al Simon didn't return and didn't return. Finally Jim Bogue decided they should go look for him. Teena and Edith found him in the cottage area talking to Agnes Jones, the adopted daughter of Jim and Marcie Jones. "This is it," Agnes told them. "Try to get yourselves out." The Bogues and Simons then decided to cast their lot with Congressman Ryan; it seemed a surer bet, at that point, than hiking to Matthew's Ridge.

Jim Bogue walked into the pavilion and told Congressman Ryan his family also wanted to leave Jonestown. Ryan said that the dump truck was filling quickly, so they might have to wait for a second load. There were now twenty defectors, in addition to the newsmen and visiting relatives.

"There won't be another load," Edith Bogue told him bluntly.

"Yes, there will, because I will stay right here with you," Ryan said.

"You are one person, and these people are many," she said, glancing around at the crowd surrounding the pavilion.

Jones walked up to Jim Bogue and threw his arm around his shoulder as if they were old buddies.

"You know you don't have to go," Jones said in a confiding voice.

Bogue just looked at the ground and shook his head.

"And if you do go, you'll be welcomed back anytime," Jones continued. "Even some of those who have lied against us have come back."

Bogue just let him talk. He had nothing more to say to him.

The sky had been swirling with dark clouds all morning and now a giant wind heaved through the pavilion, rocking the planters hanging from the rafters, and knocking over the carefully displayed crafts. It was as if all the tension in Jonestown had condensed above it, and now, on this final, horrible day, was transmogrified into its own physical force. Rain began to drill the pavilion's metal roof, silencing talk, stifling movement. A moat formed around the structure's edges.

When the rain let up, Ryan and Speier chaperoned the defectors to their cottages to retrieve their meager belongings and Jones pressed his hand to his chest and asked Marcie for a pill. She tried gently to dissuade him. Behind his shades, his eyes were glazed. He wasn't listening to her. He was planning his last sermon.

Jim Bogue searched frantically for his youngest daughter. At one point after they returned to the pavilion he'd spotted Marilee, but then she disappeared into the crowd. His companion, Luna Murral, walked up to him.

"Are you really leaving?" she asked.

"Come with us," he said.

She shook her head and walked back to her five children.

Harold Cordell saw his youngest son, fourteen-year-old James. They'd always been close. He tugged on Jimmy's arm.

"Come on, Jimmy, let's get out of here," Harold said. "We gotta go."

"No," James said without hesitation. He was raised in the church to be dedicated to the cause, and in Jonestown, he was such an avid communist that people called him "Jim Stalin." Harold offered to take Jimmy to Cuba, but still, the boy refused. He was about to tell him about the poison when his son backed away from him with a look of contempt stamped on his face. He saw his father as a deserter, and wanted nothing to do with him.

Tommy saw Brian Davis. He was standing next to his dad with his arms crossed, watching the defecting group, watching Tommy, with huge, scared eyes. This was the third act of their *Creature Feature*, when the heroes finally triumphed over the monster. They could make it this time.

He beckoned for Brian to join him. But Brian's father, a true believer, was standing right next to him, ready to grab his son's elbow and physically prevent him from doing so. Brian was only sixteen. He wasn't free to do what he wanted. He was just a kid. He looked miserable, and shook his head sadly at Tommy.

"Good-byes" and "See you laters" seemed beside the point. There was no time to waste; the departing residents sensed that the longer they tarried, the more danger they were in. The crowd seethed with fear and anger. One woman pressed a note into Beverly Oliver's hands: "Keep your damn mouth shut," it read.

Those who stayed behind blamed those who were leaving for breaking ranks and provoking Jones, yet many longed to join them. The NBC crew filmed residents as they huddled in doorways, conferring in whispers, their eyes darting back and forth, chewing their cuticles to the quick.

As the Parks family walked past the camera toward the waiting dump truck, a woman announced over the loudspeakers: "Bonnie Simon, Bonnie Simon: Please come to the radio room." The camera cut to the Simon family. Al, his father José, and Al's three kids were walking toward the dump truck. Then the camera panned to Bonnie as she rushed over to yank Alvin Jr. from his grandfather's arms. She turned to shriek at her husband, striding toward the truck with Summer in his arms and Crystal trotting beside him:

"You bring those kids back here! Don't you take my kids!"

He kept walking.

"Mother!" Bonnie called in desperation. Marceline came over to calm her and José picked up his grandson and cradled him against his chest. The camera zoomed in on their faces: the grandfather's grimly determined, the boy's eyes wide with anguish. José caught up to Al, and the two men marched shoulder to shoulder toward the truck, casting nervous glances behind them.

They almost made it.

Charles Garry intervened. Al couldn't just take the kids, he said. Congressman Ryan volunteered to stay behind to negotiate the matter.

At two-thirty, the newsmen and fourteen defectors were standing in the truck bed, anxious to go. It was still dripping rain. Stanley's friend Eddie Crenshaw was the driver. He kept getting out of the cab and going over to talk to Jones and the security guards at the edge of the playground, even as the defectors yelled for him to pull out. They worried that Jones would kill them right there. Finally, the truck started rolling, but Eddie deliberately drove the massive tires into a ditch. As they waited for the bulldozer to pull them out, shouts erupted from the pavilion. The reporters jumped out and sprinted over. They found Congressman Ryan with blood on his shirt. As he was discussing the Simon custody problem with the lawyers, a burly ex-Marine named Don Sly came up behind him and pressed a knife to his throat, shouting, "Motherfucker, you are going to die!" The lawyers pulled Sly off, and he cut his own hand during the struggle.

Jones watched the altercation as if he were in a trance. "I wish I had been killed," he muttered.

"You get that man arrested," an angry Ryan told him.

"Does this change things?" Jones asked.

Ryan said it wouldn't—as long as Sly was detained, he wouldn't recommend further investigations of the camp.

Ryan assumed that his position as a United States congressman would grant him respect and protection in Jonestown. The newsmen and relatives thought his presence would grant them safety as well. Now, as Ryan brushed himself off, Dwyer urged him to get out of Jonestown immediately. Not only might he be assaulted again, but his very presence could be a catalyst for violence; surrounding them were hundreds of people, some with openly hostile faces. Dwyer decided he'd better escort Ryan to the airstrip himself before returning to sort out the custody matter.

NBC filmed Ryan walking toward the dump truck. His face was grim. He carried his briefcase in one hand, and his soiled shirt was unbuttoned to the waist, exposing his soft white middle. A last-minute defector shuffled alongside him in a long green poncho. It was Larry Layton, Debbie Blakey's brother and a known Jones loyalist. Speier found it odd that Layton, who had sought her out a few hours earlier to state how happy he was in Jonestown, was now claiming the exact opposite. Some defectors had seen Layton whispering with Jones by the playground; the two men had even hugged. They insisted he was a plant; he wasn't even carrying any luggage, they pointed out. But the American officials had no choice but to take his declarations at face value; they offered safe passage to anyone who wanted to leave.

The six-mile drive to the airstrip took forever. Halfway out of Jonestown, over the defectors' vehement protests, the truck stopped so the NBC crew could film more b-roll. Jim Bogue told Tommy to grab his sisters and head for the jungle if anything went down. When they got to the front entrance, the gate was closed, and a security guard with a pistol hanging from his jeans hopped on the running board and ordered the passengers to spread out. It was Joe Wilson, looking for his wife, Leslie, who'd fled into the bush with their toddler son and nine others that morning. He stayed hanging off the truck, glowering at everyone, all the way to the airstrip.

There were no planes waiting for them, despite Dwyer's request. Anxiety spiked again. Don Harris took advantage of the lag to interview Ryan.

"All of a sudden we had a whole lot of people at the last minute who wanted to go, who suddenly rushed forward and said, 'We want to leave,'" Ryan said. He'd been taking down their names when Sly jumped him.

"What do you intend to do now?" Harris asked.

"Put it all together," Ryan said.

After fifteen minutes, a five-seat Cessna appeared overhead and landed. It was followed, several minutes later, by a twenty-seat Guyana Airways Twin Otter. As the defectors loaded their gear onto the planes, they noticed Layton talking to Joe Wilson. The two men shook hands under Layton's rain poncho, then Layton sat by himself with a "long, weird stare on his face," a survivor later testified. Their agitation grew as they watched the tractor trailer arrive and drive down the side of the airstrip to park 200 yards away from them. Eddie Crenshaw drove the dump truck over to it. A dozen or so Jonestown guards stood around the two vehicles surveying the departing party.

"I think we've got trouble," Harris said to his colleagues.

Speier was jotting down seat assignments on a piece of paper. There weren't enough seats to fly all thirty people out, so some reporters would have to wait until the following day, she announced. The newsmen protested; each wanted to file his story first.

Layton ambled over and insisted on being seated on the Cessna. Speier paused; that was the plane she planned on taking. She took Ryan aside and said she didn't trust Layton, so the congressman suggested she ride on the Otter instead. At the defectors' insistence, Ryan patted Layton down for weapons. He didn't find anything. Layton climbed aboard the Cessna followed by Dale Parks, his twelve-year-old sister Tracy, Monica Bagby, and Vernon Gosney.

The other defectors boarded the Otter as Speier tried to coax out an Amerindian child who'd scuttled up the gangway. The journalists stood on the tarmac, still arguing about who should get a seat, when they heard the tractor-trailer's diesel motor gunning toward them above the plane's twin engines and turned.

The tractor stopped about thirty feet away, parallel to the plane. The driver, Stanley Gieg, a nineteen-year-old from the San Francisco suburb of Walnut Creek, waved away Guyanese bystanders as six men who were hidden in the trailer bed stood up, holding guns. They jumped to the ground, and shot out the Otter's front wheel before training their weapons on people.

Tommy was sitting directly in front of the open door. "Duck down!" Harold Cordell shouted. Patty Parks, forty-four, buckled into the seat in front of Tommy, didn't move fast enough. She was hit in the back of the head, and her brain landed on the empty seat next to her. Tommy jumped up to close the gangway, putting himself in the line of fire. He knew they'd all die if he didn't. But the mechanism was too heavy. Teena rushed to help him and together they pulled it up as bullets zinged around them. When Tommy sat back down, he noticed his left calf was bleeding profusely from tiny holes riddling his flesh; he'd taken a shotgun blast, and Teena had been shot in the leg by a .22.

Outside, Ryan ran around the plane's nose and crumpled to the dirt. "I've been shot!" he yelled. He grabbed his neck and wrapped his body around the front tire, trying to shield himself from the bullets. NBC cameraman Bob Brown bravely continued to record the attack until a slug burrowed into his leg; he groaned as he was hit, and an instant later, the film dissolved into gray static. The gunmen walked among the wounded, shooting them at point-blank range, killing Bob Brown, Greg Robinson, Don Harris, and Leo Ryan—the only congressman to be assassinated while in office.

At the far end of the runway, the Cessna was also under siege. Larry Layton pulled out a .38 revolver hidden in his clothing and seriously wounded Bagby and Gosney before his gun jammed. Dale Parks wrested it from Layton and punched him in the face, subduing him. He gave the gun to Dwyer, who'd been shot in the thigh but was still mobile. The diplomat asked a bystander to drive Layton to the police station, and on the way to Port Kaituma, Layton begged, unsuccessfully, to be brought to Jonestown instead.

Witnesses would later say that as the tractor-trailer drove back to the settlement, the men riding it smiled and flashed victory signs at onlookers.

CHAPTER 27

END

After the shooters left, Tommy lowered the Otter's door and stepped cautiously down the gangway. Under the plane, bodies, blood, and brains were spewed everywhere. Some on the ground survived by playing dead when the assailants delivered the coups de grace, but they were badly wounded. The survivors started to regroup when someone yelled, "They're coming back!"

"Run!" Jim Bogue told his son. Tommy grabbed his sister Teena and sprinted toward the shade line of the jungle.

After the defectors left, Marceline got on the loudspeaker. She assured residents that everything was okay, and instructed them to return to their quarters to freshen up for dinner.

Garry and Lane dropped their shared enmity and took a walk together to discuss the day's events. Garry mentioned that he hadn't seen Gene Chaikin all weekend, and Lane told him about the drugged sandwiches, among other alarming things he'd learned from his now-client Teri Buford.

Around five o'clock, Jim McElvane and another Jones loyalist, Jack Beam, tracked down the lawyers and asked them pointed questions about the defections. Jones wanted to know if his legal team still supported him. Garry started to criticize the lack of free expression in the community when Jones's voice came over the PA system, summoning residents to the pavilion. A few seconds later, the walkways were flooded by a river of people. As they passed Garry and Lane, many smiled and called out greetings. McElvane, apparently not content with the lawyers' answers, ordered the men to accompany him to meet with the Temple leader.

He led them to a school tent. Inside, Jones sat on a carpenter's horse with Harriet Tropp beside him.

"Charles, all is lost," Jones said in a glum voice. "Every gun in this place is gone."

Garry was taken aback; he'd spent years defending Jonestown from rumors that it was an armed camp. "Jim, I didn't know you had any guns here," he said.

Jones ignored his comment. He said that the residents were upset with the lawyers because they'd insisted he welcome Ryan into Jonestown and the visit had been a disaster.

"Your life is not safe here," Jones said. "People are angry at you."

Garry thought this odd, considering the friendliness of the passing throng. Jones told his adopted Korean son, Lew, to escort the lawyers to the East House to wait until further notice. After arriving at the cottage, they grew anxious when they noticed a line of men exiting the building next door carrying weapons and boxes of ammunition and hustling back toward the pavilion. The situation grew more ominous when Don Sly—the same man who tried to stab Congressman Ryan—showed up and sat on the cottage steps, as if he were guarding them. Sly, his hand wrapped in bandages, refused to talk to them, but kept calling out to the men carrying weapons, "When do you want me up there?"

The lawyers heard Jones begin to address his people, but his voice was too distant to hear very well. They made out random words, including *death*. Sly finally stood and followed the others.

As Garry and Lane were discussing their alternatives, including fleeing into the bush, two armed men returned to their cottage. They feared the worst.

Garry recognized Poncho Johnson, the nineteen-year-old who sang "The Greatest Love of All," the previous night. As the young men walked down the pathway toward them, they laughed and kidded around.

"What's going on?" Garry asked.

"We're committing revolutionary suicide," said Poncho, grinning widely.

Garry recalled the September siege and Huey Newton's complaint that Jones didn't understand what the term meant.

"Is there no other alternative?" Lane asked.

"No," said Poncho, still smiling.

"Well, Charles and I will stay back and tell the story to the world," Lane replied. Poncho considered this for a moment before nodding his assent. The teens hugged the lawyers good-bye, and raised their fists in a revolutionary salute before turning away.

As the lawyers ran toward the jungle in their business loafers, Garry overheard a man, who appeared to be somewhere nearby, state gruffly, "Let's not be divisive," followed by three gunshots.

Hyacinth waited in her cottage for her sister to return from the meeting.

That afternoon, Zipporah had come by with the breathless news that two families were leaving with the Congressman.

"That so?" Hyacinth replied before dropping the subject. She was careful not to show her disappointment at not being among them, but had her own escape plan in the works: She was due in Georgetown to get the bottom plate of her dentures fixed, and while she was there, she planned to find her way to the American embassy.

As the sisters spoke, Jones came on the loudspeaker and ordered everyone to the pavilion. Zippy pressured her to go. "Jim is going to be awful mad if you don't," she said. When Hy refused, blaming, as always, her lame leg, Zip turned to search through her belongings. "I believe I'll wear my red sweater tonight," she said. The remark struck Hy as odd; her sister never spoke of such trivial things as clothes. She promised to tell Hyacinth all about the meeting when she returned then turned and walked out the door.

The congregation assembled. Parents held small children on their laps; older kids sought out their friends. Edith Roller no doubt sat next to Eddie Washington, in their usual spot near the front. Edith's journal ends, mysteriously, on August 31. Her activities that day were typical: She typed up a large-letter edition of the news for seniors, lectured on socialism, and lined up to have her athlete's foot treated at the sore table. The FBI never found the last three months of her journal, although agents did recover a letter she wrote Jones in September in which she complained that someone had rifled through the crate where she stored her journal and had taken part of it. Maybe one of the policemen, reporters, or soldiers who arrived on the scene after the massacre kept her final pages as a souvenir. Or perhaps Jones himself destroyed them, unhappy with Edith's frank disclosures.

As the crowd waited for Jones to appear, a young woman named Shirley Smith climbed onstage and began dancing and singing about being a freedom fighter. She appeared to have lost her mind, a witness would later say. The guards got her down.

After a long delay, Jones appeared. He climbed on stage and sat in his light-green chair, then reached over to turn on the cassette recorder, as he'd done hundreds of times before. He began speaking in the past tense:

"How very much I've loved you," he said in a weary voice. "How very much I've tried my best to give you the good life."

He told the community that one of the supposed defectors was planning to shoot the congressman's plane down, and that his action would prompt the Guyanese army to invade Jonestown. Before the soldiers came in with their guns blazing, he said, "We had better not have any of our children left."

The "death tape," as Jones's last speech became known, ran for forty-four minutes, and included more than thirty edits in which Jones stopped recording, presumably to censor voices or sounds he didn't want taped for posterity. (After one early edit, Jones warned someone called Ruby that she'd regret what she said, if she didn't die first.)

Jones's voice, at some points, is thick and slurred. Like Elmer Fudd, he lisps some words: "Suicide" becomes "thuicide," and "simple" sounds like "thimple." Most likely, he was high. His autopsy report would reveal long-term barbiturate abuse.

Stanley Clayton was stirring a pot of black-eyed peas when the alert was called. All day long folks had been coming by the kitchen—which was behind the dining tent and out of view of the pavilion—with updates: The Parks were leaving. Then the Bogues. Al Simon wanted to leave with his kids but Bonnie wouldn't let him. As the cooks bustled about, preparing the evening meal for one thousand people, Larry Schacht and Joyce Touchette came into the kitchen to retrieve a large steel drum. They were carrying boxes of Flavor-Aid, a powdered drink mix, and Stanley presumed Jones was going to stage another drill.

Around five-thirty, Lew Jones came into the kitchen and told the crew to report to the pavilion. It was the first time the on-duty kitchen workers were required to attend an emergency meeting, and Lourece Jackson, a Louisiana native who was there with her three teenagers, turned to Stanley with a stricken face.

"This is it," she said. "We gonna die."

As they followed Lew past the playground and up the walkway to the pavilion, they could hear Jones telling the assembly that enemies would soon be "parachuting in" to torture and kill them. "So my opinion is that we be kind to children and be kind to seniors and take the potion like they used to take in ancient Greece, and step over quietly, because we are not committing suicide," Jones said. "It's a revolutionary act. We can't go back. They won't leave us alone. They're now going back to tell more lies, which means more congressmen. And there's no way, no way, we can survive."

Stanley searched for Janice. She was seated toward the back, as usual. She slipped her arm through his. Her eyes were big with fear.

"Anyone who has any dissenting opinion, please speak," Jones said.

Christine Miller, sixty, a native of Brownsville, Texas, stood up. Miller, who had no kin with her and only attended Temple services in Los Angeles sporadically before coming to Guyana, had written Jones months before that she "did not find the peace she expected" in Jonestown, and asked to leave. "It seems that I'm in a cage like a bird," she wrote.

On the evening of November, 18, 1978, the outspoken Miller was the only person recorded on the death tape who opposed Jones.

"Is it too late to go to Russia?" she asked.

Jones said it was: The attack on the congressman set in motion a chain of events that would lead to the violent invasion they'd longed feared.

Miller persisted: "I feel that as long as there's life, there's hope. That's my faith. . . . I look about at the babies and I think they deserve to live, you know?"

"I agree," Jones said. "But don't they also deserve much more? They deserve peace."

"When we destroy ourselves," Miller continued, "we're defeated. We let them, the enemies, defeat us."

"We will win," Jones said. "We win when we go down."

"I think we all have a right to our own destiny as individuals," Miller insisted. "I have a right to choose mine, and everybody else has a right to choose theirs."

Lue Ester Lewis, a forty-eight-year-old Louisiana native, yelled at Miller that she was "scared to die," and was joined in heckling her by several others. Jim McElvane, the towering security chief, stepped to the microphone and ordered everyone to simmer down.

But Christine wasn't done yet. In a brave, desperate move, she appealed to Jones's paternal instinct.

"You mean you wanna see John die?"

Her audacity elicited outraged screams, but Jones hushed the crowd.

"He's no different to me than any of these children here," he said.

An old man stepped up to the microphone, crying. "Dad, we're all ready to go. If you tell us we have to give our lives now, we're ready—I'm pretty sure all the rest of the sisters and brothers are with me."

His words were roundly applauded. The tide had turned in Jones's favor. He'd been goading them toward this night for years.

The dump truck and tractor-trailer returned, speeding down the Jonestown road. A guard rushed forward to whisper in Jones's ear. He turned to the crowd.

"It's all over," he announced. "The congressman has been murdered."

There's a pause, an edit, before he speaks again, his voice now urgent: "Please get us some medication. It's simple. It's simple. There's no convulsions with it. It's just simple. Just, please get it. Before it's too late. The GDF [Guyana Defense Force] will be here, I tell you. Get movin', get movin'. Don't be afraid to die. If these people land out here, they'll torture our children, they'll torture our people, they'll torture our seniors. We cannot have this."

Eddie Crenshaw, back from the airstrip, sat down heavily next to Stanley.

"Man, they just blew Congressman Ryan away," he said, shaking his head.

Jones's aides arrived carrying the drum Stanley saw them borrow from the kitchen, and placed it on a table at the front of the pavilion. It contained a dark purple liquid that had been carefully mixed by Dr. Schacht and included grape Flavor-Aid, potassium cyanide, Valium, chloral hydrate (used to put patients to sleep before surgery), and potassium chloride (used in lethal injections to stop the heart muscle). The aides piled paper cups and packages of syringes on the table beside the drum. As nurses tore open the packets of syringes and dipped them into the deadly punch, Stanley panicked. There was a line of guards with crossbows circling the pavilion, and beyond them, a ring of men holding guns. About twenty-five armed guards, total. He noted that their weapons were trained on the residents, not on the jungle.

At the front of the pavilion Maria Katsaris stood before the mic and told residents to form lines.

"You have to move, and the people that are standing there in the aisles, go stand in the radio room yard. Everybody get behind the table and back this way, okay? There's nothing to worry about."

She asked mothers to bring their babies forward. First in line was Ruletta Paul, whose husband, Robert, hiked out that morning, leaving her and their three young sons behind. As the stunned audience watched, Ruletta picked up a needleless syringe from the table and squirted it into the mouth of one-year-old Robert Jr. before using another on herself. Her actions were calm and deliberate. She walked out of the pavilion and sat down in the adjacent field, rocking her baby. It was sunset, but the sky was gray with low-slung clouds.

Some mothers followed willingly. But others hugged their infants to their chests. The nurses tried to cajole them into surrendering their children before summoning guards to pry their babies from their arms. At the beginning of the tape, you can hear babies babbling and cooing in the background; a few minutes later, they are crying.

"There's nothing to worry about," Maria told the crowd. "Everybody keep calm and try and keep your children calm . . . and the older children can help love the little children and reassure them. They're not crying from pain. It's just a little bitter tasting. But they're not crying out of any pain."

The day before, Marcie boasted to reporters that thirty-three babies had been born in Jonestown. On November 18, 304 minors would be murdered there, 131 of them under age ten.

Jim McElvane, sensing the building unrest, again stepped up to the microphone. In his soothing baritone voice, he urged residents to quiet down before talking about his experiences as a therapist specializing in reincarnation.

"Everybody was so happy when they made that step to the other side," he assured the crowd. "If you have a body that's been crippled, suddenly you have the kind of body that you want to have."

As he spoke, kids screamed. High-pitched, terrified, inconsolable screams. They were being poisoned to death. Jones, sitting on the stage, interrupted McElvane to reassure the crowd that death was only "a little rest, a little rest."

Poisoned parents, weeping, carried their poisoned daughters and sons into the muddy field, cradling them as best they could, as their children began to convulse and froth at the mouth. They watched their kids die before beginning to strain for air themselves. The odor of burnt almonds—the telltale sign of cyanide ingestion—hung in the air.

In the pavilion, McElvane continued to tell the living how appealing death was: "It feels so good. You've never felt so good as how that feels."

A woman came to the microphone and chastised those who were afraid. "This is nothing to cry about," she said. "This is something to rejoice about. We should be happy about this."

Other residents began coming up to the microphone to say their goodbyes, but Jones interrupted them.

"For God's sake, let's get on with it," he reprimanded the crowd. "Let's just be done with it. Let's be done with the agony of it."

The screams grew louder. "Die with a degree of dignity," Jones ordered. "Lay down your life with dignity. Don't lay down with tears and agony. Stop the hysterics. This is not the way for people who are socialists or communists to die. There's nothing to death . . . Look children, it's just something to put you to rest."

A woman began to shout hysterically, apparently refusing to hand over her child. It's impossible to hear her words over Jones's voice: "Mother, mother, mother, mother, please. Mother please, please, please. Don't do this. Lay down your life with your child, but don't do this."

Stanley Clayton, sitting hip to hip with Janice, deluded himself into believing it was just another drill until a boy named Thurman Guy, fifteen, veered back into the pavilion and ran into him before collapsing against a pole. The boy was wheezing, his eyes unfocused, and he began to shake uncontrollably.

"Get him out of here!" Jones shouted, as horrified residents watched.

Stanley grabbed the boy's arms and another man lifted his legs. As they carried him into the darkening field, his body went limp, and in that moment, Stanley knew beyond a doubt that Jones was making good on his mass suicide threat. Looking around, he noticed all the other bodies. Aides were dragging small corpses into rows to make room for more Temple members.

Returning to the pavilion, he watched a foster girl named Julie Ann Runnels, twelve, refuse to drink the poison. She kept spitting it out. Finally, her court-appointed guardian, Paulette Jackson, and nurse Annie Moore grabbed her hair and pulled her head back. They poured the punch into her mouth and then covered her mouth and nose, forcing her to swallow it.

"No!" a boy shrieked loudly, somewhere near the microphone.

"Children!" Jones admonished. "It will not hurt, if you will be quiet."

They would not be quiet. Their screams grew louder, so Jones took their parents to task: "Quit telling them that they're dying. Adults. I call on you to quit exciting your children, when all they're doing is going to a quiet rest."

Their deaths were anything but quiet.

After all the kids were killed, Jones told the adults to step forward. "Where is the vat with the green C on it? Bring it here so the adults can begin."

Edith Roller certainly didn't want to die.

A few weeks earlier, Jones asked residents to answer the question: "What would I do if this was a final White Night?" Edith wrote, "I would like to teach, and write. Write about the people I have known in our country, and our cause and in the Philippines, Greece and India, all of them of great worth and charm. Some short stories, even poetry. . . . Want to do more to give children the love they need. Want to plant rows of vegetables. I would like to raise a kitten."

Edith must have stood in line with Eddie Washington. Perhaps they held hands. She must have worried about what her sisters and her friend

Lorraine would think of her when they heard the news. Most likely she drained her cup without hesitation, determined, as she'd been during the prior drill, to "be a credit to herself." One hopes she comforted herself, one last time, with poetry.

As the crowd dwindled, Jones taped one last lie for posterity: "We didn't commit suicide, we committed an act of revolutionary suicide protesting the conditions of an inhumane world."

After clicking off the recorder, he descended from his throne and started pulling stragglers toward the vat. At the same time, his wife, Marceline, walked around embracing people, saying, "I'll see you in the next life."

Janice could read it in Stanley's face: He wanted to split. But her family—her mom, two sisters, brother, and grandmother—were already dead. She'd seen their bodies lying in the field.

"I know you want to go, but I can't do it," she said. She asked him to put her in her mother's arms. At the table, she picked up a paper cup and threw it back as if it were a shot of whiskey. There was chaos at the end; no one noticed that Stanley didn't drink himself. He put an arm around her and guided her out of the pavilion. As they walked, she kept saying, "I'm okay, I'm okay." They got about five yards onto the grass when she started convulsing. He picked her up, struggling to hold her churning body. Her breath became a high squeak, and then she went slack. He found her family; her mother was lying on her back between her two sisters. He lowered Janice facedown onto her mom's chest and put one of her arms around her mom's waist before kissing her cheek and standing.

Some of the guards were eyeing him with suspicion. He walked back into the pavilion and sat down on a bench, mind racing, trying to develop a plan. A guard grabbed the man sitting next to him and shoved him toward the vat. Stanley got to his feet and began to move backward through the crowd, from side to side, biding his time. There were only about one hundred fifty people left. Many just sat on benches with vacant eyes, shell-shocked, as nurses walked among them, plunging needles into their arms. He saw one woman fight the guards; a nurse came up and injected her. An old man was led up to the table several times, and each time, he turned around and walked back to his seat. Finally he, too, was injected; Stanley watched him fall to the dirt floor, crying, alone.

Stanley walked into the field, where he saw Dr. Schacht pressing a stethoscope to people's chests to make sure they were dead. Phyllis Chaikin was helping him. When a guard asked him where he was going, Stanley said he was looking for Eddie Crenshaw; they were going to "cross over" together.

"Ed's dead," the guard said. Stanley had suspected as much. He pretended to head back to the pavilion. He came to the line of guards with crossbows and recognized a woman he was friendly with named Marie Lawrence. She looked scared.

"If you feel like a rabbit, do like the rabbits do," Stanley told her. She stepped back and drew her bow at him.

Jones told the remaining residents to exchange a final embrace, so Stanley walked to the line of guards armed with guns and started hugging them good-bye. At the end of the line was Forrest Ray Jones, the husband of Jones's adopted daughter Agnes. Stanley had his fist cocked to punch him and try to make a break for it when he noticed activity in the school tent.

"I'm gonna tell them good-bye," Stanley said, motioning toward the tent. Forrest let him through. He took a few steps and looked back. Forrest wasn't watching him, so he sprinted into the darkness. He reached a field and kept tripping over rows of vegetables, falling and cursing, and getting up and running.

When he was a safe distance away, he hid behind a bush. After a long silence, he heard cheers coming from somewhere in the settlement, perhaps from the Temple leaders, who'd retired to Jones's cabin for a final cyanide toast. He started walking back toward the pavilion when he heard a series of shots, probably someone killing the community's dogs and Mr. Muggs, the chimpanzee. He hid again. Lights blazed in the pavilion, the medical offices, and a few cabins. After another hour or so, he went to his cottage to collect some clothes and photos of Janice. Then he went to the office, which was about fifty yards in front of the pavilion, to search for his passport. He turned on the light. They were in a crate in alphabetical order, and he quickly found his. As he took it, he heard a single loud shot nearby and slapped off the light.

He crouched, breathing heavily. But there were no footsteps. No one barged through the door. After a waiting a few minutes, he got up and sprinted away.

After watching his people die in agony and indignity, Jones must have spent a few moments taking in the scene before him. The camp was quiet, except for the occasional call of night birds. As he surveyed the bodies at his feet, he surely must have recalled that Sunday in Indianapolis, decades before, when he asked his congregants to lie on the floor for him. There weren't many that day, only a dozen or so. Now almost a thousand bodies lay prostrate before him.

It would be interesting to know his last, drug-addled thoughts before he placed the barrel of his .38 Smith & Wesson revolver to his right temple and pulled the trigger. This was probably the shot Stanley heard from the office. Was Jones satisfied with his handiwork? We'll never know. He did, however, accomplish his long-cherished goal: He went down in history. Not as a great socialist leader, but as a madman, the architect of the largest mass murder-suicide in modern times.

The road out of Jonestown was the longest road Stanley Clayton would take in his life. He ran blindly in the dark, slipping in the mud and trying to keep his precious photos from getting dirty, half-expecting to hear the dump truck's diesel engine gunning behind him.

He'd lost everything. The family who'd buoyed him up, who kept him from becoming a career criminal, who taught him that black was beautiful, and, more important, that black was powerful. Certainly he'd hated many aspects of Jonestown. Jones and his guards had become cruel tyrants. But there were also all the brothers and sisters who loved and supported him, who accepted him for who he was. And Janice, with her pure heart and megawatt smile. Now they were all dead, and the only thing he had to show for his years in the Temple were a couple of photographs. Eventually, he'd lose those, too.

CHAPTER 28

BODIES

As the massacre was underway, a female radio operator in Jonestown, most likely Maria Katsaris, radioed Lamaha Gardens in Georgetown, and in a heavily coded message, passed along Jones's final order for all Temple members to kill themselves.

US Embassy Consul Doug Ellice intercepted it. He'd been monitoring radio transmissions between Jonestown and Georgetown throughout the day on November 18 to keep tabs on the congressman's visit, and he recorded several of them, including Dwyer's request for a second plane. He grew alarmed, however, when, shortly after five o'clock, the Jonestown operator grew strident and she started speaking in code. "A lot of people have seen Mr. Fraser," she said. "I think Mrs. Brownfield has offered to help . . . get S.B. to help." She repeated the peculiar message several times, and Ellice wrote it down before calling Ambassador John Burke to inform him that something strange was happening in Jonestown. The two men were puzzling over the cryptic messages when they got word of the airstrip attack.

Eventually the FBI would decipher the code: "A lot of people have died; do whatever you can to even the score. . . . Get Sandy Bradshaw to help." This was Jones's order to Temple leaders in Georgetown and San Francisco to enact the last stand and begin murdering Temple enemies—defectors, politicians, and critics—before killing themselves.

Ellice also heard the Jonestown radio operator tell Sharon Amos to take her children to see "Mr. Fraser," and Amos's reply that she didn't have any "vehicles" to do it. The Jonestown operator then switched to Morse code, tapping out "K.N.I.F.E." Amos herded her three children—Liane, twenty-one, Christa, eleven and Martin, ten—into an upstairs bathroom, where she used a butcher knife to slit her two younger kids' throats before helping Liane press the blade against her own neck. She murmured, "Thank you, Father," before collapsing. With difficulty, Liane then cut her own throat.

The killing stopped there. Although the Jonestown operator had ordered the basketball team, which was in Georgetown for a tournament and was comprised primarily of Jonestown security guards, including Stephan and Jim Jones Jr., to go to the Pegasus hotel and kill the Concerned Relatives, Stephan refused to follow the directive, and also called Temple leaders in San Francisco to dissuade them from enacting the last stand in California.

At first only 409 Jonestown residents were reported dead. US Army helicopters buzzed the jungle searching for survivors, as soldiers on board called over loudspeakers that it was "safe to come out." Back in the States, relatives grasped at straws, certain that their loved ones had managed to escape. But when the soldiers started removing the corpses, they found bodies stacked on bodies, parents on top of children. The number rose to 909.

Guyana's chief medical examiner, Leslie Mootoo, who flew up to Jonestown on November 20, estimated that at least seventy bodies showed signs of puncture wounds on their upper arms, and deduced that many residents had been forcibly injected with cyanide.

In Jones's cabin, thirteen bodies were found, including those of John Victor Stoen, Carolyn Layton and her son Kimo, Maria Katsaris, Jim McElvane, Dick Tropp, Annie Moore, and several other Temple leaders. All died from poisoning except Moore, who both ingested the cyanide and was shot in the head. Guyanese police found a .357 Ruger Magnum beside her body, along with her suicide note.

"I am at this point right now so embittered against the world that I don't know why I am writing this," it read. She called Jonestown "the most peaceful, loving community that every existed" and Jones the "most honest, loving, caring, concerned person" she'd ever met.

"We died because you would not let us live in peace," she wrote in her last sentence, believing, to the end, Jones's claims of harassment.

Dick Tropp, the former English instructor, wrote a longer note. Like Moore, he continued to spin reality even as hundreds of people agonized in death throes a few hundred yards away.

Nov. 18, 1978—The Last Day of Peoples Temple
To Whomever Finds This Note:

Collect all the tapes, all the writing, all the history. The story of this movement, this action, must be examined over and over. It must be understood in all of its incredible dimensions. Words fail. We have pledged our lives to this great cause. We are proud to have something to die for. We do not fear death. We hope that the world will someday realize the ideals of brotherhood, justice and equality that Jim Jones has lived and died for. We have all chosen to die for this cause. We know there is no way that we can avoid misinterpretation. But Jim Jones and this movement were born too soon. The world was not ready to let us live.

As I write these words people are silently amassed, taking a quick potion, inducing sleep, _relief_. We are a long-suffering people. Many of us are weary with a long search, a long struggle—going back not only in our own lifetime, but a long painful heritage. (_Please_ see the histories of our people that are in a building called teachers resource center.)

Many of us are now dead. Each moment, another passes over to peace. We are begging only for some understanding. It will take more than small minds, reporters' minds, to fathom these events. Something must come of this.

There is quiet as we leave this world. The sky is gray. People file slowly and take the somewhat bitter drink. Many more must drink. . . .

We did not want it this way. All was going well as Ryan completed [his] first day here. Then a man tried to attack him, unsuccessfully, at the same time, several set out into the jungle wanting to overtake Ryan, [his] aide, and others who left with him. They did, and several [were] killed. When we heard this, we had no choice. We _would be taken._ We have to go as one, we want to live as Peoples Temple, or end it. We have chosen. _It is finished._

Hugging & kissing & tears & silence & joy in a long line.
A tiny kitten sits next to me. Watching. A dog barks. The birds gather
on the telephone wires. Let all the story of this Peoples Temple be told.
<u>*Let all the books be opened.*</u> *This sight . . . o terrible victory.*
If nobody understands, it matters not. I am ready to die now.
Darkness settles over Jonestown on its last day on earth.

Poetic yes, but also riddled with errors, outright lies, and ignorance—willful or not. There were no soldiers poised to storm the camp; the death scene was anything but peaceful.

The police found another four bodies inside the special care unit; one of them was surely that of Gene Chaikin. One wonders what Jones's aides told the shut-in seniors and sick bay patients—that the poison was just a little medicine? One wonders whether Phyllis Chaikin stopped helping Dr. Schacht long enough to hug her and Gene's children good-bye.

Most Americans heard about Jonestown for the first time the next evening, when the networks interrupted their regular programming with special reports on the massacre. The news from Guyana was sketchy in the beginning, and so were the broadcasts, which announced that a "strange religious" cult had ambushed Congressman Ryan and his party. Over the following days and weeks, the mass murder-suicide would generate thousands of new stories worldwide, and photographs of the bodies would appear on the covers of *Time* and *Newsweek*. Both used the same headline: Cult of Death.

One reporter arriving at the scene by helicopter would say that, from the air, the colorfully dressed bodies looked like a patchwork quilt. Others were less charitable and portrayed Jonestown residents as brainwashed zombies. They were deemed monsters, and therefore deserving of their fate. It was far easier to condemn Jones's victims than to comprehend them.

In San Francisco, crowds gathered outside the Geary Boulevard Temple shouting "Baby killers!" at Temple members who'd gathered inside to comfort one other. Television crews knocked on the door, telling associate pastor Guy Young, "We heard you're going to commit suicide, and we want to film it." Some members were followed by FBI agents. Others, returning from Guyana penniless and hungry, were denied welfare and food stamps.

Guyana refused the United States' request to bury the 909 bodies *in situ*, so the Army flew in its Grave Registration Unit to retrieve them. By then the corpses had lain in the jungle sun and rain for four days and were bloated to the point of bursting. Soldiers placed them in body bags using snow shovels and loaded them into the cavernous hold of a C-141 Starlifter, which flew them to Dover Air Force base in Delaware for processing. Army forensic examiners were only able to identify 631 of the 913 dead, or 69 percent of the bodies. More than two hundred children would never be identified; their small bodies decayed faster than the adults', and many did not have dental or fingerprint records.

Of the identified dead, only about half were buried by their relatives. Some families didn't claim their dead because they were too poor to pay for transportation and interment; others were ashamed that a family member had fallen prey to a "suicidal cult."

The bodies of 408 victims are buried in a mass grave at Evergreen Cemetery in Oakland. Most of these are children; the babies were buried two to a casket. Marilee Bogue, who was last seen in Jones's cottage playing with John John and Kimo after her family left, is also buried at Evergreen, as are the three George siblings, David, Phillip, and Gabriela. After the massacre, their oldest sister, Valita, spent a day at the camp turning over bodies, but she failed to locate their remains.

The bodies of Jim and Marceline Jones were cremated, and their ashes scattered over the Atlantic.

Edith Roller, Body 89-D, was identified by a fingerprint match with her US Department of State ID card. Her sisters had her remains cremated. Sadly, just as Edith had feared, her family viewed her supposed suicide as an indication of her mental instability.

CHAPTER 29

SURVIVORS

Tommy Bogue hit the jungle with Teena and kept on running. Following at their heels were Brenda and Tracy Parks, and Brenda's boyfriend, Chris O'Neil. The small holes peppering Tommy's calf hemorrhaged blood, but adrenaline propelled him forward; he was terrified the attackers were returning to finish them off.

Remembering the skills the Amerindians taught him, Tommy led the group in circles and walked up streams to keep the trackers at bay. But he was missing the primary survival tool: a knife. Without one, he couldn't build a shelter, make a snare, or drink from the vine with the tea-flavored sap.

At the Port Kaituma rum shop where the other airstrip survivors had taken refuge, Jim Bogue told reporters he wasn't worried about Tommy. "He knows the bush," he said proudly. "He'll lead out those other kids who ran with him." He didn't know, of course, that his son was badly wounded.

By the second day, Tommy was delirious from blood loss. The kids spent most of their time hiding behind trees. Tommy would lead the group toward a light in the distance, thinking it was a way out of the jungle, only to find it was a light well created by an opening in the canopy.

On the third morning, Tommy was at a loss. He didn't know which way to go. He imagined he saw a man leaning against a tree, smoking a cigarette. He thought he saw people jumping from trees into the river. He heard bird calls and thought they were signals made by their assailants, communicating their positions to each other as they zeroed in for the kill.

The world's largest beasts no longer terrified him; his church brethren were the ones who wanted to murder him.

His leg began to smell like rotten meat. Maggots infested the bullet holes. It was hard to walk. Toward noon the group heard the faint hum of a generator, and Tommy sent the Parks girls and O'Neil to investigate it; he and Teena were too weak to walk any farther. When the trio didn't return for several hours, he feared the worst.

Then he heard the splashing of boat oars, and someone calling his name in a lilting Guyanese accent: "Tommy Bogue! Tommy Bogue!" He and Teena waded into the river and crouched behind a log. When the canoe slid into view, he recognized Sorrel, one of the Amerindians who'd taught him to survive the jungle.

His rescuers carried him on a stretcher to the Port Kaituma rum shop, and for the second time in his life, he saw his dad cry.

Hyacinth Thrash opened her cottage door on the morning of November 19 and walked out into brilliant sunshine. Usually, she heard Mr. Muggs, the chimpanzee, grunting in his cage, which was only a few yards from her cottage, but on this morning she was greeted by a deep stillness.

The evening before, she'd heard people outside her cottage calling for Rheaviana Beam, and then a gunshot. She thought Rheaviana, who'd also followed Jones from Indiana, might have been playing hooky and that the guards had fired a weapon to flush her out. But when Zipporah and her other roommates didn't return from the meeting, Hy grew worried that Jonestown had indeed been invaded by mercenaries, and she crawled under her bed to hide. It wasn't difficult for her to compact herself into the reduced space: she'd lost thirty-three pounds in Jonestown and weighed a mere eighty-nine pounds. During the long night she got uncomfortable, however, and crawled into her bed.

When she woke around six-thirty, her roommates were still gone. She got dressed and hobbled outside on her cane, then slowly descended the cottage's four stairs, cane in one hand, the other hand gripping the wooden railing.

She made her way to a neighboring senior residence and opened the door. Inside she saw a figure sitting in a chair, draped with a sheet. She could tell it was her friend Birdie Johnson, an eighty-six-year-old Mississippian, by her shoes. Hy called to her, but got no response. Behind Birdie was another draped figure in a chair, and Hy shuffled over to pull back the sheet. It was Lavana James, a seventy-four-year-old Texan. She was obviously dead. Hy looked around and saw three more women, lying or sitting in their beds, all covered with sheets. She panicked.

"They came and killed them all, and I's the onliest one alive!" she yelled in anguish.

She pinched herself to make sure she wasn't dead, too. Then she thought she heard a voice say, "Fear not; for I am with you," and recognized Isaiah 41:10, a passage she often repeated silently to comfort herself in Jonestown. She hadn't stopped believing in God during her twenty years with Jones, and now, she believed His spirit was consoling her.

She walked back to the pathway, and looked in the direction of the kitchen. The door was open, and it was empty. A tray of sandwiches sat uncovered on a table. Not knowing what to do, she returned to her cottage. She panicked again, and took a white towel and stood on her porch waving it, yelling for help. No one came. She went inside and mixed up some powdered milk the residents kept in the cottage and drank it, then sat on a chair in a daze, listening to the birds. She considered trying to hike through the jungle, but knew she wouldn't make it. As dusk approached, she finally ventured to the bathroom, where she fell asleep on the toilet. She woke at dawn and watched the sun break over the settlement, as glorious as ever, before returning to her cottage to wait, weak, confused, and frightened.

That's where a couple of astonished Guyanese soldiers found her on Monday afternoon, November 20. "Lady, what are you doing here?" one asked. They carried her to the pavilion. It looked like a battlefield. They asked her to help them identify the dead, but she couldn't stomach looking at the lifeless forms of dear friends she'd chatted with only a few days earlier.

She was able to identify her sister, however. Zippy was lying on her back in the dirt just outside the pavilion. Hy recognized her red sweater. There were too many bodies in the way to get closer to her.

Odell Rhodes, a crafts teacher who escaped by volunteering to fetch a stethoscope for Dr. Schacht before fleeing into the bush, and a few other survivors arrived to identify the dead; Hy had Rhodes write Zippy's name on a piece of cardboard and pin it to her dress. The soldiers asked her to verify the identity of Jim Jones, who was lying on the platform in the pavilion, but she refused. Although his body was only thirty feet away, she'd have to walk by so many people she knew and loved to reach him. Rhodes told her Jones's eyes were wide open, as if he were seeing something horrifying. Hyacinth took this to mean he was in hell.

The soldiers brought her to a school tent, where she encountered another elderly survivor, Grover Davis, seventy-nine, who'd survived by lowering himself into a ditch while the others lined up.

"Hyacinth, don't say nothing about Jim," Davis warned her; he still feared Jones's mythical powers.

Reporters arrived. "No comment," Hy told them. They described her as a "tiny, birdlike woman." She wanted to be left alone to think. She fretted over her sister's death; did she drink the poison willingly? She saw needles scattered about the pavilion, the tub of toxic punch. She refused to believe Zip died without a struggle. She'd later regret that she didn't examine her sister's body for needle marks. She anguished over the children; the nursery workers often paraded the toddlers past her cottage dressed in sun suits and little paper hats, and she'd wave to them from her porch.

The looting—by impoverished locals, reporters looking for an angle, soldiers wanting souvenirs—began even before Hyacinth left. She returned to her cottage after spending the night in the school tent to find her photographs splayed over the floor. Her arthritis made it hard for her to bend over to retrieve them, and the soldiers were rushing her, as the bodies had started to smell. She was forced to leave five photo albums behind: a lifetime of memories of Zippy, of their parents, of their Alabama girlhood, of their hard-won home in Indianapolis. She'd write the American Embassy and offer to pay to have the albums shipped to her, but would never receive a reply.

When she boarded a plane at the Port Kaituma airstrip for the first leg of her journey back to the United States, she hunkered down between the seats and covered her head. The other survivors laughed at her, but she'd heard about the attack on the congressman's party.

"I've made it this far," she told them. "I want to go home."

* * *

Stanley Clayton reached the house of the kiosk owner around midnight and banged on the door.

"I got a story to tell you," he told the man. "Give me a beer and a pack of cigarettes." He downed one beer and was starting the second when he announced, "Everyone in Jonestown is dead." The man snatched the bottle from his hands and accused Stanley of talking nonsense. The next morning, Stanley learned other survivors had been seen at the airstrip, and he set off down the road toward Port Kaituma, but was picked up by a patrol of GDF soldiers. Suspicious that he was still alive, they handcuffed him and brought him to the police station, where Odell Rhodes corroborated his story of Jonestown's last hours. Stanley credited his street smarts, of always being mindful of the nearest exit, with his survival. He would never again be that terrified twelve-year-old boy, locked inside the store he was robbing as he waited for the police to arrive.

Others straggled out of the bush. The police arrested brothers Tim and Mike Carter, as well as PR man Mike Prokes, in Port Kaituma. While the suicides were in progress, Maria Katsaris gave them a suitcase filled with $550,000 and told them to deliver it to the Russian embassy. It was too heavy, so they buried some of the money in Jonestown. When they reached the river, the *Cudjoe* wasn't there to take them to Georgetown. A local saw them enter a building to hide and alerted the police.

Teri Buford told reporters that Jones had set aside millions of dollars in Swiss banks to finance the last-stand plan. The government managed to freeze the church's overseas accounts, but several defectors went underground, some for decades, still worried that Jones's loyal lieutenants would kill them.

Fearing prosecution, surviving church leaders quickly purged Temple files. They burned boxes of documents in a bonfire at a San Francisco beach and used magnets to erase tape recordings. One can only wonder what damning information these contained. Afterward, most Temple leaders would disappear into the woodwork, guarding their secrets and living quiet, undistinguished lives as they successfully dodged the media spotlight.

There were a couple of exceptions. One was Mike Prokes. On March 13, 1979, Prokes called a press conference in a Modesto motel room, where he read a five-page statement defending the Jonestown "suicides" to half a dozen reporters, then walked into the bathroom and shot himself in the head.

Another was Paula Adams. After the massacre, Adams followed Ambassador Mann to Washington, D.C., and had a son with him. When she tried to leave the abusive relationship in 1983, Mann tracked her down at her new apartment, where he shot and killed her and their eighteen-month-old son before turning the gun on himself.

Charles Garry and Mark Lane emerged from the jungle on November 19, bedraggled and still bickering. During their long night together, Lane told Garry many secrets he'd learned from Teri Buford, including the plan for a mass suicide. Back in the States, Garry would accuse Lane of being "morally responsible" for the massacre because he'd fostered Jones's paranoia. For his part, Mark Lane told the *New York Times* that he was "the only person who tried to prevent the murders and tried to keep Leo Ryan from going to Guyana." He went on the lecture circuit with his "Horrors of Jonestown" talk, earning $2,750 per appearance, and wrote a book in which he still, incredibly, maintained there was a conspiracy to destroy Peoples Temple. Charles Garry, for his part, was deeply scarred by his association with the group and, after a luminous career defending progressive causes, he shunned the spotlight. He died in 1991.

FBI agents interviewed about two thousand people as they tried to determine whether there was a conspiracy to assassinate Congressman Ryan. In 1987, a Federal Court in San Francisco charged Larry Layton with aiding and abetting Ryan's murder. He spent eighteen years in prison before being paroled in 2002.

A House of Representatives investigation found fault with the US

Embassy's dealings with Jonestown on several levels. It criticized consular officers for giving the Temple an advance list of most of the people they wanted to interview, allowing Jones to rehearse residents' responses, and blamed officers for lacking "common sense" and a "healthy skepticism" when faced with Jones's staged performances and the interviewees' canned responses.

A San Francisco Superior Court appointed a local attorney, Robert Fabian, to locate and disperse Temple assets. Between overseas accounts and real estate holdings, he amassed over $10 million. The Department of Justice and the Internal Revenue Service took $1.7 million for cleaning up the bodies and for unpaid taxes. The rest was divided among more than six hundred claimants, including survivors, relatives of Jonestown residents, people who were wounded at the Port Kaituma airstrip, and the heirs of those killed in the airstrip attack. Hyacinth Thrash received $4,351. Jackie Speier received $360,000.

The ornate brick building at 1859 Geary Boulevard was auctioned to a Korean Presbyterian church, which occupied it for a decade before it was severely damaged in the Loma Prieta earthquake and torn down. Today, a branch of the United States Post Office occupies the lot.

Jonestown was slowly dismantled by neighboring Amerindians who took clothing, food, books, mattresses, lumber, and even the fence marking Lynetta Jones's grave. The Guyanese government distributed the better furniture among its ministries, as well as thousands of packets of salt and pepper, which are a novelty in that country and were still being used in government offices until recently. A fire burned down the Jonestown buildings, and gold prospectors stripped deserted vehicles of metal to build mining equipment. The site is now an empty, overgrown field, a tangle of vines and jungle flowers. A single tree marks the spot where the pavilion once stood. The earthen tunnel that once concealed "the box" is filled with roosting bats.

The Guyanese government, hoping to capitalize on the trend in "dark tourism," is considering several proposals to turn the site into a travel destination. One plan calls for rebuilding the pavilion, Jones's cabin, and several cottages and charging visitors two hundred dollars per night for the thrill of living the Jonestown "experience."

* * *

Hyacinth Thrash flew to Los Angeles to stay with a nephew. The FBI found Social Security checks belonging to her inside the safe in Jones's cabin, and she used the money to bury her sister. She dreamed of Zipporah often. Her room at her nephew's house had twin beds, and sometimes she awoke sensing Zippy's presence in the next bed. A couple of times she thought she heard Zip call her name, and once she heard her groan, as, Hy thought, she must have done as the poison killed her. She had nightmares about Jim Jones being angry that she was still alive.

A doctor prescribed sedatives to treat her anxiety. She felt ashamed of her Temple association, and refused to talk about it for many years, even with close friends and relatives. She concluded that Jones was devil-possessed and that he took advantage of unschooled blacks to gain a following. Like Job, she felt her Christian faith had been tested and restored.

Eventually, she moved back to Indianapolis to live with family there. She joined a Holiness church, and whenever she fell into a funk, she sang gospel music aloud to lift her spirits. She kept waiting for her healing. At Deliverance Temple, members prayed over her leg, and she attended the services of a healing evangelist at the Indianapolis Convention Center. She was still waiting for her healing when she died in a nursing home on November 21, 1995, at age ninety. She is buried in Indianapolis's Crown Hill Cemetery, where her mother was laid to rest seven decades earlier.

In Georgetown, Stanley Clayton made thirty thousand dollars selling his "exclusive" story to reporters. He stayed at a hotel with other survivors for several weeks while Guyanese police questioned him, and met a local woman named Patricia at the hotel bar. He married her a month later, and sent for her when he returned to Oakland. But posttraumatic stress and the hardship of adjusting to life outside the Temple were difficult for him to surmount. He couldn't hold down a job, and his new bride couldn't match his idealized vision of Janice. The couple argued constantly, and one night he hit her. She left him while he served an eight-month sentence for domestic violence.

It was downhill from there. He was introduced to crack cocaine and told, "We don't snort it no more, we smoke it." He became an addict.

To support his habit, he became a pimp. He had six women working for him at one point, and took their trick money in exchange for providing them with food, protection, and a hotel room to sleep in. When he got too old to pimp, he became homeless. He slept in neighborhood parks and "spare changed" outside restaurants.

At the time of this writing, in March 2011, Stanley was living at a shelter for the mentally disabled homeless, and was on court probation for trying to buy crack from an undercover police officer. He sorely misses his Temple family, the brothers and sisters who held him to a high standard and noticed when he failed to meet it. Nobody notices Stanley anymore. He plods around his Berkeley neighborhood in soiled clothes, unshowered, one of the city's many invisible miserables.

"There were a lot of people in the church who believed in me and supported me," he says. "I don't have that no more."

Tommy Bogue, who now goes by Thom, spent a month hospitalized in Georgetown and another month in San Francisco, after which came more months of physical therapy to regain use of his leg. He still carries shot pellets in his calf muscle; occasionally they work their way out.

Thom also had a rocky road back to normalcy. He served time for drug use, got married, had a son, and got divorced. In 1995, he met his current wife, with whom he had a daughter. They moved to Dixon, California, a small town about an hour north of San Francisco, where he opened an automotive shop. He stayed clean. Harold Cordell, whose relationship with Edith Bogue ended after several decades, works in his front office. In November 2010, he was elected to the Dixon city council, running on a platform of support for small businesses.

Jim Bogue tormented himself for years for not fleeing with Marilee when he had her at the sawmill. A few weeks after he returned to San Francisco, he was falling asleep when he believed she appeared to him.

"Dad, I just wanted you to know that everything is all right," he heard her say.

That gave him a little more peace.

* * *

He's now remarried to the love of his life, Colleen, and the couple leads a quiet existence in a small northern California town. He still tinkers; one of his latest efforts is a fuel-saving device that powers his car with hydrogen. He's sworn off church completely. "If you could show me a religion where there isn't somebody in control of the people, then I might be interested," he says. He does believe in an afterlife, however. "If Marilee could come to me like that, then why wouldn't I see her again?" he asks. He hopes he'll see his son Jonathon again, too.

His bond with Thom is tighter than ever. When they discuss Jonestown, their families press in, amazed at their stories. Father and son fill in each other's memories, and their admiration for each other is palpable.

"He's one of the strongest people I ever met in my life," Jim says of Thom. "What he went through, just because he dared."

Thom laughs at this. "I wasn't one of the strongest. I was one of the stupidest. I couldn't keep out of trouble." He concedes his experience in Jonestown made him stronger. "Life can't throw anything at me that I can't handle now," he says. "It can only get better—can't get any worse."

Neither Bogue attends the memorial service held each November 18 at the mass grave in Oakland where Marilee is buried. They view their time in the Temple as a closed room they choose not to enter. It happened, and now they've moved on.

"Why live in the past?" Thom asks.

The legacy of Jim Jones is still hotly contested. Although evidence of his charlatanism abounds, many former Temple members still believe Jones had inexplicable powers, and insist that his staged healings somehow spurred real ones. They chafe at suggestions that all of Jones's alleged miracles were fakery, and are still struggling to come to terms with the depth of their deception. Some have joined other religious movements or struggle with drug abuse, others collect cats, and one woman who lost her mother and four children fills her home with so many paintings and sculptures of African American figures that by their sheer number they create a presence. A few view media coverage of Jonestown as prurient and insensitive; they prefer to remember the church in its San Francisco heyday, when they felt empowered by a sense of unity and equality.

Today, few Americans born after 1980 are familiar with the Jonestown tragedy, although anyone with an Internet connection can listen to the haunting tape of the community's mass extinction. And while the phrase "drinking the Kool-Aid" has entered the cultural lexicon, its reference to gullibility and blind faith is a slap in the face of the Jonestown residents who were goaded into dying by the lies of Jim Jones, and, especially insulting to the 304 murdered children. As the FBI files clearly document, the community devolved into a living hell from which there was no escape.

If anything, the people who moved to Jonestown should be remembered as noble idealists. They wanted to create a better, more equitable, society. They wanted their kids to be free of violence and racism. They rejected sexist gender roles. They believed in a dream.

How terribly they were betrayed.

NOTES

All audiotapes found in Jonestown archived by the FBI; transcriptions provided by the Jonestown Institute.

All FBI documents begin with prefix RYMUR (for RYan MURder) and the digits 89-4286-.

Edith Roller's journals transcribed by Don Beck.

Audiotape transcripts were summarized and sometimes compressed for clarity. Document dates are included, if available.

CHAPTER 1: AN ADVENTURE

p. 1, **The journey up the coastline:** Thom Bogue interview with author.

p. 3, Census of temple members' entry to Guyana: RYMUR 89-4286-2018-X-5 & X-7, compiled by the Jonestown Institute (http://jonestown.sdsu.edu).

CHAPTER 2: CHURCH

p. 5, **He later described his father:** audiotape Q134.

p. 5, **like an outcast on many levels:** audiotape Q134.

p. 5, **There, a neighbor brought Jim to the local Nazarene church:** Tim Reiterman. with John Jacobs, *Raven: the Untold Story of the Rev. Jim Jones and His People* (E.P. Dutton: 1982), 17.

p. 6, **"I found immediate acceptance":** audiotape Q134.

p. 6, **By age ten, he was holding pretend services:** Reiterman, *Raven*, 23.

p. 6, **He attempted to integrate the church:** Rebecca Moore, *A Sympathetic*

History of Jonestown: The Moore Family Involvement in Peoples Temple (Edwin Mellen Press: 1985), 151–52.

p. 7, **He named the new church:** Reiterman, *Raven*, 49.

p. 8, Background on Hyacinth Thrash's life from her autobiography: Catherine Hyacinth Thrash as told to Marian K. Towne, *The Onliest One Alive, Surviving Jonestown, Guyana* (self-published: 1995).

p. 9, **forced to integrate:** Butler-Tarkington neighborhood association website.

p. 10, **A line lifted from a church newsletter:** Temple newsletter, "The Open Door to All Mankind," April, 1956: the collection of Gene and June Cordell, Indianapolis, Indiana.

p. 10, **two months after he was ordained:** Jones's Ordination certificate, RYMUR 89-4286-BB-17-cc.

p. 11, **The sisters would become part of:** Rebecca Moore, "Demographics and the Black Religious Culture of Peoples Temple," in *Peoples Temple and Black Religion in America* (Indiana University Press: 2005), 57–80.

p. 11, **When his adopted Korean daughter died:** Marceline Jones, undated, "To Whom It May Concern," RYMUR 89-4286-EE-1-I&J, pp. 73–75.

p. 11, **As his wife, Marceline, walked down the street:** Interview Jim Jones Jr.; Walter Spencer, "Human Rights Director Endures Hate Letters, Calls, Vandalism," *Indianapolis Times*, July 29, 1961.

p. 12, **When he learned that several Indianapolis restaurants:** news brief, *Indianapolis Star*, March 21, 1961.

p. 12, **Jones announced on his television program:** "White Pastor Stages Hunger Strike to Protest Restaurants' Prejudice," *Indianapolis Recorder*, January 24, 1959.

p. 12, **They tried to move him to a white ward:** Reiterman, *Raven*, 75.

p. 12, **"The Negro wants to be our brother in privilege, not our brother-in-law":** Jim Jones's letter to the editor, *Indianapolis Times*, February 24, 1961.

p. 12, **In his first weeks as commission head:** news brief, *Indianapolis Star*, March 21, 1961.

p. 12, **Led by their fearless pastor:** Thrash, *The Onliest One Alive*, 51.

p. 13, **Jones recruited Hyacinth and Zipporah:** Thrash, *The Onliest One Alive*, 59.

p. 13, **She had second thoughts about Jim Jones:** Thrash, *The Onliest One Alive*, 51.

p. 13, **One doctor told her it was a miracle:** Thrash, *The Onliest One Alive*, 51.

CHAPTER 3: REDWOOD VALLEY

p. 14, **In the Soviet Union, Nikita Khrushchev repeatedly threatened:** "Government Booklet Gives Grim Fallout Information," Associated Press, December 31, 1961.

p. 14, **He claimed to have had a vision of a mushroom cloud:** Reiterman, *Raven*, 76.

p. 14, **Where services once attracted:** Reiterman, *Raven*, 85.

p. 14, **Hy and Zippy started:** Thrash, *The Onliest One Alive*, 59.

p. 15, **As schools let out for summer vacation in 1965:** Reiterman, *Raven*, 98.

p. 15, **Relatives of the migrating members:** Gene and June Cordell, "Reflections," essay published on Jonestown Institute website.

p. 15, **All told, about one hundred fifty people:** Reiterman, 98

p. 15, **She had it surgically removed:** Thrash, *The Onliest One Alive*, 53 & 55.

p. 15, **He told Jerry Parks:** Jerry Parks interview with the author.

p. 16, **For the past ten years:** Thrash, *The Onliest One Alive*, 45.

p. 16, **They drove most of the way on Route 66:** Thrash, *The Oneliest One Alive*, 61.

p. 17, **He held services in borrowed quarters:** Reiterman, *Raven*, 100.

p. 17, **The bonds uniting them grew stronger:** Jeannie Mills, *Six Years With God: Life Inside Rev. Jim Jones's Peoples Temple* (A. & W. Publishers: 1979), 132.

p. 18, **The state paid them:** Thrash, *The Onliest One Alive*.

p. 18, **In their spare time:** Thrash, *The Onliest One Alive*.

p. 18, **Zip's original cranberry sauce cake:** Thrash, *The Onliest One Alive*.

p. 18, **They spent many pleasant afternoons:** Thrash, *The Onliest One Alive*.

p. 18, **The jarred preserves were distributed:** Thrash, *The Onliest One Alive*.

p. 18, **Al Barbero:** Harold Cordell interview with author.

p. 18, **Sheriff Reno Bartolomie:** Harold Cordell interview with author.

p. 19, **Later, he'd use stronger words:** audiotape Q953.

p. 19, **"We must have a prophet":** Jones, *The Letter Killeth*, California Historical Society, MS 3800.

p. 19, **much-hyped miracle crusade:** newspaper advertisement, California Historical Society, MS 3800.

p. 19, **He'd astound locals with his healings:** audiotape Q162.

p. 20, **"The dregs of fascist USA":** audiotape Q741.

p. 20, **They cured heroin addicts:** Neva Sly, "Four Years of Utopia, Then Prison!" Jonestown Institute.

Chapter 4: "Dad"

p. 23, **He was just your average "holy ghost man":** Harold Cordell interview with author.

p. 23, **In the spring of 1973:** audiotape Q 1059 (Part 1 of 6)

p. 24, **He combined the Apostle Paul's mandate:** King James Bible, Acts 4:31–32 and 35.

p. 24, **Karl Marx's directive:** Karl Marx, "Critique of the Gotha Program," *Die Neue Zeit*: 1890-91 Q1059, part 1.

p. 24, **They used to call him Jimba:** Lynetta Jones's "Index of Stories Written: Jimba's Life," RYMUR 89-4286-BB-18-Z, pages 2–48.

p. 24, **In Guyana, he'd tell top aides:** RYMUR 89-4286-O-1-B: An untitled collection of reminiscences by Jim Jones.

p. 25, **The data from the subsequent survey:** Mills, *Six Years With God*, 14.

p. 25, **His sunglasses:** David Wise interview with author.

p. 25, **His aides who worked in hospitals:** Peter King, "How Jones Used Drugs," *San Francisco Examiner*, December 28, 1978.

p. 25, **others feigned insomnia:** Peter King, "How Jones Used Drugs," *San Francisco Examiner*, December 28, 1978.

p. 26, **The potent sedative:** Teri Buford interview with author.

p. 26, **At the next service:** Teri Buford interview, David Wise, "25 Years Hiding from a Dead Man," Jonestown Institute.

p. 26, **He made troublemakers "drop dead":** Mills, *Six Years With God*, 13.

p. 26, **He warned a man caught cheating:** Edith Roller journal, August 10, 1975, RYMUR 89-4286-2018-HH-2-28 to 69.

p. 26, **Still weak:** Mills, *Six Years With God*, 152.

p. 27, **"Jim was shot but they couldn't kill him!":** Jim Jones Jr., interview with author.

p. 27, **he'd "neutralized" the bullet:** Mills, *Six Years With God*, 162.

p. 28, **Jones vehemently denied:** Jim Jones Jr. interview.

p. 28, **In one bizarre instance:** audiotape Q953.

p. 28, **He wondered aloud:** David Wise interview with author.

p. 28, **Shortly after the bomb scare:** Peoples Temple press release, March 13, 1974, California Historical Society, MS3800.

p. 28, **Women were subjected to a seventeen-step procedure:** "Searching Procedures–Sisters," California Historical Society, MS3800.

p. 28, **Babies were unwrapped:** "Security Notes," California Historical Society, MS3800.

CHAPTER 5: EDITH

p. 30, **After the war:** "Roller Family" history, written by her sister, Edna Garrison, Edith Roller's press release announcing her resignation (Roller family collection, shared with the author by her first cousin, Alan Rice).

p. 30, **More than four hundred students:** San Francisco State University Strike Collection.

p. 31, **And so it was:** Edith Roller's healing affidavit, RYMUR 89-4286-2018-ff-6-27.

p. 31, **She taught high school equivalency:** Email confirmation from Bridget C. Hodenfield, Human Resources, Santa Rosa Junior College, 12.17.09.

p. 31, **and apostolic socialism:** audiotape Q 1059 (Part 3 of 6).

p. 31, **It was flanked:** Marshall Kilduff and Ron Javers, *The Suicide Cult: Inside Story of the People's Temple Sect and the Massacre in Guyana* (Bantam Doubleday Dell Publishing Group: 1978), 194.

p. 32, **The plan was pure fiction:** John A. William, *The Man Who Cried I Am*, (Little Brown: 1967).

p. 32, **and instructed members:** Neva Sly, "Four Years of Utopia, Then Prison!" Jonestown Institute.

p. 33, **He called himself the "spokesman for the people":** David Wise, "25 Years Hiding from a Dead Man," Jonestown Institute.

p. 33, **at the height of Jones's power:** John M. Crewdson, "Followers Say Jim Jones Directed Voting Frauds," *New York Times*, December 17, 1978.

p. 33, **Moscone acknowledged his debt:** audiotape Q783.

p. 34, **was shocked at the change:** Guy Young interview with author.

p. 36, **Edith summarized her convictions:** Edith Roller diary, August 15, 1975, RYMUR-89-4286-2018-HH-2-28 to 69.

p. 36, **Jones rejected the article:** Garry Lambrev, "The Living Word and Me: The Limits of Anarchism in Peoples Temple," by Garrett Lambrev, Jonestown Institute.

p. 36, **For example, Jones said that true followers:** "A True Follower of This Activist Christian Ministry," from the collection of David Wise.

p. 37, **She stood up:** Roller journal September 7, 1975, RYMUR 89-4286-2018-HH-2-70 to 2-91.

CHAPTER 6: TRAITORS

p. 39, **When a man named Earl Jackson:** Jones note to "Bro Jackson," undated, RYMUR 89-4286-1099, b7c.

p. 39, **Every church member older than eleven:** Security Notes—California Historical Society, MS3800.

p. 40, **threatened to divorce him:** Reiterman, *Raven*, 121.

p. 40, **"My love will not reach you":** Roller journal, February 8, 1976, RYMUR 89-4286-2018-HH-2- 92 to 116.

p. 40, **others he pressured to abort:** Teri Buford interview with author.

p. 40, **Jones bragged about his dalliances:** Reiterman, *Raven*, 172.

p. 40, **He only made it:** Laura Kohl, Jordan Vilchez with author.

p. 41, **"but what he did is unacceptable":** David Wise interview with author.

p. 41, **Once that line was crossed:** Neva Sly, "Four Years of Utopia, Then Prison!" essay, Jonestown Institute website.

p. 41, **Adults caught smoking:** Mills, *Six Years With with God*, 208.

p. 41, **Sometimes, children would collapse:** Thom Bogue interview with author.

p. 41, **This consisted of leading them into a dark room:** Mills, *Six Years With God*, 74.

p. 42, **Those who did were called traitors:** Juanell Smart interview with author.

p. 42, **One family moved all the way to the East Coast:** Mills, *Six Years With God*, 28.

p. 42, **He likened them to the spokes and hub of a wheel:** Roller journal, August 30, 1975, RYMUR-89-4286-2018-HH-2-28 to 69.

p. 42, **"We're interested in instilling respect":** Roller journal, July 25, 1976, RYMUR 89-4286-Bulky 2018 HH-2-1 to HH-2-27.

p. 43, **Jones promised members lifetime care:** Kilduff, *The Suicide Cult*, 82.

p. 43, **Jones's aides cut words and letters from magazines:** Deborah Layton, *Seductive Poison: A Jonestown Survivor's Story of Life and Death in the People's Temple* (Anchor Books: 1999), 92.

p. 43, **"No pigs":** Example of threatening note, RYMUR 89-4286-X-3-c-1.

p. 43, **Jones's staff would leave the notes on defectors' porches:** Mills, *Six Years With God*, 58.

p. 43, **They also called in threats from pay phones:** Declarations of Teresa Buford, October 10, 1978, RYMUR-89-4286-2233-R-1-B-2 & R-1-B-3.

p. 43, **The day before Edith Roller begged:** Roller journal, February 4, 1976, RYMUR-89-4286-2018-HH-2- 92 to 116.

p. 43, **Another woman who left:** Roller journal, December 1, 1976 RYMUR-89-4286-Bulky 2018 C-1-A-7 (1) to 7 (146).

p. 43, **"You cannot escape . . .":** Roller journal, December 4, 1976 RYMUR-89-4286-Bulky 2018 C-1-A-7 (1) to 7 (146).

p. 44, **He went into hiding for twenty-five years:** David Wise interview with the author.

p. 44, **Jones advocated racial equality:** Gang of Eight letter, California Historical Society, Moore Family Papers, MS 3802.

p. 44, **Not long after the "Gang of Eight" left:** Carey Winfrey, "Why 900 Died in Guyana," *New York Times Magazine*, February 25, 1979.

p. 44, **Black Panther leader Huey Newton:** Mills, *Six Years With God*, 257.

p. 44, **"When reactionary forces crush us":** Huey Newton, *Revolutionary Suicide* (Random House: 1973), xiv.

p. 44, **Police threw tear gas:** Susan Sontag, James Baldwin, et al, "Police Shooting of Oakland Negro," *New York Times*, May 6, 1968.

p. 45, **He asked the commission members:** Laurie Efrein Kahalas, "The Notorious Incident in L.A." a/k/a "Kill the Messenger," Jonestown Institute.

p. 45, **Such an extravagant act:** Mills, *Six Years With God*, 231.

p. 45, **After a brief silence, Jack Beam:** Grace Stoen, interview with author.

p. 45, **They would all be dead within an hour:** Carey Winfrey, "Why 900 Died in Guyana," *New York Times Magazine*, February 25, 1979.

p. 45, **Some members thought he was just being theatrical:** Don Beck, Grace Stoen interviews with author.

p. 45, **Patty Cartmell:** Mills, *Six Years With God*, 311.

p. 45, **Afterward, some of those present felt proud:** Carey Winfrey, "Why 900 Died in Guyana," *New York Times Magazine*, February 25, 1979.

p. 46, **He was debating two options:** Carey Winfrey, "Why 900 Died in Guyana," *New York Times Magazine*, February 25, 1979.

p. 46, **He pursued the suicide-by-plane idea:** Teri Buford interview with author.

p. 46, **After Maria got her private pilot's license:** confirmed by Federal Aviation Administration.

p. 46, **Maria claimed that she was putting in hours:** Guy Young interview with author.

p. 46, **Soon after, however, she abruptly dropped out:** Teri Buford interview with author.

p. 46, **They described the mission's water:** "Letters from Jonestown," California Historical Society collection MS3800, Box 2, folder 44.

p. 47, **After several seconds:** FBI interview former member of Jones's Indianapolis church, December 4, 1978, RYMUR 89-4286-696.

p. 47, **"The last orgasm I'd like to have is death":** Roller journal, February, 7, 1976, RYMUR-89-4286-2018-HH-2- 92.

p. 47, **"It would be the greatest reward":** Roller journal, August 25, 1976, RYMUR-89-4286-Bulky 2018 C-1-A-3 (1) to 3 (104).

CHAPTER 7: EXODUS

p. 50, **Several times she started to tell Jones:** Thrash, *The Onliest One Alive*, 74.

p. 52, **When the worship service began:** Reiterman, *Raven*, 314.

p. 52, **He convinced *New West* to cancel the assignment:** Marshall Kilduff interview with author.

p. 53, **the calls became more menacing:** W. E. Barnes, "Yet-to-Be-Printed-Story Builds a Storm," *San Francisco Examiner*, June 11, 1977.

p. 53, **When he published this observation:** Tim Stoen, Letter to *Indianapolis Star*, October 24, 1971.

p. 54, **Meanwhile, the editor working on the series:** Reiterman, *Raven*, 216.

p. 54, **The Synanon lawsuit would end up costing:** Les Ledbetter, "Libel Suit Costs Hearst $600,000; Synanon Agrees to Drop Its Legal Action Based on Adverse News Articles," *New York Times*, July 3, 1976.

p. 54, **The impending story created such paranoia:** audiotape Q579.

p. 54, **Jones himself called friendly *Chronicle* reporters:** Katy Butler interview with author.

p. 55, **Temple aides burned compromising files:** Sharon Amos, "Trip Strategy and Problems," RYMUR 89-4286-2018-c-7-a-la.

p. 55, **and tried to make the article disappear:** Kilduff, *The Suicide Cult*, 78.

p. 55, **The media that once hailed Jim Jones as Gandhilike:** "White Pastor Stages Hunger Strike to Protest Restaurants' Prejudice," *Indianapolis Recorder*, January 24, 1959.

p. 55, **He left that same night for Guyana:** Layton, *Seductive Poison*, 111.

p. 55, **so offended by his vulgar screed:** FBI interview with ham-radio operator, March 1, 1979, RYMUR 89-4286-29-183.

p. 55, **Jones's powerful friends helped him mitigate the damage:** Letter from Lt. Governor Mervyn Dymally to Prime Minister Forbes Burnham, August 3, 1977, CHS, MS3800.

p. 55, **refusing to heed calls to investigate the Temple:** "Mayor Won't Investigate Rev. Jones," *San Francisco Chronicle*, July 27, 1977.

p. 56, **On August 21, 1977, the Temple issued an official response:** "Neo-McCarthyite Campaign Persists Against Peoples Temple," August 21, 1977, Jonestown Institute.

p. 56, **The exodus was planned down to the last detail:** Sharon Amos, "Trip Strategy and Problems," RYMUR 89-4286-2018-c-7-a-la.

p. 56, **The local press kept a close eye on the Geary Street headquarters:** Tim Reiterman, "Peoples' Temple being Evacuated," *San Francisco Examiner*, Aug 17, 1977.

p. 56, **San Francisco, nevertheless, felt the move:** Marshall Kilduff, "Peoples Temple Speeds up Its Unusual Exodus to Guyana," *San Francisco Chronicle*, August 17, 1977.

p. 56, **as entire communes were emptied in a matter of days:** Kilduff, *The Suicide Cult*, 104.

p. 57, **Fred Lewis, who was not a Temple member:** Kevin Fagan, "Haunted by Memories of Hell," *San Francisco Chronicle*, November 12, 1978.

p. 57, **"This does not seem like the sister I know":** letter to Vernetta Christian from brother in Idaho, September 21, 1977, RYMUR 89-4286-2233-EE-1C1b.

CHAPTER 8: PIONEERS

p. 59, **In July 1974, Jim Bogue boarded the *Cudjoe*:** *Cudjoe* cargo manifest, July 12, 1974, RYMUR 89-4286-2233-PP2K5.

p. 59, **Their designated captain was an Indiana native:** Vessel survey by "Nelson & Associates, Inc." Miami, Florida, June 28, 1974, RYMUR 89-4286-2233-PPP2C7.

p. 60, **in February 1976, the Temple signed a twenty-five-year lease:** Guyana Land Lease , RYMUR 89-4286-A-31-a-21a-21c.

p. 60, **Burnham was eager to use the settlement:** Paula Adams memo to Jones,

"Notes from conversation with Joe Lambert (Guyana Airlines)," February 20, RYMUR 89-4286-2233-x-3-g-2a.

p. 60, **encouraged the group to hire locals:** Hamilton Green interview with author.

p. 60, **Guyana and Venezuela were embroiled in a long-simmering territorial dispute:** Tim Merrill, ed. Guyana: *A Country Study* (Washington: GPO for the Library of Congress, 1992).

p. 60, **Venezuelan militants attacked a Guyanese border town:** "Guyanese Troops Move on Rebels; Sons of U.S.-Born Rancher Said to Be in Group," *New York Times,* January 5, 1969.

p. 60, **By placing a large community of Americans along its border:** Hamilton Green interview with author.

p. 61, **One amateur agronomist insisted on collecting all the pits and seeds:** Don Beck interview with author.

p. 61, **The settlers hired a crew of local Amerindians:** Wilfred Jupiter interview with author.

p. 63, **Like other members, the Bogues agreed to donate 15 percent of their income:** Jim Bogue interview with FBI, December 28, 1978, RYMUR 89-4286-254.

p. 64, **Jim Bogue dashed off a sentence:** Jim Bogue false confession, RYMUR 89-4286-2233-EE1AB65.

p. 67, **The United Nations classified the jungle soil as "non-productive":** Timothy Stoen memo to Jim Jones, California Historical Society, MS 3800.

CHAPTER 9: THE PROMISED LAND

p. 72, **Jones sentenced him to fifty whacks with the board of education:** Roller journal, March 3, 1976 RYMUR-89-4286-Bulky 2018 C-2-A-7

p. 72, **After Tommy broke a Temple rule by associating with outsiders:** Roller journal, May 19, 1976, RYMUR 89-4286-Bulky 2018 C-2-A-9 (1) to A-9 (143).

p. 74, **In the early days, residents ate well:** interview with Jim and Thom Bogue.

p. 74, **Other times teens brought out a boom box:** Leslie Wagner-Wilson, *Slavery of Faith* (iUniverse.com: 2009), 80.

p. 74, **Couples sneaked off to have sex:** Wagner-Wilson, *Slavery* 70.

p. 75, **the Temple released a progress report:** "Peoples Temple Agricultural Project: Progress Report, Summer 1977," Jonestown Institute.

p. 75, **five times more than the land could support:** Jim Bogue interview with author.

p. 77, **After showing the home movies:** Sharon Amos, "Strategies and Problems Since JJ Left," RYMUR 89-4286-2018-c-7-a-2a.

p. 78, **Babies slept in the nursery:** Wagner-Wilson, *Slavery*, 72.

p. 78, **Each dwelling measured fifteen by thirty feet:** "Jonestown, Guyana, "Housing site 102," RYMUR 89-4286-2018C-7-b-1.

p. 78, **The cottages were crude:** "Housing in Jonestown" Jonestown Institute.

p. 78, **Residents emerged onto the walkways in bathrobes and flip-flops:** Wagner-Wilson, *Slavery of Faith*, 72.

p. 79, **At the end of July 1977, a group of thirty-nine Temple members flew to Guyana in a single day:** Entry to Guyana, Sec 105, pp. 2–165 and Sect 106, pp. 2–202. [RYMUR 89-4286-2018-X-5 & X-7], prepared by the Jonestown Institute.

CHAPTER 10: GEORGETOWN

p. 81, **He'd used this tactic to a lesser degree in California:** Deborah Layton, *Seductive Poison*, 62.

p. 81, **sent out these "PR girls" to bedazzle influential men:** Hamilton Green interview with author.

p. 81, **Located at the end of a quiet street, 41 Lamaha Gardens:** Reiterman, *Raven*, 413.

p. 81, **the Temple women used provocative means to promote their cause:** Nicholas Horrock, "Mass Cult Immigration Violated Jones's Agreement with Guyana," *New York Times*, December 24, 1978.

p. 81, **Some men were swayed by mere suggestion:** Robert Lindsey, "State Dept. Called Lax on Mass Deaths," *New York Times*, November 30, 1978.

p. 81, **Wives grew suspicious:** Hamilton Green interview with author.

p. 82, **Jones's envoys spent most of their time on Georgetown's principal boulevard, Main Street:** Reiterman, *Raven*, 274.

p. 82, **"Don't give me your California hard sell":** Meeting with Foreign Minister Fred Wills, January 30, 1978, RYMUR 89-4286-2018-x-2-a—5

p. 82, **He asked the team to bring him a pint of milk a day:** Sharon Amos Meeting with Wills, 3.27.78, RYMUR 89-4286-2233-BB-2-222-6.

p. 82, **Jones's star performer—his "political prostitute":** Paula Adams memo on Guyanese ambassador Laurence Mann, RYMUR 89-4286-2233-BB-1-xx-14.

p. 82, **Paula was quiet and down-to-earth:** Laura Kohl interview with author.

p. 82, **entered the Temple a confused twenty-two-year-old:** Reiterman, *Raven*, 274

p. 83, **They moved into an apartment together:** Paula Adams memo on Mann, RYMUR 89-4286-2233-BB-1-xx-14.

p. 83, **he was also related to Prime Minister Forbes Burnham:** Paula Adams memo on Mann, RYMUR 89-4286-2233-Bb-1-ff-2.

p. 83, **radioed the information to Jonestown nightly:** Laura Kohl interview with author.

p. 83, **When Paula wasn't playing housemaid:** Paula Adams memo to Jones, RYMUR 89-4286-2233-BB-1-KK-1.

p. 83, **"Most of Georgetown relates on a forum of drink":** Paula Adams memo on "constructive criticism for assimilation," RYMUR 89-4286-2233Bb-1-ccc-1.

p. 83, **immigrating Temple members stopped at JFK's duty-free shop to buy bottles of single-malt whiskey:** Roller diary, January 16, 1978, RYMUR 89-4286-2018-C-2(Part I)-A-1-(1) to (8).

p. 83, **Twelve days after "John John" was born, Tim Stoen signed a peculiar document:** Timothy Stoen sworn statement, February 6, 1972, RYMUR 89-4286-FF-4-A-175.

p. 84, **One gave the Temple parental authority over John:** Undated note from Grace Stoen, RYMUR 89-4286-BB-31-a-43, Parental Consent and Power of Attorney, March 9, 1976; RYMUR 89-4286-FF-41-174.

p. 84, **A few months later, her estranged husband:** Power of attorney, September 30, 1976, RYMUR 89-4286- BB-31-a-81.

p. 84, **Mann reported the conversation to Temple leader Jean Brown:** Conversation between Jean Brown and Laurence Mann, RYMUR 89-4286-2233-FF-1-6.

p. 85, **"I consulted with my wife and my entire church before I did it":** JJ letter to Reid, September 10, 1977, RYMUR 89-4286-2233-BB-17-WW-1.

p. 85, **On Main Street, Paula Adams assured cabinet ministers:** Paula Adams, letter to Fred Wills, RYMUR 89-4286-2233-Bb-1-ww-1.

p. 85, **A staff member who was rummaging through his briefcase:** Teri Buford memo to Jones regarding the contents of Timothy Stoen's briefcase, RYMUR 89-4286-2233-BB-31-a-178.

p. 85, **before leaving, Tim Stoen returned to 1859 Geary Boulevard to try to purge any compromising files containing his name:** Layton, *Seductive Poison*, 132.

p. 87, **They left California believing they were going on a yearlong mission:** Thrash, *The Onliest One Alive*, 83.

p. 88, **It was hard for Hyacinth to navigate:** Thrash, *The Onliest One Alive*, 91.

p. 88, **Her days were largely unsupervised:** Thrash, *The Onliest One Alive*, 88.

p. 88, **Hy chose not to believe it:** Thrash, *The Onliest One Alive*, 78.

p. 88, **"And he's doing so much better because of it":** David Wise interview with the author.

p. 89, **The conversation startled many:** audiotape Q986.

p. 89, **"That's Tim's boy up there!":** Thrash, *The Onliest One Alive*, 70.

p. 89, **he told police that Jonestown was a "slave colony":** Memo to Jones from Paula Adams, RYMUR 89-4286-2233-BB-1-X-1.

p. 89, **several members jumped him before making him crawl to Jones's feet and beg for forgiveness:** Reiterman, *Raven*, 356.

p. 90, **Jones told McCoy that Broussard was a liar:** Reiterman, *Raven*, 359.

p. 90, **US embassy personnel had been making periodic checks on the American group:** Memo of Marsha E. Barnes to Ashley Hewitt regarding contacts with Peoples Temple, "The Assassination of Representative Leo J. Ryan and the Jonestown Guyana Tragedy," Report of the Committee on Foreign Affairs, US House of Representatives, May 15, 1979, p. 131.

p. 90, **the Temple had caught wind of Looman's phone call:** Reiterman, *Raven*, 360.

p. 90, **John John was trotted out, and seemed healthy enough:** Paula Adams letter to Ptolemy Reid, RYMUR 89-4286-2233-BB-1-uu-1.

p. 91, **"the government does not approve of such tactics":** Jones letter to Reid, RYMUR 89-4286-2233-BB-17-hhh-1.

p. 91, **Yet other regional bureaucrats pressured Jones:** Notes from meeting with regional officials, RYMUR 89-4286-2233-BB-2-lll-1, October 17, 1977.

p. 91, **Jones wrote Prime Minister Burnham complaining:** Jones letter to Burnham, RYMUR 89-4286-2233-BB-17-hh-1, September 26, 1977.

p. 91, **Burnham himself handed down the order validating the Jonestown**

school: Amos meeting with Wills, RYMUR 89-4286-2233-BB-2-gggg-2, March 8, 1978.

p. 91, **customs agents did a spot check on ninety crates bound for the settlement:** Reiterman, *Raven*, 355.

p. 91, **They found nothing, but passed along the tip to the International Police Agency, Interpol:** Memo on Interpol report, RYMUR 89-4286-2018-H-1-d-2.

p. 91, **Emigrating Temple members turned in their weapons before leaving:** Mills, *Six Years With God*, 57.

p. 92, **On the off chance that they did open a crate:** Reiterman, *Raven*, 354.

p. 92, **"Merry Xmas from the system!":** Sandy Bradshaw memo to Jones, RYMUR 89-4286-2233-BB-6-HHHHHHH.

p. 92, **Jonestown's arsenal would grow to include more than thirty firearms:** List of weapons/rounds, RYMUR 89-4286-H-1-C-4.

p. 92, **used to kill Congressman Leo Ryan:** Reiterman, *Raven*,355.

p. 92, **"there are enough bibles here to do a lot of praying if necessary":** Sandra Bradshaw note to Jones, "More contingency plans," RYMUR 89-4286-2233-FF-13-A-18.

p. 92, **"It is my understanding we can get as many rifles/shotguns as we wish":** Sandy Bradshaw memo to Jones, RYMUR 89-4286-2233-BB-6-J7.

p. 92, **Paula Adams, informed of Hass's arrival by embassy officials:** Kilduff, *The Suicide Cult*, 105.

p. 93, **Reid suspended protocol to allow them to be processed posthaste:** Nicholas Horrock, "Mass Cult Immigration Violated Jones's Agreement with Guyana," *New York Times*, December 24, 1978.

p. 93, **He also transferred several pesky regional officials:** Nicholas Horrock, "Mass Cult Immigration Violated Jones's Agreement with Guyana," *New York Times*, December 24, 1978.

p. 93, **he crept into the bush, then turned and aimed the .38 at Jones's cabin:** Jim Jones Jr. interview with author.

p. 93, **When Stephan Jones, who was also on the security force:** Jonestown security, original research document, Jonestown Institute.

p. 94, **No one was to surrender or be taken alive:** Barbara Walker, "The Front Line in Ballad and Thought," RYMUR 89-4286-2233-EE-1-H-24.

p. 94, **Supreme Court Justice Aubrey Bishop ordered Jones to bring John

Victor Stoen to his courtroom on September 8: Writ of Habeas Corpus ad. Subjiciendum, September 6, 1977, RYMUR 89-4286-U-1-c-1.

p. 94, **Minister of Information Kit Nascimento offered Hass his plane:** Jones letter to Reid, September 10, 1977, RYMUR 89-4286-2233-BB-17-WW-1.

p. 95, **he was certain that the Guyanese government had turned on him:** FCC audiotape #9, courtesy Jonestown Institute.

p. 95, **Jones told Jim Bogue to stay behind:** Jim Bogue, interview with author.

p. 95, **An eighty-year-old woman fell into the water and broke her hip:** Thrash, *The Onliest One Alive*, 98.

p. 95, **One of Jones's aides had thought to grab recording equipment:** audiotape Q135.

p. 95, **that the "rivers were blocked to the rest of my people":** audiotape Q135.

p. 95, **When the truck returned the women to Jonestown at dawn, she found a stranger sleeping in her bed:** Thrash, *The Onliest One Alive*, 99

p. 96, **Aides gathered the older children in the school tent:** Wagner-Wilson, *Slavery*, 90.

p. 96, **Teenage boys tried to prove their valor by charging to the front lines wielding cutlasses:** Wagner-Wilson, *Slavery*, 90.

p. 96, **When Jones wasn't ranting, he led his people in civil rights anthems:** Dawn Gardfrey, interview with the author.

p. 96, **walked down the line crying:** Barbara Walker, "The Front Line in Ballad and Thought," RYMUR 89-4286-2233-EE-1-H-24, X-3-6-16.

p. 96, **stop forwarding Social Security checks:** US Postal Service routing slip, September 9, 1977, RYMUR 89-4286-2233-Mm-3-9.

p. 96, **The move effectively cut off Jonestown's monthly income of $35,000:** FAQ "Was there Social Security fraud in Jonestown?" Jonestown Institute.

p. 96, **proof, Jones said, of a systematic plot to destroy them:** Deborah Blakey affidavit, June 15, 1978, Jonestown Institute.

p. 96, **The meeting was dramatically interrupted by a second sniper attempt:** "Temple Leader Shot at Four Times," Associated Press, September, 10, 1977.

p. 96, **700 followers:** Jonestown population censuses, Jonestown Institute.

p. 96, **slapped their palms over their mouths in an Indian war whoop:** Thrash, *The Onliest One Alive*, 109.

p. 97, **Only two people raised their hands in favor of mass suicide:** Timothy Carter, "Murder or Suicide: What I Saw," essay published on Jonestown Institute website.

p. 97, **they didn't come to the promised land to die:** Mike Wendland, "Some strange messages on radio from Jonestown," *Free Lance-Star*, January 13, 1979.

p. 97, **This time he flew up on a Guyana Defense Force plane:** Reiterman, *Raven*, 365.

p. 98, **he took a second suicide vote:** Carter, "Murder or Suicide: What I Saw," Jonestown Institute.

p. 98, **he radioed Marceline in San Francisco:** Reiterman, *Raven*, 367

p. 98, **"That chap [Idi Amin] seems to be able to stand up for what he believes":** audtiotape Q135. The transmission was illegally broadcast outside ham bands, but was recorded by a Florida man, who told the FBI he thought a missionary outpost was under attack.

p. 98, **Jones then gave his San Francisco aides a chilling ultimatum:** Blakey, *Seductive Poison*, 131.

p. 98, **In a taped message for Reid, Jones distorted the suicide vote:** audiotape Q800.

p. 98, **a little over two hours to find Reid:** Teri Buford memo to Jones, RYMUR 89-4286-2233-BB-7-K-1.

p. 98, **They popped tranquilizers:** Buford memo to Jones, RYMUR 89-4286-2233-BB-7-J-1.

p. 98, **Marceline Jones, two aides, and Temple lawyer Charles Garry flew to Chicago:** Miscellaneous information, RYMUR 89-4286-2233-BB-17-aaa-1.

p. 98, **his wife assured the visitors that the Guyana Defense Force wouldn't attack Jonestown:** Reiterman, *Raven*, 370.

p. 99, **"We tried to get an arrest warrant for Jones":** Kilduff, *The Suicide Cult*, 108.

p. 99, **Jones gave various triggers for the plan:** Teri Buford, interviews with author.

p. 99, **Teri Buford would later claim that Sandy Bradshaw:** Doyle McManus, "Ex-Aides of Jones Trade Bitter Charges," *Los Angeles Times*, December 22, 1978.

CHAPTER 12: BULLETS TO KILL BUMBLEBEES

p. 100, **"Should anything happen that would kill Jim":** Buford letter to Pat Richartz, October 9, 1977, RYMUR 89-4286-2233-BB-7-D10.

p. 100, **Garry's secretary, Pat Richartz, fired off a six-page response:** Reiterman, *Raven*, 374.

p. 101, **Debbie Blakey, who was in the room, later informed Jones of her actions:** Debbie Blakey letter to JJ, January 11, 1978, RYMUR 89-4286-2233-PP1A10.

p. 101, **US Consul Richard McCoy dismissed the stunt as a "psychological ploy":** "State Dept. Had Called Suicide Threat a 'Ploy,'" Associated Press, December 6, 1978.

p. 101, **Guyanese Ambassador Laurence Mann grew irritated at the letters flooding his office:** Notes on a conversation between Ambassador Mann and Paula Adams, RYMUR-89-4286-2233-Bb-1-ggg.

p. 101, **including a massive sugar strike that was crippling Guyana's fragile economy:** "Plot Seen in Guyana Strike," Associated Press, October 26, 1977.

p. 101, **he told Jones's representatives to direct all communication to his inferior:** Jones letter to Reid, October 9, 1977, RYMUR 89-4286-2233-BB-17-gg-1.

p. 102, **Others secretly wondered why Jones . . . didn't use his paranormal powers to save them:** Wagner-Wilson, *Slavery,* 88.

p. 102, **why the enemy would hike through the virtually impassable jungle:** Laura Kohl interview with author.

p. 103, **The family was further weakened when their children were moved:** Jim Bogue interview with author.

p. 103, **His letter is remarkable for its bluntness:** Undated letter from Gene Chaikin to Jones, RYMUR 89-4286-EE-1-C-10 ff.

p. 104, **he soon started complaining of a host of mysterious ailments:** Gene Chaikin letter to Phyllis Chaikin, 10.4.78, RYMUR 89-4286-BB-10-d-8.

p. 104, **Jones assigned school secretary Inez Wagner to seduce and spy on him:** Charles Garry deposition, Peoples Temple v. Attorney General of California, December 30, 1981.

p. 105, **"No one ever intended to die":** Reiterman, *Raven*, 376.

p. 105, **Jones casually mentioned that he'd once had to "fuck" sixteen people in one day:** Charles Garry deposition, Peoples v. Attorney General of California.

CHAPTER 13: RUNAWAYS

p. 106, **"No one leaves until all are here," Jones announced:** Roller journal, March 18, 1978.

p. 107, **"Well, Steve, I've been here seventy-two days":** Steve Addison note to Jones, May 28, 1978, RYMUR 89-4286-2233-EE-2-a-2.

p. 110, **reached over to switch on the tape recorder:** Q933, prepared by the Jonestown Institute

p. 112, **permitted the boys to be physically restrained by chain to prevent them from running away:** Release to chain Brian Davis and Tommy Bogue together, RYMUR 89-4286-2233-FF-1-55.

CHAPTER 14: CONCERN

p. 114, **The group persisted, trying to break the cipher:** Reiterman, *Raven*, 409.

p. 114, **She promised not to criticize the Temple:** Letter from Yulanda Crawford to JJ, RYMUR 89-4286-2018-X-2-b-1.

p. 115, **"We know you live on a ranch by yourself":** Reiterman, *Raven*, 384.

p. 115, **but at the US Embassy:** Maria Katsaris telegram to State Department, September 28, 1977.

p. 115, **It was a bald-faced lie:** Gene Chaikin note to Jones, RYMUR 89-4286-2233-BB-10-X.

p. 115, **Undeterred, Katsaris flew to Washington, D.C.:** Stephen Katsaris affidavit, Jonestown Institute.

p. 115, **and paid him a three-thousand-dollar bribe to arrange a meeting with Maria:** Mike Geniella, "Relatives were frustrated by lack of action," *Santa Rosa Press Democrat*, November 13, 1988.

p. 115, **He couldn't help wondering if she'd been coached:** Reiterman, *Raven*, 387.

p. 116, **They'd given their two teenaged sons permission to go to Jonestown:** Reiterman, *Raven*, 389.

p. 116, **but they hired an attorney to demand the return of seventeen-year-old William:** Letter from Roger Holmes to Guyana Embassy, Oct. 20, 1977, RYMUR 89-4286-2233-BB-10-f.

p. 116, **Billy was quickly flown to Georgetown and married off:** Jones letter to Reid, October 26, 1977, RYMUR 89-4286-2233-BB-17-bbb-1.

p. 116, **The trip . . . cost them a small fortune:** Reiterman, *Raven*, 389.

p. 116, **McCoy tried to arrange a meeting between Billy and his parents:** Reiterman, *Raven*, 389.

p. 117, **white woman who was conversant in the Hericlitean philosophy:** Edith Roller San Francisco State College master's thesis, "The Myth Awry," filed May 1966.

p. 117, **she commanded her to stay in her room:** Roller journal, August 15, 1977, RYMUR 89-4286-Bulky 2018-HH-2-117 to -128.

p. 117, **The tension came to a head one night:** Roller journal, November 7, 1977, RYMUR 89-4286-Bulky 2018-C-3-A-6 (2) to -6 (101).

p. 117, **When a Temple secretary told her to prepare to leave for Jonestown:** Roller journal, December 1, 1977, RYMUR 89-4286-Bulky 2018-C-3-A-7 (1) -A-7 (3) to -A-7 (81).

p. 118, **She was forced to repeat the sordid story at various services for new ears:** Roller journal, November 16, 1977, RYMUR 89-4286-Bulky 2018-C-3-A-6 (2) to -6 (101).

p. 118, **Her three younger sisters had kept each other abreast:** Roller journal, August 16, 1977.

p. 119, **Dorothy phoned Edith to deride:** Roller journal, August 17, 1977.

p. 119, **A few hours after her death:** Jones comments to Jonestown community after the death of his mother, December 9, 1977, RYMUR 89-4286-O-1-B, 1-19.

p. 120, **"Anyone knows you can't shoot anything with a pistol from two hundred yards!":** Reiterman, *Raven*, 395.

p. 120, **Jones abruptly asked his followers:** audiotape Q 998.

p. 121, **residents who didn't raise their hands:** Planning Commission meeting, December 5, 1977, RYMUR 89-4286-2018C-11-D-16b.

p. 121, **He directed the medical team to research ways to kill everyone:** Schacht note to Jones, January 6, 1978, RYMUR 89-4286-2233-EE-1-5-57.

p. 121, **"It would be terrorizing for some people if we were to have them all in a group and start chopping heads off":** Manner of suicide, Annie Moore: RYMUR 89-4286-2233-EE-1-M-77.

p. 122, **"It might be advisable to blindfold the people":** Note to Dad from Phyllis Chaikin, RYMUR 89-4286-2233-EE-Ic28b.

p. 122, **"If some asylum could be arranged for our children":** "Marceline commitment statement on death," RYMUR 89-4286-2018-NIC 31d.

p. 122, **Michigan native Shirlee Fields, forty, who worked as a dietician:** Roller journal, February 14, 1978, RYMUR-89-4286-2018- C-3-A-2- (I) to (127).

p. 122, **"This would be a different way to commit revolutionary suicide":** Shirlee Fields note to Jones, 89-4286-2233-EE-1-F-12.

p. 122, **Temple leader Jean Brown pushed to send more ammunition down:** Peoples Temple v. Atty. General of California, deposition of Teri Buford, August 3, 1979.

p. 123, **the group sang odes to socialism and Jim Jones:** Peoples Rally, December 25, 1977, RYMUR 89-4286-2018c-11-d-12hh.

p. 123, **he tried to kill himself with a cutlass:** Reiterman, *Raven*, 396.

p. 123, **During his confrontation Jones told him he should be shot through the hips:** Q938.

p. 124, **"and you know how I love donuts!":** Rose McKnight letter home, Jonestown Institute website.

CHAPTER 15: CONTROL

p. 125, **"This creates for us an atmosphere of insecurity":** Jones letter to Reid, October 15, 1977, RYMUR 89-4286-2233-BB-17-ee.

p. 125, **his Georgetown attorney advised him not to leave the project until the arrest order was canceled:** Jones letter to Burnham, October 19, 1977, RYMUR 89-4286-2233-BB-17-ff.

p. 125, **The decree nullified all previous documents granting guardianship to Jim Jones:** Order re Child Custody, Superior Court of the State of California in the City and County of San Francisco, RYMUR 89-4286-2233-BB-31-b-58.

p. 125, **If Jones didn't comply, he wrote:** Joseph Freitas letter to Wills, November 25, 1977, RYMUR 89-4286-2233-KK-3-A-1.

p. 126, **The head of the Temple PR crew in the capital, Sharon Amos:** Sharon Amos letter to Burnham, January 4, 1978, RYMUR 89-4286-2233-BB-2-55-1.

p. 126, **she was very careful not to use the word *suicide*:** Richard McCoy deposition, United States of America v. Peoples Temple.

p. 126, **At a January 7 hearing:** Unsigned January 27, 1978, State Dept. Memo, Committee Report, p. 129

p. 126, **the Guyanese government seemed to be cooperating with the Stoens:** Peoples Rally notes, January 8, 1978, RYMUR 89-4286-2018-C-11-d-2a.

p. 126, **He picked people out of the crowd to ask their opinion:** Peoples Rally notes, January 7, 1978, RYMUR 89-4286-2018-C-7-C-12a.

p. 127, **Security guards nuzzled those who refused to raise their hands with their guns:** Julius Evans, Peoples Temple v. Attorney General of California, April 5, 1982, CHS 3800, 2039 box 113.

p. 127, **After a while, Jones's obsessive suicide talk lost its shock value and began to bore them:** Thom Bogue interview with author.

p. 127, **Everyone he talked to that day:** United States of America v. Peoples Temple, Deposition of Richard McCoy, vol. 1.

p. 127, **Jones suggested it was because they weren't busy enough:** Peoples Rally, December 20, 1977, RYMUR 89-4286-2018C-11-d-14c.

p. 128, **Jones himself slept in most days:** Teri Buford interview with author.

p. 128, **"Hitler did his indoctrination speeches":** Planning Commission meeting notes, December 5, 1977, RYMUR 89-4286-2018-C-11-d-16e.

p. 128, **his voice droned on for most of the day:** Bea Orsot letter to Jones, December 30, 1977, RYMUR 89-4286-2233-FF-5-8-B.

p. 128, **Whenever Jones was speaking, everyone else was expected to stop talking and listen:** Teri Buford interview with author.

p. 128, **"whatever your reasons, it is driving me nuts":** Tropp letter to Jones, RYMUR 89-4286-2233-FF-5-r-3.

p. 128, **residents would be tested on the content of his rambling broadcasts:** Peoples Rally, RYMUR 89-4286-2018-C-11-d-10d, December 28, 1977.

p. 128, **African Americans, who comprised nearly 70 percent of the community:** Rebecca Moore, "Demographics and the Black Religious Culture of Peoples Temple," in *Peoples Temple and Black Religion in America*, edited by Rebecca Moore, Anthony Pinn, and Mary Sawyer (Indiana University Press: 2005), 57-80.

p. 128, **He said black children were being castrated:** "News," May 7, 1978, RYMUR 89-4286-2233 EE-1-I&J-22.

p. 128, **blacks were "better off during slavery":** Wesley Breidenbach note to Jones, RYMUR 89-4286-2233-EE1A363a.

p. 128, **scientists had engineered a way to kill off minorities:** Lucille Taylor note to Jones, RYMUR 89-4286-2233 EE-1-7-71.

p. 129, **"I like to do a critical reading of the news":** Ron Talley note to Jones, RYMUR 89-4286-2233-T-107.

p. 129, **The Voice of America broadcasts he heard:** Harold Cordell interview with author.

p. 129, **Then he forbade writing nonmembers altogether:** Roller journal, February 7, 1978.

p. 129, **"We're not so much worried about *incoming* mail as we are *outgoing* mail":** audiotape Q 588.

p. 129, **he withheld hundreds of letters both to and from residents:** Letter information, RYMUR 89-4286-2233-EE-5-A.

p. 130, **Jones ordered everyone to write their families upbeat letters:** Letter information, RYMUR 89-4286-2018-C-7-Q-la.

p. 130, **Mentioning that it rained every day could get a letter nixed:** Terry Carter letter to her dad, RYMUR 89-4286-2233-EE-1-1&J-29.

p. 130, **One recipient complained that the letters appeared "as if they had been written by machines":** Accusation of Human Rights Violations by Rev. James Warren Jones, April 12, 1978, Jonestown Institute.

p. 130, **"have been written according to rules and saying only approved-of things":** Larry Tupper letters, RYMUR 89-4286-2233-EE-1-T134.

p. 130, **her misspellings were crossed out and corrected in someone else's handwriting:** Letter censorship, FBI interview with subject, November 21, 1978, 89-4286-152.

p. 130, **Others noticed that Jonestown letters arrived unsealed:** RYMUR 89-4286-2233-EE4X.

p. 130, **or that the page bottoms were cut off:** Gieg correspondence, RYMUR 89-4286-2233-Ee-1-G-64.

p. 130, **Jones insisted that all letters home be written in front of censors:** Q271.

p. 132, **The letter was also a no go:** Edith Roller letter to Jim Randolph, February 1, 1978, RYMUR 89-4286-2233-EE-1-R-30.

p. 132, **Bates confided to Edith that she'd suffered from various illnesses since she arrived in Jonestown:** Roller journal, January 29, 1978.

p. 132, **If someone dared move her shoes:** Laura Kohl interview with author.

p. 133, **"I am having as little communication with Bates as possible":** Roller journal, December 16, 1978

CHAPTER 16: RELEASE

p. 136, **He didn't see any weapons:** Memo of Frank Tumminia re trip to Jonestown February 2, 1978, Committee Report, p. 137.

p. 136, **Jones micromanaged every detail of their tour:** Roller journal, February 2, 1978.

p. 137, **eighty-three-year-old Texan named Katherine Domineck complained:** Roller journal, February 2, 1978.

p. 138, **the chickery was only producing an average of 270 eggs per day:** Q 240.

p. 138, **At the weekly agricultural meeting:** Q 240.

p. 138, **The committee recommended cassava:** Roller journal, March 21, 1978.

p. 138, **there would be no vegetable harvest for thirty to sixty days, except for cassava leaves:** Roller journal, March 14, 1978.

p. 139, **he dispatched the "Jonestown police":** Roller journal, January 28, 1978.

p. 139, **they wouldn't get another chicken dinner for two months:** Roller journal, February 2, 1978.

p. 139, **Farmers gave them bruised and overripe produce:** Laura Kohl interview with author.

p. 139, **some desperately hungry people resorted to stealing food:** Roller journal, February 26 and March 10, 1978.

p. 139, **Others swiped food from the plates:** "Letters to Dad" self-criticisms, and confessions of stealing, RYMUR 89-4286-2233-ff-5-b-1.

p. 139, **he sipped cold drinks and chewed ice to ward off heat as his congregation sweltered:** Q641.

p. 140, **the way to control people was to "keep them tired and poor":** Teri Buford interview with author.

p. 141, **The child "screamed and cried as Stephan said he would tell the snake to bite him":** Roller journal, February 26, 1978.

p. 141, **ordered the snake to be hung around the neck:** Q 781.

p. 141, **As guards hung them upside down:** Sid Moody and Victoria Graham, "Chaos, God of Disorder, Ruled Jonestown," November 26, 1978, Associated Press.

p. 141, **principal Tom Grubbs, suggested a new method of behavior modification:** Grubbs memo to "Dad" on behavior modification, RYMUR 89-4286-2233-EE-1-G-53.

p. 142, **would only be at the project for six to eight weeks:** Q 881.

CHAPTER 17: DRILL

p. 143, **The ham patched Schacht through to his neighbor:** FBI interview with Richard Hayman, RYMUR 89-4286-368, November 25, 1978.

p. 143, **The *Washington Star* published a story on the birth:** Mary Ann Kuhn

"A Potomac Doctor Helps Deliver Twins 2,000 Miles Away," *Washington Star*, February 16, 1978.

p. 143, **Ambassador Laurence Mann honored Greenfield:** Mike Byrne, "Ham Operator Helps Ob. Gyn. Consult with Physician in Jungle on Emergency C-Section," *Ob.Gyn. News*, Vol. 13. No. 8.

p. 144, **the birth story was a complete fabrication:** Leslie Wilson interview with author.

p. 144, **Vigilantes fired shotguns at their house:** "No Vigilantes Needed or Wanted," *Houston Chronicle*, Friday, March 8, 1968.

p. 144, **he told his friends that the FBI:** Sherri Tatum interview with author.

p. 144, **he had a vision telling him to go to California:** FBI interview with subject, RYMUR 89-4268-636.

p. 144, **stepladder of injection marks scarring his forearms:** Carlton Goodlett, "Notes on Peoples Temple," Jonestown Institute.

p. 144, **He wrote his family:** Mona Schacht letter to Larry Schacht, July 6, 1978, RYMUR 89-4286-2233-EE-1-s-198.

p. 144, **administered various narcotics to the Temple leader:** FBI interview, RYMUR 89-4286-925.

p. 145, **Jones feared Schacht wouldn't return to the settlement:** FBI interview with Mark Lane.

p. 145, **Schacht's questions were so simplistic:** Robert C. Smithwick, W6CS amateur radio operator interview with author.

p. 145, **He was always behind on his appointments:** Schacht memo to Jones, RYMUR 89-4286-2233-EE-1-5-114.

p. 145, **"I am a pisser when I wake up":** Schacht note to Jones, RYMUR 89-4286-2233-EE-2-r-148.

p. 145, **His one free day each week was Wednesday:** Schact memo to Jones, RYMUR 89-4286-2233-EE-2-A-1-mmmm.

p. 146, **he'd succeeded in producing a culture that looked like the botulinum bacteria:** Schacht botulism experiment notes, no FBI markings.

p. 146, **"I need a good book on forensic medicine":** Schacht, "Progress report," RYMUR 89-4286-2233-EE-1-5-178.

p. 146, **"I am quite capable of organizing the suicide aspect":** Schacht note to Jones, January 6, 1978, RYMUR 89-4286-2233-EE-1-5-57.

p. 146, **Symptoms, including slurred speech, weak muscles:** National Institutes of Health data.

p. 146, **staphylococcal toxin's worst effects:** Center for Disease Control.

p. 147, **the angry reader accused the Temple of aggressive self-promotion:** Mary Ann Connors Letter to Reid, February 21, 1978, RYMUR-89-4286-2233-BB-17-XX-1.

p. 147, **"Who are they to drive around town with a foreign license plate":** Temple leaders meeting with Jennifer Small of Radio Antilles, March 8, 1978, RYMUR 89-4286-2233-BB-2-ggg-2.

p. 147, **"Why in hell's half acre . . . ":** Letter from Sharon Amos to Burnham and Reid, RYMUR 89-4286-2233-BB-2-KKK-3.

p. 148, **"It's all over, they're coming in right now to kill us":** Debbie Blakey deposition. Peoples Temple v. Attorney General of California July 12, 1979.

p. 149, **warned that anyone who tried to flee would be shot:** Debbie Blakey deposition. Peoples Temple v. Attorney General of California July 12, 1979.

p. 151, **to learn which of his followers would obey him:** Debbie Blakey deposition. Peoples Temple v. Attorney General of California July 12, 1979.

p. 152, **"One day we are drinking a death potion":** Note from Maria McCann, February 17, 1978, RYMUR 89-4286-2233-EE-1-R-46.

p. 152, **"[she] was afraid to go to sleep because she was afraid she wouldn't wake up":** Carol Dennis note to Jones, RYMUR 89-4286-2233-FF-5-d-7.

CHAPTER 18: HYACINTH

p. 153, **The sisters laughed about it:** Thrash, *The Onliest One Alive*, 97.

p. 153, **"I ought to kill everyone last one of you":** Thrash, *The Onliest One Alive*, 102.

p. 154, **Her sons urged her to quiet down:** Thrash, *The Onliest One Alive*, 103.

p. 154, **hoped that the trouble between Reverend and Mrs. Jones would lead to the failure of the project:** Thrash, *The Onliest One Alive*, 102.

p. 155, **she began to suspect that he wasn't going back either:** Thrash, *The Onliest One Alive*, 107.

p. 155, **"What did God ever do for us?":** Thrash, *The Onliest One Alive*, 101.

p. 155, **Jair Baker got caught writing "Jesus Saves":** Planning Commission meeting, December 5, 1977, RYMUR 89-4286-2018-C-11-d-16c

p. 156, **an elderly male resident who'd just died made the mistake of calling out to Jesus:** Q182.

CHAPTER 19: STANLEY

p. 157, **she was attracted to "flowers, trees, nature's beauty":** Zippy Edwards note to Jones, RYMUR 89-4286-2233-FF-5-a-3.

p. 157, **sometimes, they did:** Note to dad from Scott T., RYMUR 89-4286-2233-EE-2-ij-11.

p. 158, **he was feeling randy:** Stanley Clayton interview with the author.

p. 159, **"Go ahead and kill me":** Stanley Clayton interview with the author.

p. 160, **his fantasies about black women:** Schacht note to JJ, RYMUR 89-4286-2233-EE-1-5-112.

p. 160, **Dr. Schacht "was introduced" into Janice:** Roller journal, April 10, 1978, RYMUR 89-4286-Bulky 2018-C-2-A-2, pages 1–148.

p. 160, **"I want to die a revolutionary death":** audiotape Q635.

p. 161, **He proceeded to fart, burp, piss:** audiotape Q638.

p. 161, **"The only fuck I want right now is the orgasm of the great fucking grave":** audiotape Q636.

p. 161, **sometimes talked about high-tailing it out of Jonestown:** Stanley Clayton interview with the author.

CHAPTER 20: RELATIVES

p. 163, **The FCC's rules forbid business communications:** Wireless Communication Bureau's Code of Federal Regulations.

p. 163, **Jones would "rather have his people dead than live in the United States":** Yulanda Williams affidavit.

p. 164, **The next day, a group of about fifty people:** "Peoples Temple in Guyana is 'prison,' relatives say," Bob Klose, *Press Democrat*, April 12, 1978.

p. 164, **"An Accusation of Human Rights Violations by Rev. James Warren Jones":** List of demands of Concerned Relatives, April 11, 1978, d-20.

p. 164, **"I will not be writing you anymore":** "Peoples Temple in Guyana Is 'Prison,' Relatives Say," Bob Klose, *Press Democrat*, April 12,1978.

p. 165, **That night, an agitated Jones summoned the community to the pavilion:** White night meeting as described in tapes Q 635, Q 636, Q637, Q 638 Q 639, Q594.

p. 165, **"nearly all of your goddamned relatives, have signed a petition":** Q635.

p. 165, **describe how they'd torture their family members:** Q594.

p. 166, **the press release much debated by Temple leaders:** Q635-639.

p. 166, **Harriet Tropp, in the Jonestown radio room, read a statement:** Q 736.

p. 166, **"Patrick Henry captured it":** PT press release, April 18, 1978, RYMUR 89-4286-2018-I-1.

p. 166, **But listen carefully to the tape:** Q736.

p. 166, **Of the sixteen people who raised their hands:** Rally notes, "thinks will live a long time," RYMUR 89-4286-2233-EE-10-14.

p. 166, **shots from automatic weapons rang out in the darkness:** Roller journal, April 22, 1978.

CHAPTER 21: THE EMBASSY

p. 169, **Jones brushed their comments aside:** Roller journal, May 13, 1978.

p. 169, **the tape would be released to the world press after they died:** Q245.

p. 169, **"I hope it will be an inspiration":** Q245.

p. 170, **"I figured if we just quit arguing with him, we could get some sleep":** Harold Cordell interview with author.

p. 170, **"In view of the death of myself, and the destruction of my life's work":** letter written on May 13, 1978, signed "Rev. James Warren Jones," California Historical Society MS3800 XX.

p. 171, **Back home in San Francisco:** Affidavit of Deborah Layton Blakey, RYMUR 89-4286-B-2-d-3.

p. 171, **He found it impossible to believe that nine hundred people would line up and kill themselves:** United States of America v. Peoples Temple, Deposition of Richard McCoy vol. 1.

p. 171, **"The more 'secretive' we need to be":** Harriet Tropp note to Jones, May 1978, RYMUR-89-4286-2233-EE-1-T-64.

p. 172, **prompting Jones to place her on his list of enemies:** Roller journal, May 20, 1978.

p. 172, **Temple members surrounded her on the street:** Reiterman, *Raven*, 420.

p. 172, **Georgetown officials did little to reassure her:** UPI, "Ukiah Reporter under Protection," May 27, 1978.

p. 172, **Lindsay never cleared customs:** National Enquirer letter to Gene Chaikin, June 22, 1978, RYMUR-89-4286-2233-NN-1-CC.

p. 173, **"cyanide may take up to three hours to kill":** Schacht memo on cyanide, RYMUR-89-4286-2233-EE-1-5-55x.

p. 173, **enough poison to kill 1,800 people:** "Laboratory Dept." Order RYMUR 89-4286-2233-00-3-E2.

CHAPTER 22: THE WIDENING GYRE

p. 174, **Some tried to gain favor by informing on people who didn't smile:** Bob Davis note to Jones, June 25, 1978, no FBI#.

p. 174, **Larry Schacht reported patients who took pain poorly:** Schacht note to Jones, RYMUR 89-4286-2233-FF-5-b-8.

p. 174, **Jones himself sometimes administered pain tests:** Roller journal, February 14, 1978.

p. 174, **Some residents informed on themselves:** Roller journal, May 4, 1978.

p. 175, **Bea Orsot, told Jones about Grubbs's private fears, dreams, and sexual proclivities:** Orsot note to Jones, May 28, 1978, RYMUR 89-4286-2233-EE-1-D-2-a; Orsot note to Jones, July 8, 1978, RYMUR 89-4286-2233-EE-2-M-5; Orsot note to Jones, July 10, 1978, RYMUR-89-4286-2233-EE-2-m-3B.

p. 175, **Grubbs would find himself in trouble:** Grubbs note to Jones from extended care unit, October 27, 1978, RYMUR 89-4286-2233-FF-2-29-A.

p. 175, **a juvenile court in Oakland sent him to a foster family that belonged to Peoples Temple:** Vince Lopez, Jr., background notes courtesy of James Polk, NBC.

p. 175, **He was one of twenty-two foster kids sent to Jonestown:** California Attorney General investigation/James Polk, NBC.

p. 175, **"The woodshop wants to know":** Memo to JJ from Geraldine Bailey, June 10, 1978, RYMUR 89-4286-2233-EE-1AB-32-a,.

p. 175, **Jones gave Vince the chance to dance his way off the learning crew:** Q597.

p. 176, **Jones didn't drink the milkshakes himself:** Memo to Jones, November 5, 1978, RYMUR 89-4286-2018-NIA4-3B.

p. 176, **Joyce Parks would regularly sedate troublemakers:** Bob Kice, Tuesday Day Helper Report, September 12, 1978, RYMUR 89-4286-2018-C-11-b-7B; Day Helper Report, September 29, 1978, RYMUR 89-4286-2018-C-11 -A-15B.

p. 176, **residents who were in danger of being confined to the SCU:** Medical department instructions from Jones, RYMUR 89-4286-2018-J-3-e-la.

p. 176, **Eavesdropping ham-radio operators:** FBI interview of ham radio operator, November 29, 1978, RYMUR 89-4286-590.

p. 176, **Sedatives were always requested in one thousand doses:** List of requested medical supplies, RYMUR89-4286-2018-E-3-A-2-170.

p. 176, **Jean Brown couldn't find injectable tranquilizers:** Jean Brown memo to Jones, October 2, 1978, RYMUR-89-4286-2233-BB-29-XXX-1.

p. 176, **"The only way it can be gotten is if you get a personal prescription":** Jean Brown memo, 10.2.78, BB-29-XXX-1.

p. 176, **buy all the tranquilizers and disposable syringes she could get her hands on:** Traffic from Georgetown, October 11, 1978, RYMUR 89-4286-2018-E-3-A-2-194, Georgetown traffic, October 18, 1978, E-3-A-2-160.

p. 176, **she'd located 100 vials of Thorazine:** Georgetown traffic, October 12, 1978, RYMUR 89-4286-2018-E-3-A-2-192.

p. 177, **every resident continually sedated for two years:** Department of Justice memo.

p. 177, **"I feel awful":** Shanda James note to Jones, RYMUR 89-4286-2233-EE-2-L-22.

p. 177, **swallowed a handful of oral contraceptives to avoid getting pregnant:** Teri Buford interview with author.

p. 177, **rash of violence, runaway attempts, and mental breakdowns:** Q265.

p. 177, **reprimanded for singing slave songs:** Roller journal, August 25, 1978.

p. 177, **residents' apathy was just as serious as the garden infestation:** ACAO/Steering, October 3, 1978, RYMUR 89-4286-2233-PP3AF5.

p. 177, **leadership considered different ways to motivate people:** Steering Notes, July 31, 1978, RYMUR 89-4286-2233-PP3D1.

p. 178, **handing out wooden beads as merit badges:** ACAO/Steering notes, October 3, 1978, RYMUR 89-4286-2233-PP3AF5.

p. 178, **"It will provide a kind of psychological balance":** Tropp note to Jones, May 1978, RYMUR 89-4286-2233-EE-1-T-64.

p. 178, **a five-year swine breeding plan:** Jonestown Farm Swine Breeding Program RYMUR 89-4286-2018-C-8-a-43a.

p. 178, **a new school:** Jonestown Community School, Primary Division, Report of July 7, 1978, RYMUR 89-4286-2018-C-12-c-1.

p. 178, **a 100-acre citrus orchard:** Gene Chaikin, "Projected 100-acre citrus orchard," June 30, 1978, RYMUR 89-4286-2018-C-8-a-42a.

p. 178, **"make the place more liveable":** ACAO & Steering combined minutes, October 3, 1978, RYMUR 89-4286-2233-PP-3-A-F1.

p. 178, **"a perfect reminder of what you have taught us":** Liz Ruggiero note to Jones, October 25, 1978, RYMUR 89-4286-2233-EE-1-R-34.

p. 178, **"I am very impatient with you that still fear death"**: Q220, late summer 1978, Lee Ingram note to Jones, RYMUR 89-4286-2233-EE-1-I&J-154.

p. 178, **Jonestown library stocked five hundred copies of *The Question*:** Box 3, "Books for the Jonestown Library," No FBI markings.

p. 179, **"You would rather kill yourself first":** Deborah Touchette deposition, Peoples Temple v. Attorney General of California.

p. 179, **"I'm a mutation that dropped off some asteroid":** Roller journal, May 15, 1978.

p. 180, **Several onlookers chided Edith for not hitting her hard enough:** Roller journal, April 4, 1978.

p. 180, **Lucas, seventy-four, confided in Edith that she was lonely:** Roller journal, May 15, 1978.

p. 180, **"we have orders to report all negative comments":** Roller journal, May 17, 1978.

p. 180, **members signed a release promising to "work diligently" at the settlement and "to keep a cheerful and constructive attitude":** Release signed by Zipporah Edwards, April 12, 1977, California Historical Society, MS 3800, folder 1108, 11B.

p. 180, **she promised to send him a "box of jewelry" each month:** Lovie Jean Lucas note to Jones, undated RYMUR 89-4286-2233-EE-3-KKKK-2.

p. 180, **Danielle Gardfrey, thirteen, was assigned to the learning crew:** Roller journal, August 4, 1978.

p. 181, **"Sometimes I feel like getting away from it all":** Brenda Warren note to Jones, RYMUR 89-4286-2233-FF-11-A-9.

p. 181, **"a chowder of fish heads and greens":** Roller journal, March 2, 1978.

p. 181, **"curried chicken necks":** Roller journal, April 21, 1978.

p. 181, **a few slices of watermelon or pineapple:** Roller journal, May 12 and 31, 1978.

p. 181, **the farm would only produce enough beans to feed residents every third day:** "Anticipated Harvest," July 15–January 15, RYMUR 89-4286-2233-PP-8-n-3.

p. 181, **Bogue suggested visitors bypass the fields altogether:** Analysts Meeting Follow-up, August 11, 1978, RYMUR 89-4286-2018-C-8-a-21a.

p. 181, **Jones complained constantly about how much it cost to feed residents:** Roller journal, February 7, 1978.

p. 181, **far from enough to sustain one thousand people:** Patty Cartmell note to Jones, RYMUR-89-4286-2018-N-I-A30-a.

p. 182, **Doing so would take energy away from him:** Teri Buford interview with author.

p. 182, **she'd be willing to return to her Bechtel job:** Edith Roller memo to Jones May 28, 1978, RYMUR 89-4286-BB-31-a-62.

CHAPTER 23: ESCAPE

p. 184, **She thought about taking up her cane:** Thrash, *The Onliest One Alive*, 94.

p. 184, **"I am blessed to be here":** Zipporah Edwards note to Jones, RYMUR 89-4286-2233-EE-1-E-10-b.

p. 185, **Jones had engineered such mishaps:** Grace Stoen interview with author, November 18, 2009. Jones would have wives drug husbands to make them think they were having a heart attack and bring them back into the fold.

p. 186, **who flirted openly with other men:** Bonnie Simon "Dear Dad note," RYMUR 89-4286-2233-EE-1-5-132.

p. 186, **"the lives of my kids meant more than mine":** Al Simon note "To Dad," April 9, 1978, RYMUR 89-4286-2233-EE-1-5-11.

p. 186, **Bogue sent Jones periodic updates:** Gold Prospecting Report, James Morrell, May 7, 1978, RYMUR 89-4286-2233-PP-8-a-104.

CHAPTER 24: CHAOS

p. 189, **rehearsed the answers to questions Freed might ask:** Q279.

p. 190, **Cottage supervisors coached residents:** Undated list of questions/responses for guests, RYMUR 89-4286-2018-C-8-a-34-e and c-8-a-14d.

p. 190, **Jones's lieutenants went from cottage to cottage:** ACAO, House Drill, August 7, 1978, RYMUR 89-4286-2233- PP3AD1.

p. 190, **"It's important that we all appear happy and exhibit satisfaction":** Roller journal, August 27, 1978.

p. 190, **"Everyone is to smile constantly and make the victory sign":** Minutes from peoples rally RYMUR 89-4286-2018-c-8-a-28a.

p. 190, **even scripted the escorts' seemingly spontaneous jokes:** Preparation for Freed Visit, RYMUR 89-4286-2018-c-8-a-15b.

p. 190, Details about Freed's trip to Jonestown: Don Freed, interview with author.

p. 191, **she struggled to keep up with Freed's jumbled stream of thought:** Roller journal, August 22, 1978.

p. 191, **Freed told the crowd that Tim Stoen was a CIA agent:** Roller journal August 15, 1978.

p. 191, **she also noted . . . what he and the other Temple leaders were eating:** Roller journal, August 24, 1978.

p. 192, **proceeded to interrogate him over a September afternoon:** Reiterman, *Raven*, 435.

p. 192, **Mazor had a reputation as a con man:** "Report to Adult Authority," Parole report for Joseph A. Mazor, December 16, 1970, RYMUR 89-4286-2018-S-1-0-1a.

p. 192, **repeated the fallacious expedition story to Jones's lieutenants:** Reiterman, *Raven*, 439.

p. 192, **Jones never left his cabin during the day:** Robert Scheer and Henry Weinstein, "Lane Talks of Temple Connection," *Los Angeles Times*, December 6, 1978.

p. 192, **behavior didn't stop Lane from promising the Temple leader that he'd get to the bottom of the conspiracy:** Deborah Touchette deposition.

p. 192, **a coordinated campaign to destroy Peoples Temple:** "Counteroffensive program," September 27, 1978, RYMUR 89-4286-2233-NN-6, A1.

p. 192, **he and Don Freed held a press conference:** Press conference transcript, October 3, 1978

p. 193, **embarrassed by the success of the socialist experiment:** "Peoples Temple Colony 'Harassed,'" *San Francisco Examiner*, October 4, 1978.

p. 193, **accuse them of being CIA agents:** KSAN Radio New Broadcast October 3, 1978, RYMUR 89-4286-2233-BB-7-D-3.

p. 193, **San Francisco's largest paper was part of the vast plan to destroy him:** Richard Tropp letter to *San Francisco Chronicle*, November 1, 1978, RYMUR 89-4286-2233--NN-6-P.

p. 193, **Charles Garry thought Mazor's jungle tale was "bullshit":** "Reports," Jean, October 23, 1978, RYMUR 89-4286-2233-BB-7-A-49.

p. 193, **he'd once been a member of the service group himself:** Law Office Report #50, August 16, 1978, RYMUR 89-4286-2018-B4B, (15a1).

p. 193, **Only the FBI sent him its information on Jim Jones:** Charles Garry deposition, Peoples Temple v. Attorney General of California, December 30, 1981.

p. 193, **suggested Garry might also be "in the pay of the CIA":** Roller journal, February 25, 1978.

p. 193, **Jones hired Lane as a red herring:** FBI interview with Garry, December 4, 1978.

p. 193, **Garry would accuse Lane of being "morally responsible" for the mass deaths:** Diane Alters, "Garry Labels Lane Catalyst for 900 Jonestown Deaths," McClatchy Newspapers Service, September 20, 1979.

p. 194, **"mixture of Moon and Manson":** Draft of Gordon Lindsay article for the *Enquirer*, RYMUR 89-4286-2018-I-l-c-1p.

p. 194, **"I ain't dealing with 'old toupee Garry' now":** Q265.

p. 194, **Lane would say Lindsay's article was "absolutely, 100 percent true":** John Crewdson, "Mark Lane and Peoples Temple: A Cause to Back, Then Condemn," *New York Times*, February 4, 1978.

p. 194, **Residents signed a petition:** Petition to immigrate to the USSR, undated, RYMUR 89-4286-2018-G-1-c-9.

p. 195, **"Are we or are we not welcome in the Soviet Union?":** Message from Jim Jones, undated, RYMUR 89-4286-2018-G-1-b-3a.

p. 195, **"The Temple thinks every movement of the moon deals with it":** Sharon Amos meeting with Russian embassy, October 20, 1978 RYMUR 89-4286-2018-G-1-b-1a.

p. 195, **Although Buford sent numerous memos to Jones supporting the "last-stand" plan:** Buford Memo to Jones, RYMUR 89-4286-2233-BB-7-W.

p. 195, Details on Buford's relationship with Jones: Teri Buford interview with author.

p. 196, **it only cost $500 to hire a hit man:** Teri Buford deposition, United States of America v. Peoples Temple

p. 196, **Lane was constantly coming on to her:** "Stateside traffic," October 8, 1978, RYMUR 89-4286-2233-PP-9-h-1.

p. 196, **He had a mysterious ailment that gave him 106-degree fevers:** Message from Jim Jones, undated, RYMUR 89-4286-2018-G-1-b-3a.

p. 196, **He had a bad heart:** Untitled, undated, RYMUR 89-4286-2018-G-1-9-6.

p. 196, **He had lung cancer:** 10.8.78, Russian Embassy, October 8, 1978, RYMUR 89-4286-2018-G-1-e-2a.

p. 197, **The medical department had even sent diseased cells:** Visit to Russian Embassy, October 13, 1978, RYMUR 89-4286-2018-G-1-b-7a.

p. 197, **the Soviet Union would not allow the group to immigrate:** Meeting

at Russian Embassy: October 24, 1978, RYMUR 89-4286-2018
-G-1-f-a.

p. 197, **She later publicly apologized:** Roller journal, May 15, 1978.

p. 197, **Marcie wasn't told of his first mass suicide threat:** Teri Buford memo
to Jones, RYMUR 89-4286-2233-BB-7-J-6.

p. 197, **she made it abundantly clear that she was opposed to killing children:**
Marceline Jones note to Jones, RYMUR 89-4286-2233-EE-1-K-1.

p. 197, **Jones recorded a private message of "utmost gravity":** Georgetown
traffic, October 8, 1978, RYMUR 89-4286-2018-E-3-A-2(208).

p. 197, **Mingo rummaged through papers on his desk:** Mingo visit, October 9,
1978, RYMUR 89-4286-2018-D-2-K-19a.

p. 197, **Mingo canceled his weekly meetings with Sharon Amos altogether:**
Georgetown radio traffic, October 21, 1978, RYMUR 89-4286-2018-E-
3-A-2-140.

p. 197, **He told his followers that he had lung cancer:** Roller journal, August 8,
1978

p. 197, **complaints must stop:** Follow-up notes from Peoples Rally, August 8,
1978, RYMUR 89-4286-2018-c-8-a-23a.

p. 198, **aside from a urinary tract infection:** Schacht note to Jones, RYMUR
89-4286-2233-EE-1-5-210.

p. 198, **they refused to commit their promises to writing:** Sharon Amos,
"Mingo Visit," October 9, 1978, RYMUR 89-4286-2018-D-2- K-19a.

p. 198, **Goodlett suspected Jones was suffering from manic depression:** *The
Need For A Second Look At Jonestown*, edited by Rebecca Moore and
Fielding M. McGehee III (Edwin Mellen Press: 1989).

p. 198, **He reassured Jones that he wasn't dying:** "Notes on Peoples Temple" by
Carlton B. Goodlett, Jonestown Institute.

p. 198, **"If you can't convince him, then take him":** Guy Young interview with
author.

p. 198, **Sometimes he even sounded some words out:** Q216.

p. 198, **he ordered nearly twenty people to be medically sedated:** Reiterman,
Raven, 468.

p. 198, **"No, Jim! That's *not* necessary!":** Harold Cordell interview with
author.

p. 198, **He stationed armed guards outside his door:** 10.16 Q384, Job Description,
Internal Security Patrol, RYMUR 89-4286-2018—c-11-b-16cc.

p. 199, **He carried a .357 magnum revolver in his waistband:** List of guns by carrier, RYMUR 89-4286-2018-H-1-c-4.

p. 199, **according to a memo she sent him:** "Analysis of Future Prospects," Carolyn Layton memo to Jones, RYMUR 89-4286-2018-X-3-e, pp. 32a-32e.

p. 199, **in Jonestown's last weeks:** Fielding McGehee, interview with author.

CHAPTER 25: NOVEMBER

p. 200, **Sam Houston was worried about them:** House of Representatives Committee on Foreign Affairs Staff Investigative Report, May 15, 1979.

p. 200, **Justice Aubrey Bishop, quit the case after receiving phone calls:** Nicholas Horrock, "Guyana Orders Custody Case Inquiry," *New York Times*, December 7, 1978.

p. 200, **Chief Justice Harold Bollers didn't reassign it:** Georgetown feedback, October 2, 1978, RYMUR-89-4286-2018-E-3-A-2(234).

p. 200, **as the court had done with the arrest warrant:** Meeting with Registrar Barnwell, RYMUR 89-4286-2233-NN-2-rrr-1, October 18, 1978.

p. 201, **he was prepared to retrieve his son by force if necessary:** US Embassy Log 587, October 3, 1978.

p. 201, **On November 1, the congressman sent Jones a telegram:** Ryan telegram to Jones, November 1, 1978, RYMUR 89-4286-2233-AA-1-b6.

p. 201, **refused to allow the crew entry to Jonestown:** Letter to NBC, November 4, 1978 RYMUR 89-4286-2233-AA-1-y-1.

p. 201, **"The Committee does intend to leave as scheduled":** Ryan letter to Lane, November 10, 1978 RYMUR 89-4286-2233-AA-1-h-1.

p. 201, **That would create a snowball effect:** Georgetown radio traffic, November 12, 1978 RYMUR 89-4286-2018-E-3-A-2(25).

p. 202, **it would be a "grave mistake":** undated, RYMUR 89-4286-2018-E-3-4-2(72).

p. 202, **He was irritated by the stunt:** Georgetown Traffic feedback, October 10, 1978, RYMUR 89-4286-2018-E-3-A-2(202).

p. 202, **they didn't see "barbed wire":** House of Representatives Committee on Foreign Affairs Staff Investigative Report, May 15, 1979, 143.

p. 202, **congressman's staff was more concerned about travel logistics:** Jackie Speier deposition, Peoples Temple v. California Attorney General, January 26, 1982.

p. 203, **he intended to stay down there "as long as it takes":** Marshall Kilduff,

"Ryan to Visit Rev. Jones' Jungle Refuge," *San Francisco Chronicle*, November 8, 1978.

p. 203, **they would suffer the consequences:** Q175.

p. 203, **The Temple leader could barely walk:** Reiterman, *Raven*, 468.

p. 203, **"I will see you in the grave":** Q313.

p. 203, **He placed multiple orders for the poison:** Lab orders, RYMUR 89-4286-2233-EE-8-5-19, 00-3-UUU2, 00-3-BBBB2.

p. 203, **his autopsy detected large levels of Thorazine:** Schacht autopsy, AFIP#1680274.

p. 204, **Harold Cordell witnessed a large drum of chemicals arrive aboard the** *Cudjoe:* Harold Cordell interview with author.

p. 204, **They schemed and schemed:** Harold Cordell interview with the author.

p. 204, **The young woman didn't answer:** Thrash, *The Onliest One Alive*, 97.

p. 204, **she was too poor to feed them:** Valita George interview with author.

p. 205, **he was prepared to make a great sacrifice:** Q314.

CHAPTER 26: RYAN

p. 206, **revoke the visas of the other reporters:** Georgetown, November 14, 1978, RYMUR 89-4286-2018-E-3-A-2(15).

p. 206, **to find their reservations canceled:** Reiterman, *Raven*, 482.

p. 206, **restamped their passports:** Reiterman, *Raven*, 483.

p. 207, **whom Jones had summoned to Guyana the previous day:** Stateside Feedback, November 13, 1978, RYMUR 89-4286-2233-AA-1-hh-1.

p. 207, **Jones was too ill to do so:** Reiterman, *Raven*, 484.

p. 207, **he was worried about the mental health of the Jonestown residents:** Georgetown traffic, November 16, 1978, RYMUR 89-4286-2018-E-3-A-2(5).

p. 207, **Jones held a rally:** Q50.

p. 207, **he refused to sit next to him:** Garry FBI interview.

p. 208, **"Very well":** Garry deposition.

p. 208, **Temple members stood beside it:** Dwyer deposition.

p. 209, **Carter walked away:** Dwyer deposition.

p. 209, **they weren't even permitted to leave the airstrip:** Reiterman, *Raven*, 489.

p. 209, **Temple leader wouldn't let him into Jonestown:** *New York Times*, November 20, 1978.

p. 209, **Logs had been deliberately strewn across the road:** Dwyer deposition.

p. 209, **"I hope to God I have done the right thing":** Dwyer deposition.

p. 210, **they'd be on the floor, he warned:** Q050.

p. 210, **Jones had said she was a CIA agent:** FBI interview with Beverly Oliver, December 7, 1978, SJ 89-123.

p. 210, **she made weird comments about the guests' food being poisoned:** FBI interview with Anthony Katsaris, December 8, 1978, SJ 89-123.

p. 210, **nod their head if they wanted to leave:** Dwyer deposition.

p. 210, **supposedly sick or otherwise unavailable:** Speier deposition.

p. 210, **these, as ordered, were duly handed to Temple censors:** Letters brought in by Ryan, RYMUR 89-4286-2233-AA-1-e-1.

p. 211, **"Sometimes I feel like a dying man":** Reiterman, *Raven*, 493.

p. 211, **"I only said it is better that we commit suicide than kill":** Reiterman, *Raven*, 498.

p. 211, **Anthony Katsaris invited Maria to take a stroll:** FBI interview with Anthony Katsaris, December 8, 1978, SJ 89-123.

p. 211, **Marceline interrupted Ryan's interviews:** Q048.

p. 212, **"Help us get out of Jonestown":** Reiterman, *Raven*, 503.

p. 212, **Gosney, a former heroin addict:** CNN transcript of interview with Vern Gosney.

p. 212, **Dwyer went to bed . . . feeling satisfied:** Dwyer deposition.

p. 212, **Jones gave the residents a free day:** Edith Bogue, FBI interview.

p. 212, **and prescribed Valium by Dr. Schacht:** "Gene Chaikin medical chart," RYMUR 89-4286-2233-BB-10-d-6, "Orders," BB-10-d-1.

p. 212, **Ryan had visited Gene:** Dwyer deposition.

p. 213, **he jumped to the conclusion that the inhabitants were being held against their will:** Krause, *The Guyana Massacre*, 67.

p. 213, **reporters noted that the living space was crammed:** Reiterman, *Raven*, 509.

p. 214, **a group of children watched *Willy Wonka*:** Reiterman, *Raven*, 505.

p. 214, **"Please leave us":** NBC footage.

p. 214, **to call for a second plane:** Q1289.

p. 214, **"You held us here as slaves":** Gerald Parks interview with author.

p. 216, **"Try to get yourselves out":** Edith Bogue's notebook detailing last days of Jonestown (Bogue family collection).

p. 217, **Jones pressed his hand to his chest:** Reiterman, *Raven*, 513.

p. 217, **He was about to tell him about the poison:** Harold Cordell interview with author.

p. 218, **"Keep your damn mouth shut":** FBI interview Beverly Oliver.

p. 218, **chewing their cuticles to the quick:** NBC footage.

p. 218, **Jones would kill them right there:** Interviews with Harold Cordell, Jim and Thom Bogue.

p. 219, **"Motherfucker, you are going to die!":** Tim Carter, Guyanese inquest.

p. 219, **"I wish I had been killed":** Dwyer deposition.

p. 219, **he wouldn't recommend further investigations of the camp:** Garry deposition.

p. 219, **Dwyer urged him to get out of Jonestown immediately:** Dwyer deposition.

p. 219, **It was Larry Layton:** NBC footage.

p. 220, **then Layton sat by himself with a "long, weird stare":** Dale Parks deposition.

p. 220, **"I think we've got trouble":** Reiterman, *Raven*, 525.

p. 220, **the congressman suggested she ride on the Otter instead:** Jackie Speier deposition.

p. 221, **He grabbed his neck:** Dwyer deposition.

p. 221, **NBC cameraman Bob Brown bravely continued to record the attack:** Reiterman, *Raven*, 530.

p. 222, **Dale Parks wrested it from Layton:** Reiterman, *Raven*, 533.

p. 222, **The diplomat asked a bystander:** Joel Edwin Clementson interview with author.

p. 222, **flashed victory signs:** Carlton Daniels interview with author.

CHAPTER 27: END

p. 223, **Lane told him about the drugged sandwiches:** Lane, 159.

p. 224, **Jones sat on a carpenter's horse with Harriet Tropp beside him:** Garry deposition.

p. 225, **"Let's not be divisive":** Garry deposition.

p. 226, **someone had rifled through the crate:** Edith Roller note to Jones, September 10, 1978 RYMUR 89-4286-2233-EE-2-pg-9.

p. 226, **She appeared to have lost her mind:** Tim Carter, Guyana inquest.

p. 226, **His autopsy report would reveal longtime barbiturate abuse:** Autopsy report by prosecutor Kenneth Mueller, Dover Air Force Base.

p. 227, **"It seems that I'm in a cage like a bird":** Christine Miller to Jones, RYMUR 89-4286-2233-EE-2-l-5B.

p. 229, **and included grape Flavor-Aid, potassium cyanide, Valium, chloral hydrate:** report of Guyanese medical examiner, Leslie Mootoo.

p. 229, **She walked out of the pavilion:** Rhodes inquest.

p. 229, **pry their babies from their arms:** Stanley Clayton interview with author.

p. 229, **304 minors would be murdered there:** The Jonestown Institute.

p. 230, **The odor of burnt almonds:** Tim Carter, SDSU.

p. 231, **Aides were dragging small corpses into rows:** Rhodes inquest.

p. 231, **forcing her to swallow it:** Stanley Clayton interview with author.

p. 231, **"I would like to raise a kitten":** Edith Roller note to Jones, RYMUR 89-4286-2018-C-5-a-8.

p. 232, **"I'll see you in the next life":** Stanley Clayton interview.

p. 233, **pressing a stethoscope to people's chests to make sure they were dead:** Guyanese Inquest, Odell Rhodes, SC interview.

p. 234, **he got up and sprinted away:** Clayton Inquest.

p. 234, **he asked his congregants to lie on the floor for him:** FBI interview former member of Jones's church RYMUR 8/75.

p. 234, **revolver to his right temple:** Guyanese inquest testimony Leslie Mootoo ruled suicide.

p. 234, **This was probably the shot Stanley heard:** Vernon Gentle/Leslie Mootoo inquest, Odell Rhodes.

CHAPTER 28: BODIES

p. 235, **As the massacre was underway:** Jonestown radio operator Mike Carter at Guyanese Inquest.

p. 235, **"Brownfield has offered to help":** Q1290 recorded by Douglas Ellice on 11.18.78.

p. 235, **to enact the last stand and begin murdering Temple enemies:** "Grand Jury Hears Aide to Jim Jones; Lawyer says 'Crimes' Are Outlined," John Crewdson, *New York Times*, December 20, 1978.

p. 236, **The Jonestown operator then switched to Morse code:** Raven, 522.

p. 236, **Liane then cut her own throat:** Raven, 545.

p. 236, **showed signs of puncture wounds on their upper arms:** "Ex-Aide May know of Temple Millions," John Kifner, *New York Times*, December 1, 1978.

p. 236, **both ingested the cyanide and was shot in the head:** Annie Moore autopsy report.

p. 236, **found a .357 Ruger Magnum beside her body:** Cecil Roberts, Assistant Commissioner of Crime, Guyanese Inquest.

p. 236, **along with her suicide note:** "Moore suicide note," RYMUR 89-4286-1894.

p. 237, **wrote a longer note:** Dick Tropp, "Last words," condensed version, RYMUR 89-4286-X-1-a-54

p. 238, **looked like a patchwork quilt:** Chris J. Harper, "What I Saw," *Time*, December 4, 1978.

p. 238, **shouting "Baby killers!":** Nora Gallagher, "Jonestown: The Survivors' Story," *New York Times* Magazine, November 18, 1979.

p. 238, **"We heard you're going to commit suicide":** Guy Young interview with author.

p. 238, **were followed by FBI agents:** Guy Young interview with author.

p. 239, **placed them in body bags using snow shovels:** Jeff Brailey, "Policing Up the Bodies." The Jonestown Institute spent a day turning over bodies.

p. 239, **only able to identify 631 of the 913 dead:** RYMUR memorandum, FBI, RYMUR 89-4286-2370, November 9, 1979.

p. 239, **babies were buried two to a casket:** Fielding McGehee interview with author.

p. 239, **was last seen in Jones's cottage:** Tim Carter, excerpt from unpublished book, Jonestown Report no. 9, Jonestown Institute.

p. 239, **spent a day at the camp turning over bodies:** Valita George interview with author.

p. 239, **an indication of her mental instability:** "Discovering Aunt Edith Through Her Journals," Miranda Smith, Jonestown Institute.

CHAPTER 29: SURVIVORS:

p. 240, **"He'll lead out those other kids who ran with him":** Reiterman, *Raven*, 551.

p. 241, **carried him on a stretcher to the Port Kaituma rum shop:** Bernard Conyers interview with author.

p. 241, **she'd heard people outside her cottage calling:** Thrash, *The Onliest One Alive*, 110.

p. 241, **she'd lost thirty-three pounds in Jonestown:** Thrash, *The Onliest One Alive*, 126.

p. 242, **They carried her to the pavilion:** *New York Times*, November 29, 1978.

p. 243, **Jim Jones, who was lying on the platform in the pavilion:** Vernon Gentle, Detective Inspector of Police, Guyanese Inquest.

p. 243, **but she refused:** Thrash, *The Onliest One Alive*, 118.

p. 243, **Grover Davis, seventy-nine, who'd survived:** *New York Times,* November 29, 1978.

p. 243, **a "tiny, birdlike woman":** *New York Times,* November 30, 1978.

p. 243, **but would never receive a reply:** Thrash, *The Onliest One Alive*, 136.

p. 244, **a suitcase filled with $550,000:** Reiterman, *Raven*, 563.

p. 244, **A local saw them enter a building to hide:** Carlton Daniels interview with author.

p. 244, **Jones had set aside millions of dollars in Swiss banks to finance the last-stand plan:** John Kifner, "Ex-Aide May Know of Temple Millions; Lawyer Says Woman Has Data on $8 Million in Foreign Banks and Alleged Death Squad," *New York Times*, December 4, 1978.

p. 244, **several defectors went underground:** John Crewdson, "Ex-Aide Links Threats and Violence to Jones Adviser," *New York Times*, December 22, 1978.

p. 244, **church leaders quickly purged Temple files:** Guy Young interview with author, Fielding McGehee interview with author.

p. 245, **he shot and killed her and their eighteen-month-old son:** Nancy Lewis and Joanne Ostrow, "Slain Bethesda Woman Linked to Cult Chief, Guyana Envoy," *Washington Post*, October 26, 1978.

p. 245, **Lane told Garry many secrets:** Charles Garry, FBI interview, SF 89-250C131, 11.29.78, Garry deposition, Peoples Temple v. Attorney General of California, December 30, 1981.

p. 245, **Garry would accuse Lane of being "morally responsible" for the massacre:** Diane Alters, "Garry Labels Lane Catalyst for 900 Jonestown Deaths," McClatchy Newspapers Service, September 20, 1979.

p. 245, **"the only person who tried to prevent the murders":** John M. Crewdson, "Mark Lane and Peoples Temple: A Cause to Back, Then Condemn," *New York Times*, February 4, 1979.

p. 245, **earning $2,750 per appearance:** Reiterman, *Raven*, 579.

p. 245, **charged Larry Layton with aiding and abetting:** Katherine Bishop, "1978 Cult Figure Gets Life Term in Congressman's Jungle Slaying," *New York Times*, March 4, 1987.

p. 245, **House of Representatives investigation found fault with the US Embassy's dealings:** House of Representatives Staff Investigative Group, May 15, 1979.

p. 246, **Hyacinth Thrash received $4,351:** Thrash, *The Onliest One Alive*, 134.

p. 246, **Jackie Speier received $360,000:** Moore, *A Sympathetic History,* 354.

p. 246, **and charging visitors two hundred dollars per night for the thrill of the Jonestown "experience":** Gerry Gouveia interview with author.

p. 247, **she used the money to bury her sister:** Thrash, *The Onliest One Alive,* 123.

p. 247, **she heard Zip call her name:** Thrash, *The Onliest One Alive,* 128.

p. 247, **he took advantage of unschooled blacks:** Thrash, *The Onliest One Alive,* 132.

p. 247, **she sang gospel music aloud to lift her spirits:** Thrash, *The Onliest One Alive,* 127.

p. 247, **she attended the services of a healing evangelist:** Thrash, *The Onliest One Alive,* 131.

p. 247, **It was downhill from there:** Stanley Clayton interview with author.

p. 248, **Tommy Bogue, who now goes by Thom:** Thom Bogue interview with author.

p. 248, **Jim Bogue tormented himself for years:** Jim Bogue interview with author.

ACKNOWLEDGMENTS

First and foremost I want to thank those Jonestown survivors who shared their experiences with me. Thom and Jim Bogue were exceedingly gracious with their time and hospitality, and answered my questions with patience and good humor. Stanley Clayton helped me understand the draw of Peoples Temple for a marginalized kid from Oakland, and how, even in the worst times, he felt sustained by this fellowship. Harold Cordell, Leslie Wagner-Wilson, Jordan Vilchez, Laura Kohl, Teri Buford, Don Beck, Dawn Gardfrey, Guy Young, Jerry Parks, Yulanda Crawford, Grace Jones, and Garry Lambrev all offered keen anecdotes and insight that helped complete the narrative.

Fielding "Mac" McGehee and Rebecca Moore of the Jonestown Institute for their tireless efforts to humanize Jones's victims and to provide researchers with accurate material and direction.

I'll never visit Indianapolis again without thinking of Hyacinth Thrash, whose memoir, *The Onliest One Alive*, was so helpful to me, or enter a World Market store without remembering Edith Roller, who also loved shopping there. I hope that someday the last months of her diary will be recovered.

Other sources to whom I'm indebted include Marshall Kilduff, who, in many ways, laid the groundwork for this book; author Donald Freed; former FBI agent Barry Mones; and, in Guyana, Valita George, Bernard Conyers, Carlton Daniels, Joel Edwin Clementson, Raschid Osman, Wilfred and Benjamin Jupiter, Gerald Gouveia, and Hamilton Green.

My publishing team at Free Press, Dominick Anfuso and Leah Miller, who kept the manuscript from suffocating in details and helped me find the natural arc of the story. Free Press publisher Martha Levin for granting me extra time to get the job done.

Kim Witherspoon, my wonderful agent, who was always responsive and supportive, as an agent should be.

My family. I was pregnant as I wrote this book, and my daughter Davia Joy was born in the middle of it. I'm forever grateful to my husband, Tim Rose, who took on the bulk of night feedings and daily care so I could write. My older daughter, Tessa Liberty, kept me from straying too far into the Jonestown darkness with her playfulness and affection. My family continually reminded me, as I worked with such tragic subject matter, how precious life is.

INDEX

abolitionist movement, 92
Adams, Paula, 82–83, 85, 91, 92, 98,
    115, 194, 245
African Americans, 6–7, 9
    discrimination against, 16–17,
        20–22
    Peoples Temple and, 11, 32, 50,
        128, 133, 137, 174
    violence against, 27, 32, 44–45
Alleg, Henri, 179
amateur (ham) radio, 2, 46, 55, 68, 81,
    83, 85, 98, 101, 114, 118, 129,
    130–31, 143, 145, 151, 162–63,
    165, 176, 198, 235–36
Amerindians, 33, 67, 70, 73, 75, 91,
    108, 144, 185, 204, 221, 240,
    241, 246
Amin, Idi, 98
Amos, Christa, 236
Amos, Liane, 236
Amos, Martin, 236
Amos, Sharon, 126, 147, 170, 195,
    196, 197, 202, 207, 235–36

Anaesthesia and Intensive Care, 173
Angelou, Maya, 134
Annibourne, Neville, 208, 209, 212
apostolic socialism (divine socialism),
    24, 31, 32, 36, 40, 44, 47
Army, U.S., 236, 239
Assemblies of God, 10

Bagby, Monica, 212, 221, 222
Baker, Jair, 155–56
Baldwin, Mary, 181
Banks, Dennis, 33
Bates, Christine, 48, 49, 77–78, 132,
    133
Beam, Jack, 42, 45, 178, 223
Beam, Rheaviana, 241
Bechtel Corporation, 29, 36, 117, 118,
    134, 182
Beecher, Henry Ward, 92
Bible, 7, 29–30, 155, 242
    Jones's disenchantment with,
        18–19, 50, 88
Bishop, Aubrey, 94, 97, 126, 200

A Thousand Lives
Julia Scheeres

Reading Group Guide

Introduction

In this heart-wrenching account of the largest mass murder-suicide in history, Julia Scheeres uses recently declassified documents to paint a harrowing portrait of the 1978 Jonestown Massacre in Guyana. *A Thousand Lives* follows five individuals who joined Peoples Temple, a progressive church founded by the charismatic yet unstable Jim Jones, and wound up trapped in a jungle compound with a leader bent on killing them. A story of broken trust and psychological warfare, *A Thousand Lives* deftly and poetically reveals how a congregation's dream of Eden turned into an inescapable Hell.

Topics and Questions for Discussion

1. Why did you choose to read *A Thousand Lives* with your book club? How much did you already know about the Jonestown Massacre? Did you know that there were survivors?

2. Discuss and compare Edith Roller's, Hyacinth Thrash's, Stanley Clayton's, and Jim Bogue's different reasons for joining Peoples Temple. What brought each of these individuals to Jim Jones's congregation? What commonalities do you see in their motivations for becoming part of the "socialist" movement?

3. Did you find any merit in Jones's initial, singular view of socialism? Do you think he ever really supported these ideals? Was the Temple, in any of its incarnations, ever indicative of an egalitarian society?

4. Why do you think so many Temple members in Guyana denied Jones's mistreatment and instability to Consul McCoy in their private

talks? Did they all fear reprisals from the Jonestown community? Do you think some of them were truly happy?

5. Discuss Jones's many deceptions—from his fake healings, to fraudulent miracles, to his "practice" white nights in Guyana. Why do you think so many followers were swayed by his displays?

6. What do you make of Edith Roller's ultimate death? Discuss her frank diary entries and love of poetry and literature. What do you imagine the missing final months of her journal might say about her experience?

7. Discuss the relationships forged in Guyana. Consider the following relationships in your response: Tommy Bogue and Brian Davis; Stanley Clayton and Eddie Crenshaw; Jim Bogue and Al Simon; Edith Roller and Eddie Washington; and Hyacinth Thrash and Zippy Edwards. What forged these bonds in the violent climate of Jonestown? What tested them?

8. The very notion of "family" is a challenged and warped concept in Jonestown. How do you define family? Are any of the Jonestown residents able to maintain traditional family structure?

9. In the introduction, Scheeres writes: "Learning about other people's lives somehow puts your own life into sharper relief." Did reading *A Thousand Lives* do so for you? How?

10. Do you agree with Charles Garry that Mark Lane is "morally responsible" for fostering and aggravating Jones's paranoia? Why or why not?

11. Would you take part in "dark tourism" if the Guyanese government were to reconstruct the Jonestown pavilion and make the locale a museum? Why or why not?

12. The people of Jonestown sought to create a paradise free of racism, violence, and disparity. Though their dream was wildly betrayed, reflect on your vision of utopia. What does your perfect society look like?

1. Visit www.juliascheeres.com to browse photos, home movies, documents, and audio recordings from Jonestown. Discuss how these primary sources enhance or affect your reading experience of *A Thousand Lives*.

2. Read Julia Scheeres's first book, *Jesus Land*—a memoir about her relationship with her adopted brother and their time spent in a Christian reform school in the Dominican Republic. How do themes of religion, race, and "cult" mentality differ from or align with *A Thousand Lives*?

3. One of Jones's psychological tactics was to expose his followers to books and movies that reinforced his own depressive, nihilistic outlook. These included *No Blade of Grass*, a sci-fi movie about the collapse of civilization; *Night and Fog*, a documentary on Nazi medical experiments; and *The Question*, a journalist's account of being tortured by the French military for supporting Algerian independence. Watch or read any one of these works and try to imagine what it must have been like for the denizens of Jonestown to supplement their real horror with bleak works of art.

ABOUT THE AUTHOR

Julia Scheeres is the author of the *New York Times* bestselling memoir *Jesus Land*. She lives in Berkeley, California, with her husband and two daughters and is a member of the San Francisco Writers' Grotto.

Tommy Bogue

Zipporah Edwards

Marceline Jones

Janice Clayton

Carolyn Layton

Christine Bates

Mike Prokes

Marilee Bogue

Paula Adams

Monique Bacon

Harriet Tropp

Dick Tropp

Michael Rozynko

Eddie Crenshaw

Larry Schacht

Phyllis Chaikin

Vera Talley

Maya Ijames

Anne Moore

Tom Partak

Rose McKnight

Ron Talley

Eddie Washington

Katherine Domineck

Norya Blair

Dana Truss

Irvin Perkins

Leanndra Dennis McCoy

Jair Baker

Shanda James

Alleane Tucker

Michaeleen Brady

Brenda Warren

Crystal Simon

Lovie Jean Lucas

Jimmy Cordell

Garry (Poncho) Johnson

Jim McElvane

Thurman Guy

Julie Ann Runnels